Interfaith Inclusion

——INTERFAITH——
INCLUSION

THE UNIVERSITY RELIGIOUS CONFERENCE AND THE PURSUIT OF A PLURALIST AMERICA

Lois Nettleship

University Press of Kansas

Published by the University Press of Kansas (Lawrence, Kansas 66045), which was organized
by the Kansas Board of Regents and is operated and funded by Emporia State University, Fort
Hays State University, Kansas State University, Pittsburg State University, the University of
Kansas, and Wichita State University.

Library of Congress Cataloging-in-Publication Data

Names: Nettleship, Lois, author
Title: Interfaith inclusion: the University Religious Conference and the
pursuit of a pluralist America / Lois Nettleship.
Description: Lawrence: University Press of Kansas, 2025 | Includes
bibliographical references and index.
Identifiers: LCCN 2025008550 (print) | LCCN 2025008551 (ebook)
ISBN 9780700640676 cloth
ISBN 9780700640683 epub
Subjects: LCSH: University Religious Conference (Los Angeles, Calif.) |
University of California, Los Angeles—Religion | Religious institutions—California—
Los Angeles | Interfaith worship—California—Los Angeles | Religious pluralism—California—
Los Angeles | Cultural pluralism—California—Los Angeles | College students—Religious life—
California—Los Angeles | BISAC: RELIGION / Religion, Politics & State | HISTORY / Social History
Classification: LCC BV1430.U55 N48 2025 (print) | LCC BV1430.U55 (ebook)
LC record available at https://lccn.loc.gov/2025008550
LC ebook record available at https://lccn.loc.gov/2025008551

British Library Cataloguing-in-Publication Data is available.

Jacket design by Karl Janssen
Jacket photograph: Six members of the URC Panel of Americans seated outside the University
Religious Conference Building, 1947. Marian Hargrave Private Papers.

To my husband, William

Contents

A photo gallery follows page 150.

Acknowledgments

Writing this book has been a humbling experience. It has heightened my awareness of how much I owe to those who have gone before me: the professors and mentors who have encouraged and inspired me and the numerous scholars whose works have given me their insights and made my own work possible.

Some of those professors and mentors have passed on. But their spirit remains. Their wisdom and example are still with me. They are: Bert James Loewenberg, Charles Trinkaus, Helen Merrill Lynd, Lindsey Pherigo, James Shenton, and Hugh Speer. Stephen Yeo, still with us, is the one who taught me about the profound connection between nineteenth-century British social reform and religion.

Many students have given me hope and renewal over the years, and a few stand out: Deanna Marquette and Julie Metzler in Kansas, and in California, James Skee and Janet Tanner, now a scholarly author, who helped me preserve my interviews.

The friends and colleagues who have contributed to this book include Susan Brown Tucker, who introduced me to the Kansas City Panel of American Women, which led me to study its predecessor, the Panel of Americans, at the University Religious Conference at UCLA, and Emily Rader, who introduced me to the URC Trialogue program. Before that, two friends welcomed me, a naive New York City girl, to the wild prairies of Kansas: the late Thomas Barr of the Kansas State Historical Society and Reed Whittaker Jr. of the National Archives. They called me KIN, a Kansas Improved New Yorker.

Pat and David Brodsky and Becky and Paul Clervi made my Midwestern research trip a pleasure with their friendship and hospitality. Richard Rupple encouraged me to write this book, as did Robert Adzema, even when the going got tough. Michael Steiner boosted my spirits with his comments on some of the chapters of my book and his supportive suggestions. Benjamim Hubbard talked to me at length about interfaith programs in Orange County and about the Iowa School of Religion, where he studied. As a guest in the History Reading Group, led by Margaret Nash at UC Riverside, I received helpful feedback, not only from her but also from her students. For many years the gemütlich Women's History Reading Group has sharpened my wits through lively discussions. My dear friend Karen Lystra, a published scholar and a woman of sparkling intellect, curiosity and generous heart, was a constant source of wisdom for me as I wrote this book.

My special thanks to the following URC participants who generously agreed to be interviewed by me about their experiences at the University Religious Conference. Some of them also gave me related documents. I shall always be grateful to them: Bill Burke and Jean Burke and their daughter Sharon Burke, John Burnside, Diane Donoghue, Luke Fishburn, Irvin Goldring, Marian Hargrave, Gilbert Harrison, Robert Hine, Joan Meyersieck Rosen, and Martin Rosen. I am especially grateful to Marian Hargrave for her ongoing support. She has been an untiring cheerleader for this book and gave me copies of dozens of documents about the URC.

The librarians at the University of Iowa Special Collections and University Archives were most accommodating, efficient, and understanding in filling my requests relating to the manuscript collection of Ora D. Foster. I am most grateful to them for their help. The librarians at the Charles E. Young Library, Special Collections, University Archives, and Oral History Program at UCLA expeditiously filled my requests pertaining to Adaline Guenther. My thanks to them. The staff at the University Archives at the Miller Nichols Library at the University of Missouri at Kansas City provided me with the materials I requested relating to the Student Panel of Americans. My thanks to them, as well.

My thanks above all to the board of trustees and the religious leaders of the University Religious Conference who over the years generously made available URC records for me to research and photograph. These rich and unarchived records include Annual Reports, Budgets, correspondence, and more. I could not have written this book without access to them.

David Congdon has been a wonderful editor and a stalwart champion of my book. I greatly appreciate his efforts on my behalf. Also, I would like to thank the readers whose suggestions have strengthened this book and the helpful staff at the University Press of Kansas.

My father, Charles Shankman, always had a twinkle in his eye and a funny story to tell. My mother, Ethel Bernstein Shankman, was more serious but a hippie at heart. Both of them were the children of immigrants and were glad to be Americans. They taught me to be grateful. My late brother, Al Shankman, always took pleasure in my successes. My brave daughters, Elizabeth Nettleship and Anna Nettleship, never cease to amaze me with their pioneering spirit and creativity. They are lights of my life. My husband, William Nettleship, has been my soulmate for more than half a century. The conversation we began at Columbia on the Upper West Side of Manhattan continues today in California, and we are still going strong. He has helped me in countless ways, the least of them being the thousands of photographs he took of the documents that are a major source for this book.

Introduction

Education and Pluralism

Let us declare that we can do this by acknowledging and not denying our pluralism
. . . our bitter contradictions, our victories and humane gifts to the world.
—*David W. Blight,* New York Times, *July 18, 2020*

Something caught Muriel Clark's eye one day on campus at UCLA. "The thing that made me walk all the way down to the village and climb the stairs to the second floor was a little folder I picked up on the library table on campus," recalled Clark in the 1950s. "It had a picture of a Methodist church, a Lutheran church, a Jewish synagogue, and a Catholic church on the front. I was completely stunned—in my little hometown of Hardy, Nebraska, there had been two churches—a Methodist and a Lutheran and we were adept in cutting each other's throat at every opportunity." The folder was from the University Religious Conference (URC), an extracurricular interfaith center for UCLA students, located within blocks of the campus. Clark decided to join.[1]

How strange and liberating the URC folder must have appeared to Clark, a young woman reared in a world of religious friction, characteristic not only of life in some American small towns but present in medium and large cities, too. Melting away such friction and replacing it with bonds of inclusion, shared ideals, and common cause are elusive goals, no less today than in Clark's world of the 1930s and 1940s. This is not to suggest that among the founding documents and legal precedents of the United States, none gave voice to such goals. But bringing them into focus and translating them from abstractions into practical, concrete actions is a different matter.

During the course of the twentieth century, the URC developed programs to further fellowship among university students of various religions, and later, among university students of various races and ethnicities. *Interfaith Inclusion* argues that building bonds of inclusion among diverse groups in American society was the work not only of prominent politicians, intellectuals, religious leaders, writers, missionaries, civil rights activists, and others in the spotlight but also of grass roots amateurs and volunteers with a practical bent and a sense of fairness and civic duty. Those amateurs and volunteers included URC students, other university and college students, high school pupils, teachers, and counselors, and suburban housewives and mothers. Some of them had experienced exclusion. Others had not. Many of them told personal stories in public that revealed their human side. All of them participated in projects that carried a message of American inclusion. Few know that the URC was a major source of those projects and the connections among the participants. Few know that the inclusive multifaith origins of the URC were modeled on policies of the War Department during the First World War. Few know of its spread from UCLA to other institutions of higher education in California, or of its spread in a changed form to universities and communities nationwide and its program of summer travel to India, where URC students broadened their embrace of inclusion.

This book is a narrative history that recounts how the URC programs of student action became vehicles for student bonding and religious sentiment. Through interviews and primary sources, the book reveals the interactions, experiences, and perceptions of Catholic, Jewish, Protestant, nonreligious and other URC students. It also brings to light the aims and plans of the adult religious, academic, and community leaders who helped to establish and direct the URC. The book begins by looking at the background of interfaith fellowship in the context of the First World War, which contributed to the founding of the URC in 1928 as a multifaith institution, and to its predecessor, the Iowa School of Religion (ISR) at the University of Iowa in 1927. The ISR was the first tri-faith school of religion at an American state university.[2] The book then switches focus to URC student programs of inclusion. By telling the URC story, its origins and legacies, and demonstrating how multifaith equality and inclusion were at its core, I seek to build upon the historical literature on American religion and university education, to enliven it, and to interpret and frame important issues and ideas, some of them raised by other scholars.

Various books written about the First World War have studied American military interfaith cooperation and policies of ethnic pluralism and discussed how they were used in the war effort.[3] Scholars have also looked at the establishment of a professional tri-faith military chaplaincy and tri-faith Commission on Training Camp Activities that furthered wartime religious cooperation.[4] *Interfaith Inclusion* shows that these wartime military policies left a legacy that influenced the ISR and the URC.

Other scholars have looked at the history of American religion in civilian life. K. Healan Gaston, for example, traces the history and significance of the term "Judeo-Christian," commonly used during and after the Second World War, and its tri-faith antecedents, before and after the First World War, suggesting that these terms marked anti-secular movements.[5] Although begun in part as an institution to combat student secularism and materialism, by 1935, seven years after its founding, the URC attracted students who were leaders, rather than those who were religious, and developed programs of social service that were outside the scope of conventional religion. My book argues that as an educational and religious institution, the URC sought to stimulate student discussion and dialogue and to further diverse student opinions and critical thinking. Anti-secularism, in the conventional sense, faded as a major URC goal, while inclusion through social service projects gained prominence.

Numerous scholars have argued that American religious pluralism was a Jewish project.[6] They view Jewish Americans as both insiders and outsiders who saw pluralism as a way to reconcile assimilation with maintaining Jewish identity. *Interfaith Inclusion* demonstrates that certain Protestant individuals and institutions also played a major but different role in shaping American religious pluralism.

Strengthening this line of argument, Davis Mislin examines religious cooperation among Protestants, Catholics, and Jews in the 1920s, tracing its roots back to the nineteenth century. The protagonists were principally drawn from different Protestant denominations but occasionally included Catholic and Jewish communities too. Mislin's study discusses the postwar Committee on Goodwill, organized by the Federal Council of Churches of Christ, the Amos Society, and the American Association on Religion in State Colleges and Universities (AAR). Although he discusses the connection between the AAR and the ISR, he omits the URC.[7] *Interfaith Inclusion* contrasts the ISR and the URC, showing how the URC was less academic than the ISR and relied less upon a formal course of religious study and more upon extracurricular interfaith student religious programs emphasizing service and cooperation.

Scholars generally think of the National Conference of Christians and Jews (NCCJ), established in 1927, and its founder, Everett R. Clinchy, as central to solidifying an enlarged American religious identity that included Protestants,

Catholics, and Jews.[8] The URC, although hardly known, also worked for decades on this tri-faith goal, from the 1920s to the 1970s. In fact, the URC teamed up with the NCCJ and functioned as its Southern California branch from the mid-1930s through the Second World War. Like the NCCJ, the URC portrayed Jews and Catholics as sympathetic figures and legitimate Americans who should be treated as equal to Protestants. Unlike the NCCJ, however, the URC began dealing with racial issues from 1935, when it launched a program of summer camps for disadvantaged children, many of them African American or Mexican, and some of them Native American. In addition, in the later 1930s, Tom Badley, who went on to become the first African American mayor of Los Angeles (from 1973 to 1993), joined the URC. More than that, for a time he lived in a small dormitory in the URC building in Westwood, flouting existing racial restrictions in the neighborhood. He became a close friend of Adaline Guenther, then the assistant executive secretary of the URC. They remained close friends until she died in 1975, and he gave a eulogy at her memorial service.[9] The URC also developed student panels that offered public programs on racial, ethnic, and religious inclusion beginning in 1942.

Related books look at expanding American acceptance of immigrant and marginalized groups in the 1920s, and thereafter. For example, Diana Selig looks at the cultural gifts movement (CGM) and discusses its history, ideas and programs. The CGM and the URC resembled each other in their goal of expanding acceptance of groups considered alien by many Americans. Begun after the passage of the Reed-Johnson Act of 1924 that severely restricted immigration, and continuing to the Second World War, the CGM developed programs, distributed materials, and worked with teachers and administrators nationally to teach school children, from kindergarten to high school, about the cultural gifts given to them by recent immigrant groups and marginalized minority groups.[10]

Also in the field of education, Jeffrey E. Mirel studies the public schools over several decades, including the 1920s, and focuses on four American cities. In part, he examines civic education in the 1920s, also called civic Americanization (CA), and argues that it led to patriotic pluralism, a realization by recent immigrants "that the best way to defend their cultural distinctiveness was to become patriotic Americans committed to defending democracy."[11] Different as they were, the CGM, CA, and the URC all used education to oppose the exclusion and bigotry of the 1920s. Although the CGM, CA, and the URC worked separately, they each sought to create a context for accepting diversity at a time when numerous white Protestant Americans were rejecting the changes brought about by the First World War and the recent arrival of some fifteen million immigrants, mostly Jewish and Catholic, from Eastern and Southern Europe.[12] Just as the CGM and CA saw immigration as a positive influence on American culture, the URC saw the First World War as providing a usable model for promoting fellowship among students of different faiths.

A pivotal figure in the development of interfaith cooperation during the First World War and in the decade after the war was Ora D. Foster, Congregational minister and YMCA war worker. Foster's background and education, as well as his experience working with the military during the war, fitted him to collaborate with Catholic and Jewish clergy and scholars to develop interfaith organizations.

Like other liberal academics and religious leaders of the day, he saw science and religion as compatible and feared that the teaching of religion by the churches was falling behind the teaching of the sciences by the faculties at universities, thus aggravating what he saw as cynicism, materialism, and secularism in the postwar generation of university students.[13] Foster came out of the war with a sense of urgency and mission about raising the level of religious teaching to that of the sciences and of bringing religion to secular universities to help restore the moral compass of postwar university students. After the war he worked with those of various faiths and like mind to achieve these goals.

As a Wilsonian progressive, Foster looked to service, organization, efficiency, morality, and self-improvement as means of accomplishing positive change. He agreed that good government, education, expertise, the rule of law, and international cooperation could better civilization. Foster also shared some of Wilson's blind spots. An intellectual like the twenty-eighth president, Foster was at times rigid and looked down on those of lesser education who disagreed with him, as we shall see in the next chapter. Although not an active racist like Wilson, Foster appears to have accepted the demeaning racial stereotypes of the day, despite his great admiration for George W. Carver, likely because of his scientific talents and his deep Christian beliefs. An opponent of the Ku Klux Klan and hardly a xenophobe, Foster nevertheless kept his focus on building support for interfaith institutions in higher education, rather than on immigration. Most remarkable, from the perspective of *Interfaith Inclusion*, was the fact that Foster was a religious seeker who found wisdom in other religions, perhaps *more* wisdom at times, than in his own Protestantism. His relationship with religious men, especially Jewish and Catholic religious men of intellectual stature, led to his stubborn advocacy for Jewish and Catholic men having an equal place with Protestant men, at least as much as possible, in the projects he undertook.

Inhabiting a man's world, Foster took easily to being away from women. He was a man's man who valued masculinity, vigor, physical strength, and fellowship among men and hardly thought about women at all. Having given up the life of a parish minister, he took up the more itinerant existence of an academic, an organizer, and a war worker. Although married and the father of three daughters, he spent most of his time away from home, traveling around Europe in connection with his wartime religious work. When he returned, he traveled widely for the Council of Church Boards of Education (CCBE), an organization of more than twenty Protestant boards of education, with the goal of coordinating their programs. While working for the CCBE Foster traveled nationally to help organize the AAR and to help establish what became the ISR and the URC.

Foster was born in 1877 and raised in rural Indiana. He and his family belonged to the Church of the Brethren, which recognized him as an able young person and educated him at Brethren schools. After receiving art training, Foster earned an A.B. degree in classical languages at Manchester College, where he taught Latin. After Manchester, he left the Brethren schools and attended the Oberlin Graduate School of Theology, where he studied divinity and philosophy and received a bachelor of divinity and a master of arts in 1909. He briefly attended the University of Chicago, after which he attended Yale University. There he taught Greek and received a PhD in biblical languages and literature in 1912.[14]

As a result of the years Foster spent at Oberlin and Yale, he left behind the pietistic world of the Church of the Brethren. He came to embrace a wider world of Protestant intellectual ferment and biblical studies at a time when science and academic rigor were being brought to bear on religious thought. In this period, he encountered the ideas of some of the best academics of the day. One of them was Congregationalist author and educator Henry Churchill King, who had taught mathematics, philosophy, and theology at Oberlin, and was president of Oberlin when Foster studied with him. King introduced

Foster to the work of Episcopalian Andrew Dickson White, a nineteenth- and early twentieth-century academic, diplomat, politician, and the first president of Cornell University.[15]

White and King influenced Foster's emerging liberal Protestant views. White's two- volume *History of Warfare of Science with Theology in Christendom*, published in 1896, defended the compatibility of science and religion. It took the position that modern science was compatible with religion when freed from theological dogma. Other Protestant educators, academics, and reformers at the time held similar views, among them philosopher John Dewey.[16] Charles Eliot, president of Harvard, and Daniel Coit Gilman, president of Johns Hopkins, saw science as indispensable to morality.[17] White's chapters on astronomy, geology, and medicine heightened Foster's interest in the natural sciences, and he was impressed with the argument that "true religion and science are allies in their war against the divisive theology."[18] King and White had convinced him "to put more dependence in approaching the Creator through scientific research than through obscurantist theologians." Foster left Oberlin convinced of the connection between science and religion and between academic and religious learning.[19]

Foster's years at Yale developed his scholarship of biblical languages and gave him ongoing experience teaching Greek. His doctoral dissertation, "Literary Relations of the First Epistle of Peter," was a linguistic analysis that examined Greek and other ancient languages associated with the Bible. In short, Foster's academic training at Oberlin and Yale gave him new and broader knowledge of the role of science, history, and linguistics in understanding religion.

After graduating from Yale, Foster became a Congregational minister and served a parish in Portchester, New York, and then in Madison, Wisconsin, near the university. There he encountered the impressive Jewish psychology professor Joseph Jastrow, likely the first Jew Foster came to know. Soon thereafter Foster gave up the life of a minister for the life of an academic, teaching for three years at the YMCA College in Chicago.[20]

The time Foster spent in Chicago brought him in contact with more Jewish scholars: physics professor and Nobel Prize winner Albert A. Michelson, who was on the faculty at the University of Chicago, and Emil G. Hirsch, the principal rabbi at the city's Temple Sinai. Foster admired both of them. In particular, the sense of kinship he developed with Hirsch was striking. Hirsch introduced Foster "to the thinking and work of a rabbi." "No few times, was I at his feet." "[He] had about him a cosmic atmosphere" and "begot in me a deeper respect for and ever warmer attraction to not only him but also the people of his race." His "mammoth library filled with immortal tomes of the ages," his "encyclopedic mind," and "profundity in knowledge of Semitic languages and literature, the Talmud and Rabbinical lore" appear to have made a mark on the still impressionable Foster, who was almost forty years old at the time.[21]

Years later, when he looked back on his time with Hirsch, Foster recalled, "An hour with him in his office at the Temple came at a pivotal point. . . . Who could have better prepared me for later interfaith thinking and relationships? Without the contacts with these Jewish scholars, I do not see how I could have worked so naturally and easily in later years with so many of the greatest Jews of my generation," Foster reflected on the time he had spent with Jastrow, Michelson, and Hirsch. "Their Moses, Amos, Micah, Hosea, yes their Jehovah, were also mine; while my Jesus and Paul were by blood and basic teaching by no means alien to them." Foster experienced "a feeling of oneness with them," and his bond with Hirsch was unusual, especially in the prewar period, when Protestants were dominant in the United States and confident of their superiority over other religions.[22]

Hopes of Christianizing the Jews held sway in some Protestant circles, sometimes in subtle ways. For example, according to historian Robert Handy, the prominent Protestant social gospel leader Walter Rauschenbusch attempted to win over Jews by "broaden[ing] the concept of Christianization" and "magnify[ing] the person of Jesus Christ . . . exalt[ing] his moral teachings apart from the trapping of institutional religion."[23] Protestant outreach at the time "exuded a tacit or explicit religiocultural triumphalism . . . identifying American nationalism with evangelical Christianity and American democracy with the Protestant temper," wrote Jewish historian Bennie Kraut.[24]

Given what Kraut saw as the sense of Protestant "triumphalism," its commanding majority, and cultural domination in American society at the time, Foster stood out among Protestants in his willingness to regard Jews as legitimate fellow seekers, and he was atypical in seeking out contemporary Jews as a source of wisdom. His empathy with them prepared him to become an advocate for expanding religious inclusion when he joined the American war effort with the YMCA, after three years of teaching with the YMCA in Chicago.

Despite his background in the Church of the Brethren, a pacificist denomination, Foster supported the war. Like Woodrow Wilson, "who furnished the key for placing the war on a holy plane—to make the world safe for democracy," Foster saw the war in religious terms. Other religious leaders who supported the war included Samuel McCrea Cavert, assistant secretary of the General Wartime Commission of the Churches; Frank Mason North, president of the Federal Council of the Churches of Christ; and Harry Emerson Fosdick, a well-known theologian from Union Theological Seminary.[25] Moreover, Harry Emerson Fosdick, and others like William Adams Brown, and William Herbert Perry Faunce, saw building Protestant religious fellowship as a central issue of the war. Foster did too.[26] His prewar experiences with Jewish men had prepared him to go beyond Protestant ecumenism, however, and his experiences in the war and thereafter gave him further opportunities to embrace and apply religious inclusion on a deeper level.

The First World War is the starting point for *Interfaith Inclusion*. In its early chapters, I demonstrate how the war furthered cooperation and fellowship among participants of different religions and provided the personal contacts and models that Foster used to organize Comrades in Service (CIS). The organization began as a Protestant YMCA program for training recruits and evolved into a tri-faith partnership of military and civilian personnel at the end of the war. CIS provided religious, educational, and health services, first for the military at home, and later, for soldiers and sailors stationed abroad. Foster's experiences with the CIS and the common wartime sacrifice of Catholic, Protestant, and Jewish military personnel led him to attempt duplicating in civilian life the interfaith fellowship, cooperation and service he had known in the war. After the war, Foster—along with other allied Protestant, Jewish, and Catholic religious, community, and academic men, some of whom he knew from the war—formed the AAR, with developing interfaith institutions at state universities.

Notwithstanding Foster's pioneering activities, the historical literature has paid little notice to them, to the institutions he helped to found, to those who for decades directed them, or to the grassroots projects that followed. Scholars of the history of pluralism have focused on the NCCJ and its founder, Everett Clinchy. Others have paid attention to the intellectual Horace Kallen, credited with originating the concept of cultural pluralism, and Will Herberg, popular religious sociologist and author of *Protestant-Catholic-Jew*. Moreover, the literature on the First World War has largely ignored the bonding of Catholics, Jews, and Protestants in common sacrifice and wartime fellowship and how that legacy influenced Foster in helping to found the CIS.[27] This book seeks to recover that almost forgotten story.

The manuscript collection of O. D. Foster's papers at Special Collections and University Archives at the University of Iowa Library documents that the URC and its various subsequent programs were themselves descendants of War Department policies of religious pluralism in the First World War. Researching these materials made it clear that Foster's experiences in the First World War influenced him to help establish CIS as a tri-faith organization that promoted interfaith projects in civilian life. The collections at Iowa included materials on CIS, the AAR, the founding of the ISR, and the URC.

Interfaith Inclusion sees Foster's crowning achievement as helping to found the URC as a successful multifaith institution based on interfaith fellowship. The main part of the story, however, unfolds after Foster's departure in 1928, and thus the book looks at how URC students of diverse religions bonded together and continued to expand upon those ties to include students of diverse racial and ethnic backgrounds as well.

I found most of the records on the URC student activities, unarchived, in the files at the URC building, since torn down, as well as at UCLA Special Collections and University Archives, and in other archives and private collections. In addition, many of the voices of the URC students were expressed in the personal interviews I conducted with former URC members. These sources revealed that cooperative service projects helped the URC students develop a sense of fellowship more effectively than conventional churchly institutions and religious programs. As service activities increasingly came to propel the religious vision of the URC, connections to traditional religious organizations and conventional religious activities lost ground.

Two graduates described the purpose of the URC as "a vehicle and a symbol of the trials and glories of the brotherhood of mankind."[28] *Interfaith Inclusion* brings to light these URC student experiences, how they reflected and shaped their values, and also on a broader scale, how those values took on national and international scope in URC programs and were handed on as legacies to other organizations that continued through the 1990s.

URC executive secretary Thomas Evans accumulated years of experience with social projects over the decades as a former YMCA student leader and came up with scores of suggestions for similar community social projects in the 1930s. Evans also began applying ideas derived from John Dewey, from the sciences, and from then-current ideas in progressive education. He hosted wide-ranging, democratic, collaborative student discussion sessions based on science and problem solving. These ideas were gaining ground in YMCA circles and among liberal Protestant leaders in the late 1920s and 1930s. The rationale for these sessions was that they would lead students to "creative social thinking" that could be tested in the real world.[29]

Adaline Guenther was a force of brilliant dynamism at the URC, at a time when few women had the opportunity to exercise such influence over university students, many of them male.[30] Not only did she call upon her prodigious skills as an organizer and her magnetism with students to implement some of the social programs first suggested by Evans but she also continued the salon-like discussions among URC members that he had begun. When he could no longer host them, she took them over and gave them even more cachet, entertaining the students in her own living room. She held these gatherings for more than a decade after succeeding Evans as executive secretary of the URC in the mid-1940s. Under the leadership of Evans and Guenter, URC activism and salon-like discussions became effective means of building fellowship among students of different faiths and of none.

In addition, Evans and Guenther undertook cooperative ventures with the NCCJ; later, Guenther undertook cooperative ventures with the American Jewish Committee. Both of those organizations had their own tradition of religious pluralism and social reform, and cooperation with them enlivened URC programs.

The settlement house movement was a favorite institution of Evans and other progressives like Foster, as it was for leaders of the cultural gifts movement.[31] Settlement houses were places of residence for well-educated volunteers, university and college students or recent graduates, or young professionals. The residents sought to help their neighbors who lacked basic social services and cultural amenities. The first settlement house, Toynbee Hall, was founded in the Whitechapel neighborhood of East London in the 1870s, by Anglican clergyman Samuel Barnett. Like the URC, it began as a religious endeavor and gained a following primarily through programs outside conventional religious channels but with strong religious undercurrents.

After the founding of Toynbee Hall, the settlement house movement spread in Britain and to the United States. Located in urban centers, American settlement houses tended to serve immigrant neighborhoods. Typically founded and led by a well-educated social reformer or clergyman who lived at the settlement house along with well-educated, middle-class, resident volunteers, these associations sought to improve the social conditions of the population living nearby, through social, health, and cultural programs, and to learn about their immigrant neighbors.[32]

One of the best-known leaders of the American settlement house movement was Jane Addams of Hull House, located in Chicago's Nineteenth Ward. Addams directly influenced Thomas Evans, who knew her and also E. C. Moore, provost of UCLA when the URC was established. Moore and his wife had been settlers at Hull House.

The URC was not a settlement house, but it developed a similar spirit and a few similar programs, such as neighborhood social service and cultural events. The URC used some of those programs to give scope to student and graduate activism on campus, and in the larger community. Like the activities of the settlement houses, as *Interfaith Inclusion* demonstrates, those community activities reflected the views of privileged people who thought they could lead the way for people less privileged than themselves. Nevertheless, most of the URC students were far from rich. In fact, that is why some of them attended UCLA, which, at the time, had no tuition and limited fees. As students, they had few resources to spare, and many of them held jobs after school. Despite this, the URC sought to develop a practical sense of public service among the students, which at times came to resemble a sense of noblesse oblige.

As an educational institution, the URC undertook community programs not only to aid less privileged neighbors but primarily to have the university students experience fellowship with other students by working together on common service projects. Like the settlement house social reformers, the URC students and their religious leaders had confidence that American institutions could be shaped to reflect what they took to be American values of fairness, decency, and public service.

Evans and Foster were liberal Protestants, as were many of the supporters of the IRC and the UCR. Even before the 1920s, we can trace a division in American society between those "ecumenical" or modernist Protestants and those who subscribed to a literal reading of the Bible. At the time, liberal Protestants supported the teaching of Darwinian evolution and science generally, biblical scholarship, and linguistic analysis. Like other liberal Protestants of the day, Foster saw science and scholarship as compatible with religion. He accepted the apparent contradictions they presented and incorporated them into his broad understanding of the Bible. A priority of liberal Protestants was to accommodate to the modern world while fundamentalist and similarly minded Protestants favored adherence to earlier religious traditions.[33]

By and large Jewish groups echoed similar divisions between modernizers and traditionalists. American Jews, for instance, were broadly divided into three separate groups: Reform, Conservative, and Orthodox. Reform and some Conservative Jews tended to be more receptive to tri-faith cooperation than the others, including most Orthodox Jews. The latter tended to be more suspicious of ploys to convert Jews to Christianity or were more concerned with exclusively Jewish issues and had little interest in cooperating with those outside the fold. For the most part, they were from the lands of the Austrian and Russian Empires and had arrived in the United States more recently than had the Reform Jews, most of whom had emigrated in the mid-nineteenth century from the older German speaking lands. Overall, Protestant outreach appealed mainly to liberal Reform Jewish "cooperators."[34] It seemed to promise them legitimacy and parity with Protestantism. Still other Jews included free thinkers, secularists, or atheists who resisted fitting into the Orthodox, Conservative, or Reform branches of Judaism.[35] For Jews of all persuasions, however, good will movements that called for cooperation and fellowship among Protestants, Catholics, and Jews, at times aroused suspicion of hidden motivations to convert Jews to Christianity. Small wonder that some caution, hesitancy, and ambivalence persisted among Jews and Jewish communities overall when it came to certain good will efforts in American society.[36]

For their part, Catholic lay communities had numerous internal divisions, reflecting ethnic origins, levels of education, and length of time present in the United States. The Catholic bishops were divided on the issue of supporting cooperative efforts with Jews and Protestants. Most of them opposed such cooperation. Both those who supported such efforts and those who opposed them seemed closed to compromising with their Roman Catholic coreligionists. Another major divisive issue for Catholics was whether to support public higher education. Although Catholic parochial education was already being implemented, the increasing number of Catholic students at public universities divided Catholics in America on whether any support should be given to students at those universities and, if so, how much. At the turn of the century American Catholics, like Protestants and Jews, faced divisions within, often between modernizers and traditionalists. The Catholic modernizers supported Americanism, that is, full Catholic participation in American life. The Catholic traditionalists advocated separation from American life and what they saw as an unwelcoming society with too much individualism and materialism.

The First World War appeared to have settled the matter in favor of the Catholic modernizers. The term Americanism "reappeared in Catholic discourse in the context . . . [of] World War I," wrote historian Philip Gleason, himself a Catholic, who concluded that the division was bridged "in favor of the modernizing reformers." The war also led to the founding of the National Catholic War Council, which, after the war, continued as the National Catholic Welfare Conference and "gave the church a more effective voice in Public affairs," and "a new era of purposeful Catholic participation in American life."[37]

Yet those opportunities for participation in American civilian life seem to have created ambivalence for some Catholic religious leaders and writers in their conflicting desires for separation from American culture and for assimilation.[38] Such ambivalence was reflected in the behavior of the Catholic hierarchy, which shifted back and forth on its position of cooperating with Protestants and Jews, although, as we will see, while the hierarchy mostly opposed these united efforts, some individual lay Catholics did not.

Prominent American Protestants were also disoriented and conflicted by the prospect and then the experience of the war. American icons ranging from pragmatic intellectuals like John Dewey to political leaders like Woodrow Wilson were ambivalent about whether or not America should join the conflict. This ambivalence contributed to contradictions and inconsistencies. Although Dewey had shown "increasing impatience with pacifists" in 1916, and wound up supporting American entry into the war in 1917, he warned that "national hesitation must not be ended" and that America must pressure the allies to fight for "Democracy and Civilization." Not unlike Dewey, Wilson came to see the violence of war as a necessary price to pay in order to preserve civilization and democracy. His speech to Congress in April of 1917 portrayed America as a disinterested protector of democracy, a war aim that had an altruistic cosmic dimension. As such his speech was "a genuinely great and stirring expression of the best qualities of . . . the civilization of the United States in the recent past," wrote intellectual historian Henry F. May.[39]

The League of Nations, the international body that Wilson proposed, reflected an international dimension that was shared by religious Wilsonian progressives like Foster. The idea that collective security and negotiation could largely replace war and ultimately bring world peace also appealed to others who thought that perhaps war itself could be outlawed.[40] Still others saw the League of Nations as part of Wilson's (and America's) Christian religious mission.[41] Wilson himself "believed that *America's* history offered salvation to the world," wrote historian David Kennedy.[42]

Some religious leaders saw the war as an apocalyptic event and harbored visions of overcoming long-standing sectarian divisions. "In the fusing fires of battle, Presbyterian, Methodist, Episcopalian, Unitarian, and even Catholic, Protestant and Jew have been melted, and now flow into a single flaming stream," declared an article in the *Methodist Review* of 1919. "Man after man has returned from the front to tell us that the denominational church is dead."[43]

The common wartime participation and sacrifice of Protestants, Catholics, and Jews in the American military and the apparent destruction of the barriers that had divided them led Foster to build on the good will that he had experienced before and during the war and had embodied in CIS. Like other Wilsonian progressives, Foster had high hopes following the defeat of Germany. Could tri-faith inclusion be within reach? At least on Foster's part, replicating the wartime bond of tri-faith inclusion at state-supported universities appears to have taken on missionary proportions, no doubt necessary for what turned out to be a complex and daunting task.

Even the founding of UCLA was in part a response to the First World War. Its principal founder, E. C. Moore, later to become the provost of UCLA, was influenced by the war, although not a participant in it. The war caused him to emphasize the importance of public elementary school teachers, since he thought that they, more than anyone else, were the ones to teach children the facts and skills that set the foundation for democratic values, ideals, and social relations. Contrary to German elementary education, which, he argued, had taught children the foundation for obedience, atheism, authority, and power, American teachers needed to have a grounding in the liberal arts, in classical civilization and the ethics of Western religion.[44] Moore sought to fill the need for such study by remedying the recent decline in the teaching of the liberal arts at American Normal Schools (schools for training teachers). Within these institutions, the liberal arts were then being replaced with industrial training, home economics, and vocational subjects.[45]

As the former president of the California Normal School, he was convinced that teacher training needed to include a program of three to four years studying the liberal arts at a university. Such a program came to be offered at UCLA, which was originally founded to train teachers. Moore thought that a revival of the liberal arts was necessary, since teachers would become an important civilizing influence upon youth and would have the power to deter future wars. Moore was not alone. With the wartime destruction of Europe, other educators too, came to see American higher education as the surviving carrier of civilization and began offering courses in Western civilization at various universities at this time.[46]

Like E. C. Moore, Foster believed that public education could play a vital role in transmitting democratic values. Also, like Moore, he came to that conclusion as a result of the war. Once the URC was established and Foster left the scene, his ideas were shaped and reshaped in the hands of others, notably Thomas Evans, Adaline Guenther, and the students who participated in the URC. In their hands, Foster's vision grew beyond crossing faith boundaries to crossing racial and ethnic boundaries as well. As one URC graduate put it, "Out of the diversity of backgrounds, interests, religions, talents, could come the mutual respect and the common searching which is such a precious and essential aspect of the democratic way of life, and I think many of us, probably most of us . . . came out of it different people. Better people, if you will."[47]

CHAPTER ONE

Religious Cooperation in Wartime

Founded as it is, on the highest ideals of comradeship and service, it has been a large factor in helping the morale of the troops.

—*John J. Pershing, commander in chief, American Expeditionary Force, writing about Comrades in Service, letter reprinted in* Tribune (Chicago), *June 18, 1919*

Wartime Military and Pluralism

Like many Americans, President Woodrow Wilson viewed the United States as a Protestant nation when it entered the First World War in April of 1917. But the exigencies of the war conflicted with this view. American entry into the war required building an effective, mass army out of a diverse group of recruits. Previously, the United States had a small professional army, which now needed to be expanded. Of necessity, Catholic and Jewish recruits, many of them recent immigrants or the children of immigrants (primarily from Southern and Eastern Europe), were drafted and ultimately comprised more than one fifth of the wartime troops. Unlike the European armies, which had separate units for specific religious and ethnic groups, the newly professionalized American army integrated recruits of differing religious, geographic, and ethnic backgrounds into common units. That modern army eventually grew to four million service members.[1]

In order to maintain high troop morale and moral standards, the War Department organized the Commission on Training Camp Activities (CTCA), a partnership of the military and civilian organizations, then called welfare organizations, to provide religious, educational, recreational, health, and kindred services for the military. At first, Wilson named the Young Man's Christian Association (YMCA), an interdenominational Protestant organization, as the only member of the CTCA. The religious diversity of the recruits, however, along with pressure exerted by Catholic and Jewish interests, led him and Secretary of War Newton Baker to expand CTCA membership to include Catholic and Jewish organizations. Eventually, the CTCA came to include not only the YMCA but also the Jewish Welfare Board (JWB), the Knights of Columbus (KofC), the Salvation Army (SA), and the Young Women's Christian Association (YWCA), as well as the War Camp Community Service and the American Library Association.[2] The commission encouraged the member organizations to cooperate with each other, which included such practices as having diverse religious groups share worship space when needed.[3]

Responding to ethnic differences among the immigrant recruits, the War Department also devised several special developmental programs, some taught in immigrant native tongues. Although those programs were intended to train the recruits for military service and to build their American identity, they also allowed the recruits to retain some of their cultural traditions, when necessary. The ultimate goal was for the immigrant recruits to serve as *American* soldiers, not as Poles, Italians, or other foreigners, and for immigrants and native-born alike to be regarded and treated as Americans soldiers.[4]

Another part of creating this new wartime military involved professionalizing the chaplaincy, and for the first time, accepting chaplains into the military. The Army granted chaplains military officer ranks and set standards for their acceptance. The large number of Catholic and Jewish troops, and the shortage of chaplains, made it necessary for the War Department to simplify religious identities into three broad categories: Protestant, Catholic, and Jewish, and when necessary, to require chaplains to minister to adherents of these religions. When the chaplains ministered to those of religions other than their own, they were not to proselytize but to abide by the relevant religious practices.[5] This tri-faith policy not only seemed to indicate the importance of religious observance in military life and the desire of the military to have soldiers practice religion to save them from immoral behavior—it also officially recognized that Catholic and Jewish recruits from Europe were important to the war effort.[6] Moreover, these recruits were placed in white units served by white chaplains. This practice per force granted them white status despite the prevalence at the time of racial hierarchies that placed them near the bottom or outside the white category.[7] During this era, most Americans in the military and in civilian life identified as white Protestant, and many of them still regarded Catholics and Jews as outsiders, as the rise of the Ku Klux

Klan and the increase of nativism and bigotry in the postwar era and the 1920s demonstrate.

Notwithstanding the wartime military expansion of American religious and ethnic identity among the European-born recruits, strict racial barriers remained and excluded American soldiers of African background. The racial divide separated white troops and their white chaplains from African American troops and their African American chaplains. More than 370,000 African Americans served in the First World War, almost half of them in noncombatant units at home. About another two hundred thousand served in France, alongside French troops in combat units. There they were welcomed, issued weapons, and honored for their service. When these soldiers returned home, however, they were often met with violence, as race riots took place in about a dozen cities, from Chicago to Omaha and from Washington, DC, to Tulsa. The abusive attitude of white military officers toward African-American soldiers revealed in this chapter align with the racial segregation practiced in the First World War military.[8]

The YMCA at Camp Custer

Comrades in Services began as a YMCA training program at Camp Custer, Michigan. Eventually it developed into an interfaith partnership between the military and various civilian organizations, reaching its full development in Europe at the end of the First World War. Its founding began soon after O. D. Foster arrived at Custer in the fall of 1917. This development was partly a reflection of Foster's prior experience in reaching out to people of religions other than his own, partly an attempt to further wartime religious cooperation, and partly a response to several attempts by the YMCA to dominate the other member organizations of the CTCA. Taking advantage of its wider name recognition, broader public acceptance, larger following, greater funding, and longer history, as well as an earlier and larger presence in the training camps, the YMCA attempted to evangelize the recruits in the training camps. But there were occasions when the YMCA overplayed its hand, one of which occurred at Camp Custer, located in Battle Creek, Michigan.

Hundreds of sergeants fumed when a farewell dance, their first scheduled dance at Camp Custer, was cancelled at the last minute—not by the military but by the YMCA. The dance was to be held in February 1918, at Liberty Auditorium, a YMCA building at the camp. The YMCA camp secretary A. L. Parker, a fundamentalist Methodist opposed to dancing, argued that certain YMCA officials and supporters "would never consent to such usage of a YMCA building." In response, Major General James Parker, the camp commandant, leased another auditorium for the dance, located off the base in downtown Battle Creek. That auditorium would also be used for basketball games, boxing tournaments, and events that might otherwise have been held at Liberty Auditorium. Not only the commandant but certain Y officials also favored holding the dance. "Many of us disapprove of smoking . . . but you will notice that the boys smoke to their heart's content in the 'Y' huts," one of those Y officials declared. "If we barred the smokes, we'd be barring the boys, whom we are here to serve."[9]

This was not the only such dispute over restrictions and YMCA domination. In fact, the dance incident occurred at Custer about the same time as the YMCA was conducting a campaign to evangelize the recruits. Many of the latter stayed away from the evangelical rallies, the YMCA Bible classes, and the Y huts, where they had previously come to relax, socialize, read magazines, play music, and write letters. "'Too narrow minded for us,' is the explanation given by many men now when asked . . . why they have ceased to come to the huts," reported the Detroit Free Press.[10]

Ora D. Foster was the YMCA religious director at Camp Custer at the time. He would later write, "This was the time that the Billy Sunday type of leadership at [YMCA] General Headquarters was strong, and that spirit permeated the proposed Y program, particularly the religious phase of it." (Without question, Foster's view of the Bible was broader than that of his supervisor, A. L. Parker.[11]) Thus, A. L. Parker supported the YMCA evangelical program of "saving souls in Army Camps," which was to be accomplished by having the staff at the camps distribute "war-roll cards" to the trainees. Printed on the cards was the following pledge: "I hereby pledge my allegiance to the Lord Jesus Christ as my Savior and King and by God's help will fight His battles for the victory of His Kingdom."[12] Each trainee was to sign the card and carry it with him. "These cards were seen as the evidence of 'soul saving' and the number of cards signed was to be reported to . . . the Y headquarters."[13]

The evangelical campaign was floundering. To invigorate it, A. L. Parker invited Theodore S. Henderson, the Methodist bishop of Detroit, to conduct mass meetings of the troops in the YMCA Liberty Auditorium. Here war-roll cards were handed out, signed, and collected. "Continuous advertising [of the meetings] was carried on all week" and "the Divisional band played 'Onward Christian Soldiers' . . . as it marched around the camp and to the open double doors of the huge auditorium." Meanwhile, Parker had instructed Foster "to bring an armload of war-roll cards" to the meetings. Despite the fanfare, the meetings were poorly attended, with only about eight hundred troops showing up, and the auditorium less than one third full. Once the meetings began, "two by two, three by three, the men left the hall," Foster recounted.[14]

After one of the disappointing meetings, Parker proceeded to the base hospital with Foster following behind. There, one of the beds caught Parker's attention. On it "lay a pale, emaciated boy of apparent Italian lineage." Parker asked him, "'Are you a saved man?' Looking puzzled, the boy made no reply. He then asked, 'Do you know Jesus Christ?' Clearly the boy was non-plussed—no doubt because he was surely of Catholic parentage. By this time men all over the ward were rising on their elbows in wonderment. Undaunted," Foster explained, "Parker, still having received no vocal response from the boy, and being convinced that the boy wasn't a saved man . . . fell upon his knees by the side of the bed and earnestly plead[ed] with God 'to have mercy on this lost soul.'"[15]

Foster's education and past experience had inclined him to reach out to those of other faiths, but such attitudes were out of favor with the evangelical leadership at YMCA headquarters, and with his boss, A. L. Parker. "I . . . was caught in between and thus left in none too good odor with my superior Y officers," Foster wrote. "Here was my first real head-on with Y institutionalism."[16]

Starting CIS

Foster's position as YMCA religious director at Custer was to supplement the work of the Protestant military chaplains with civilian-led YMCA religious programs for the twenty thousand troops of the Eighty-Fifth Division stationed there. A number of other Protestant religious leaders were also stationed at the camp: four military chaplains, six YMCA workers of several denominations and about twenty civilian camp pastors also of several Protestant denominations. Except for the chaplains, the Protestant religious leaders were sent by the individual churches, the Federal Council of Churches of Christ, and the YMCA. Also present at Custer were a "young, highly educated [and] amiable Rabbi," three Catholic military chaplains, and a secretary of the Knights of Columbus who came to see if he could get around YMCA opposition and set up civilian programs for the Catholic trainees.[17] The war had brought new, inexperienced staff to Custer and created a confusing situation for religious leaders. "Here was I a man of two score years challenged to get this medley of well-intentioned men into a working team. We had 'to learn to fight the war while preparing for it,' and consequently had 'to feel our way through chaos toward order," Foster recalled.[18]

Foster's most daring goal comprised promoting fellowship among the leaders of the various faiths at Custer. He invited the chaplains, the camp pastors, the YMCA religious workers, the local representatives of the KofC, and the rabbi to meet together; the Custer Religious Conference emerged from these meetings. This quasi-governing council met once a week to exchange ideas about the religious programs at the camp. Foster also cultivated a personal friendship with the rabbi and the secretary of the KofC. Interfaith lunches were held, too. For example, the religious workers of all three faiths met regularly at a "good fellowship lunch": "[They] meet every Thursday at noon in a luncheon conference [where] . . . they all loosen up, and laugh a great deal . . . [and a] splendid spirit of fellowship is the big factor in keeping all forces happy and contented. They all feel they are here for service to the soldiers." Some of the religious groups began opening up their activities to others. On Sunday evenings the Methodists offered a ten-cent supper to soldiers of all faiths. On occasion, the Episcopalians opened their doors to all the troops at Custer as well.[19]

In addition to helping organize the Custer Religious Conference, Foster helped organize Comrades in Service, an interfaith organization for the Custer trainees. It included the Jewish, Catholic, and Protestant recruits. As a voluntary, grass-roots organization, the CIS was open to any company of trainees that voted to participate. Each participating company could choose which of the YMCA religious, educational, physical, and entertainment activities to pursue. The CIS comprised Jewish, Catholic, and Protestant subcommittees offering appropriate religious activities to serve their coreligionist recruits, and its company-level organization helped religious leaders find out how many trainees of their flock were in each participating company, a fact they otherwise would not have known.[20]

CIS expressed a progressive outlook, similar to that of Foster himself, of Director of the War Department Newton Baker, and of Raymond B. Fosdick, Baker's assistant. Moreover, despite the fundamentalist religious outlook of A. L. Parker and the YMCA headquarters in New York City at the time, the YMCA at Custer supported the progressive values of the CIS in the secular realm. These values included character building, self-improvement, responsible citizenship, moral training, service, and education.

For example, the YMCA education department at Custer sponsored CIS classes in various subjects, from mathematics and engineering, to French, English, and history; at times, the department arranged a school for illiterates and for elementary education, and lectures for the CIS members on such progressive topics as world government and temperance. The YMCA physical well-being department organized boxing and wrestling contests. It organized baseball teams for the CIS, taught hygiene, or what today would be called sex education, while the entertainment department organized such activities as outdoor movies, company stunts, glee club concerts, and regimental sing-songs. These entertainments attempted to obviate the need for female company and encourage male bonding, generally useful in a military context and in keeping with the then-contemporary emphasis on masculinity.[21]

As a YMCA program, CIS often used the six Y "huts," small buildings the YMCA had built at the camp, for many of its activities. In most ways, CIS was typical of national YMCA programs and values. Contemporaries wrote, "There is a new organization at Camp Custer that already is accomplishing wonders for the moral and spiritual betterment of the men." Moreover, "The members [of the Comrades] were pledged to no creed except a promise to encourage clean stories, clean speech and clean sports in their barracks." They have become "one of the most vital and important moral forces on the grounds." According to an overly enthusiastic article in *Trench and Camp*, the YMCA National War Work Council's weekly newspaper, soon after the Comrades appeared, "gambling, swearing, telling of perverted stories and other mal-practices had stopped in scores of barracks. In the place of these are additional pianos and 'victrolas.'" The title of the article, "The White Comrade," highlights the racial segregation then practiced by the YMCA and the military.[22] Although CIS also served African American recruits, the ubiquitous racial segregation prevented common bonds from developing between them and the white recruits.

The pressures of military life and preparation for war required high morale and esprit de corps. If nothing else, the presence of white Catholic, Jewish, and Protestant trainees in the same unit made religious inclusiveness a practical matter for building unit cohesion, solidarity, common purpose, and a sense of American patriotism. As an organization open to trainees of three different faiths, it was vital that CIS offer not only sports, educational classes, and entertainments but also religious activities that respected the faiths of the recruits in each company. A most important goal was that religious diversity not divide the recruits and that other activities *outside* of institutional religion build strong bonds of fellowship among them. Building such bonds was necessary for building an effective military unit.[23] CIS "grips Private Brown who is a Methodist, as well as Private Rosenstein who is a Jew, and Private Murphy who is a Catholic and Corporal Blank who belongs to no church and disapproves them all," reported "The White Comrade" in *Trench and Camp*.[24] Foster agreed. He later wrote that one of the best things about CIS was how "differences in religious connectedness were taken for granted, respected." In his view, the Comrades furthered a new spirit of respect and legitimacy for white Catholics and Jews, as well as for white Protestants.[25]

In addition to his openness to tri-faith diversity, Foster advocated "super-denominationalism" and appeared to support secularism. In February 1918, he gave a speech that asked, "How could you think of a Baptist Christ or a Congregational Christ? Religion has too long been interpreted from the standpoint of creed. . . . Now at Camp Custer," he continued, "we have touched the spirit of super-denominationalism. We have come to judge men by what they 'do' and 'are' rather than what they believe." He proclaimed, "I cannot conceive of a religion tied up in forms. . . . Personally I feel just as religious in handing a postage stamp to a soldier at Camp Custer as I do on my knees in a downtown church."[26]

Leaving Camp Custer

The YMCA evangelical campaign was in full swing at Custer in February 1918. The movement stood in opposition to the spirit of religious cooperation, respect for religious diversity, and super-denominationalism embodied in the Custer Religious Conference, CIS, and in Foster's February speech. All of this undoubtedly contributed to his conflicts with A. L. Parker and with the leadership at YMCA headquarters in New York City. Foster left Camp Custer in March 1918, likely forced to resign as YMCA religious director.[27]

Exactly what led to his dismissal is unclear. The key problem may have been a conflict of authority with the YMCA national headquarters over the soul saving campaign. Perhaps it was Foster's February speech supporting "super-denominationalism" or his general attitude of independence. Perhaps it was a personality conflict between Foster and Parker, or a conflict over liberal versus fundamentalist religious views that had been brewing ever since Foster first came to Custer six months earlier. Parker was a prominent, well-to-do Methodist from Detroit, a plastering contractor before his war service with the YMCA, and likely had had little formal education. As we have seen, he was a fundamentalist. Foster, on the other hand, was highly educated and sophisticated. He was an academic and a religious leader who did not like taking orders from someone he considered to be inferior to him in education, especially someone who held what he regarded as intolerant, simplistic religious beliefs.

No doubt, Foster's outspoken liberal religious beliefs contributed to his dismissal. A newspaper sub-headline at the time announced, "Friends of Dr. Foster Say He Was 'Canned' for Being Too Liberal." A subheading in the same article states, "Bible Class Causes Row." According to the article, "It has been common knowledge that the theories of Dr. Foster and Mr. Parker have not agreed since the camp began." Foster "was inclined to a liberal interpretation of the Scriptures which would bear a scientific test," whereas Parker "was more inclined to accept literally all the contents of the holy book." As an example of their opposing views, "it was alleged that when Foster was teaching a Bible class, he mentioned that the Bible was "contradictory and could be interpreted in . . . different ways," to which Parker replied, "nothing in the Bible is contradictory" and that the Bible "could only be interpreted but one way."[28]

The hostility between Foster and Parker came to a head, however, over another issue: holding the dance at Custer. While Parker was in Chicago on YMCA business he got wind of the fact that the commandant of the camp, Maj. Gen. James Parker, was planning a farewell ball for the Custer sergeants about to go to the front. It was to be held at the base, at Liberty Auditorium. An article at the time reported that "Mr. [A. L.] Parker opposes dancing as a pastime." and went on to detail how the dance incident "knocked the props from under several hundred soldiers, who, none too friendly to the 'Y' in civil life, had just begun to concede that as an adjunct to the army it was worthy of even an agnostic's admiration. Now they are suspicious again." The dance incident took a toll on YMCA religious activities at Custer, affecting "the evangelistic meetings" and Bible classes and all the activities "that smacked of the religious element."[29]

Although Foster personally approved of the dance, he insisted that he was not the one who gave permission for the event; it is unclear who did. Perhaps no YMCA worker did, and the commandant took the initiative on his own. Parker, nevertheless, believed that Foster was responsible and requested that YMCA headquarters launch an investigation of Foster's alleged insubordination. YMCA headquarters sent two representatives to Custer to investigate. They spent three days there, during which Foster claimed "he never even had a glimpse" of them. After they left, Parker offered Foster a promotion overseas if he would leave Custer at once, quietly and without incident. Foster agreed, and the matter was settled.[30] Nevertheless, suspicion of Parker's motive remained. "Promotion to France 'Camouflage' Is Hint Secretary Parker Denies" cried the sub-headline of an article in the *Detroit Free Press*. According to the article, Foster's removal confirmed his [Foster's] fears "that he would be made the 'goat'" and "a strong suspicion exists that the farewell dinner for Dr. Foster prior to his 'departure for France' was camouflage to cover his exit."[31]

Notwithstanding A. L. Parker's likely disapproval of Foster, it seems clear that there were others at Custer who were sorry to see Foster leave the camp and wanted to honor him. Foster's inclusive approach was appreciated by many at Custer and even by some in positions of authority in the YMCA, despite his rocky tenure and early departure. Commandant Maj. Gen. James Parker and his staff, including the officials at the Base Hospital, as well as the members of the Custer Religious Conference and the officers of CIS all came to the surprise party banquet given for Foster. It was held at the Officers' Mess at the base Divisional Headquarters the night before he left. More than fifty people came to the dinner and toasted him. Several of them delivered after-dinner speeches. According to reports, "All of the speakers emphasized the harmony existing in the religious work circles at the camp and paid a high tribute to the character and ability of Dr. Foster in directing all this work to a common end." One of them, a former classmate of Gen. John Pershing at West Point, Brig. Gen. Julius H. Penn, presented Foster with a watch and "expressed wonder, admiration and pleasure of the unity of effort of so many organizations in camp with widely different beliefs. . . . He spoke with great feeling of his friendship for Dr. Foster." Foster was also presented with a letter signed by twenty-eight Custer chaplains, pastors, and YMCA secretaries (including A. L. Parker) praising him and quoting from the farewell speech of Gen. Julius H. Penn. The staff of *Trench and Camp* also paid tribute to him: "Dr. Foster loved every person in this camp and was personally anxious for the welfare of all."[32]

Soon after he left, Foster was on a troop ship bound for France. As time went by, he came to see the conflict at Custer "not so much between men as to the periods—todays and yesterdays—in which we were living. Our worlds were scarcely tangent, and even the words we used carried different connotations to us."[33] Foster saw himself living at a time when religious cooperation would expand beyond Protestant interdenominationalism, and viewed the war as an opportunity to bring about a new and expanded sense of religious brotherhood. He regarded the evangelistic program of the YMCA as an example of "narrow, sectarian thinking, backward looking and out-of-date." He dismissed the account the YMCA later gave, namely that "secretaries were instructed not to offer the war roll pledge to audiences nor to make public appeal for signatures, nor urge it upon individuals." According to Foster, this was "a 'post-eventum' means of getting around the storm that was turned against . . . the uses of the War Roll Cards."[34]

The YMCA was a large and complex organization that hurriedly added many thousands of new staff members during the war. The new staff included Protestants of various religious persuasions: some were liberal Protestants like Foster, others fundamentalists like A. L. Parker and likely uncomfortable with Foster's broad embrace of liberal religion. Notwithstanding likely opposition from some fundamentalist quarters, the YMCA continued to support CIS, even after Foster left for France.

During the time that Foster was at Custer, the CIS program had expanded to other training camps in the United States. Indeed, the YMCA had an interest in expanding it, for several reasons. The program was popular with the troops; it taught YMCA values; it made use of all four of the YMCA departments, and it contributed to a sense of *esprit de corps*. In fact, after Foster left Custer, the National General Headquarters of the YMCA appointed a full-time staff member to promote CIS in the training camps throughout the United States.[35]

Later, the International Committee of the YMCA recommended that CIS be extended throughout the US Army and Navy abroad.[36]

On the day he left, Foster was honored again, this time at a luncheon. After that he was taken to the train, where the Divisional Band assembled to see him off. "The sound that lingers still in my heart is that of the touching bugle call that followed the train till I could hear it no longer," he wrote years later.[37]

Building Support for CIS Abroad

In the fifteen months he spent with the American Expeditionary Force (AEF) in France, Foster met prominent leaders—military, religious, political and academic—and was able to broaden the structure and influence of CIS. His time at Custer had given him practical experience working with Catholic and Jewish trainees and religious leaders. He had been able to translate his inchoate sense of sympathy with them into a practical organization that sought to respect their varied religious beliefs. Now in his YMCA work with the AEF in France, Foster had more scope for expanding CIS than he had had at Custer.

A change of command soon after Foster arrived in France gave him opportunities to increase his influence. Henry Churchill King, Foster's mentor at Oberlin, took over the position of YMCA religious director of the entire AEF. King then reassigned Foster to Paris, to an office adjoining his own. Here Foster worked alongside King as his assistant. From this position he had ongoing contact with all the YMCA regional heads in Europe and could promote CIS throughout the AEF.

His new position in Paris and close association with King brought Foster not only wider influence and contacts but also a larger conception of CIS. Foster and King discussed expanding the Comrades beyond the structure of the YMCA, where it would have had to remain a Protestant organization. Foster wrote, "Around a Y.M.C.A. Hut, . . . [with] a distinctly Y.M.C.A. Program . . . the Catholic and Hebrew Boys would not have the most satisfactory program presented" [and] "might not find so much that was familiar to him as he might wish."[38] Around this time, Foster came to envision the Comrades as an umbrella interfaith organization that included Jewish and Catholic members playing major roles. The membership of this new conception resembled the membership of religious organizations in the CTCA. Foster had in the back of his mind a system of governance whereby the YMCA, JWB, the KofC, and the Salvation Army would become full-fledged members of the CIS governing board. He ultimately envisioned that all three of those welfare organizations could serve on an equal footing with the YMCA and that each of the four would have a vote roughly equal to the others, regardless of the size of their following.[39]

While Foster was thinking about these changes, he was called to meet with Charles H. Brent, Episcopal chief of Army chaplains of the AEF. Brent had heard of Foster from King and officers at Custer and offered him a regional chaplaincy in the Third Region, the largest region in France. Instead of accepting the offer, Foster proposed expanding CIS into an interfaith organization and including the military as part of its official structure.[40] If this were to happen, Foster thought, CIS could gain additional recognition and support. Military chaplains and other officers could supply the general CIS membership with new leadership and role models. Such a structure could enhance the interfaith character of the Comrades with Protestant, Catholic, and Jewish chaplains and military officers in the lead. They could help build programs with interfaith appeal and promote them to the troops.

It is noteworthy that Foster turned down Brent's offer of a regional chaplaincy in the largest region in France. This seems to indicate that he was more interested in the academic and organizational side of religion than in the practical day-to-day pastoral side of ministering to soldiers. Perhaps that is why he gave up the two different parish ministry positions he had held some five or six years earlier. It may be that Foster had greater interest in being with men of intellectual stature than in caring for soldiers or families. It appears most likely that above all, Foster wanted not only to be with men of intellectual stature but also in fellowship with men of other faiths and in a position to promote religious tolerance and cooperation.

Foster now had to consider how to retain the YMCA as a member of an expanded interfaith CIS. Retaining the participation of the YMCA, with its large membership, financial support, and wide recognition, was crucial to the success of any future iteration of the Comrades. Foster believed that reducing the dominant role of the YMCA by adding the military, as well as Catholic, Jewish, and other organizations, was necessary for expanding interfaith equality and military cooperation. Yet the YMCA would undoubtedly reject its diminished status, Foster feared. He was convinced that men like Edward Carter and Fletcher Brockman, part of the YMCA professional hierarchy, would be hostile to the plan. They "had the whip hand and intended to keep it" and would see the new plan as "institutionally suicidal." They "ambitiously sought to be dominant over all other agencies . . . in principle and program as . . . in numbers," Foster thought.[41]

And so Foster turned to Henry Churchill King for help. King successfully persuaded the YMCA hierarchy to accept the plan and remain in the Comrades. "They would then and there have killed the Comrades—so far as Y cooperation was concerned, had it not been for the powerful influence of King—of course they had to think a bit as to the effect it would have had with Pershing and Brent," Foster later wrote. In his view, King was the one who saved the day. "The ONE man inside the Y, and he not a professional Y man, that saved official Y cooperation. . . . [It] was Henry Churchill King and NO other."[42]

The YMCA agreed to take its place as just another participant in the Comrades, alongside the other religious welfare organizations. It was no longer the only supporter of CIS in service and no longer paid Foster's salary. Its CIS dues were higher than those of the other religious welfare organizations because of its larger membership.[43] There were some downsides: Foster complained about ongoing personal harassment and retribution behind the scenes by Y officials and about how the YMCA had to be dunned to pay its assessed dues.[44]

While King was working on retaining the support of the YMCA, Foster was working on gaining the support of the other religious welfare organizations. He first approached Edward L. Hearn, the overseas commissioner of the Knights of Columbus. Anxious and self-conscious about the red triangle on his sleeve, a symbol of the YMCA and widely regarded as a mark of hostility to the KofC, Foster found Hearn polite and cordial, if cautious. He was busy and invited Foster to return later, which Foster did. Hearn then appointed a representative to work with Foster in CIS.[45]

Next Foster met with Rabbi Hyman G. Enelow, of the reform Temple Emanu-El in New York City, who was then serving in France as the overseas commander and general field secretary of the JWB. Foster took an immediate liking to Enelow and found him receptive. "Two minutes with him made me sure that here is an understanding soul who would soon be at one with King and Brent in spirit," he recalled.[46]

The Salvation Army was another religious welfare organization that served at the front, and as such Foster invited it to join the Comrades. He seems to have admired Salvationist Lieutenant Colonel William S. Barker and was able to persuade him to participate in CIS.[47]

Brent was an ecumenist, open to broad-gauge religious inclusion. As an Episcopalian missionary in the Philippines, he had baptized and confirmed Pershing when both men served there before the First World War. As such, the two shared a spiritual bond.[48] In fact, it was General Pershing who, as commander in chief of the AEF, had invited Brent to become the chief of chaplains. Once Brent consented to Foster's suggestion, Foster was hopeful that with Brent on his side, perhaps General Pershing, who had just fortuitously walked into Brent's office, would also become a CIS supporter. "What a colossal idea I had sold those men, who trusted me enough to gamble with me on it," Foster recalled. "We were destined . . . to become evermore faithful Comrades with each other in the Service of God, Country and Ecumenicity." Foster hoped that with Brent on board, the idea of expanding and transforming CIS into a state interfaith movement would "be gaining ground in high places."[49] Foster's hopes were well-placed and Brent agreed to join as president.

As chief of Army chaplains, Brent asked members of the Chaplains' Corps and others in the military to serve in the Comrades. His recruitment efforts, as well as those of King and Foster, were successful. The new, expanded CIS could now look to the YMCA, the KofC, the JWB, the Salvation Army, and the military as partners. Foster hoped that CIS could now openly promote interfaith cooperation and accord the three new members the same level of public respect and legitimacy typically accorded to the YMCA.[50]

The Comrades built a new organizational structure to reflect its new interfaith character. Its central council and staff were drawn from the military and the constituent religious welfare organizations. Charles Brent was president; vice presidents included E. C. Carter of the YMCA, E. L. Hearn of the KofC, Rabbi H. G. Enelow of the JWB, and Colonel William Barker of the Salvation Army, as well as four members of the military drawn from the three religious groups. "Every member . . . [will] share with the entire body any such perplexities as might . . . make the Comradeship here any less complete," stated one of the Comrades' founding articles [so that] "absolute confidence and faith in each other . . . may be maintained." This article acknowledged "the novelty and difficulty inherent in bringing together those of different faiths," and the CIS goal of creating honest fellowship among them.[51]

The restructured Comrades came into being in December of 1918, over a month after the Armistice, and soon thereafter moved its headquarters from the Religious Department of the YMCA in Paris to Brent's office at the Elysee Palace Hotel in the same city. The Comrades later moved to another office within the hotel, this one donated by General Pershing. With the occupation of Germany, the CIS also set up a satellite operation for the troops in Coblenz, the following May.[52]

Interfaith Bonding and the Comrades

As an interfaith organization, the CIS could now spread an explicit interfaith message that demonstrated the equality and fellowship of Jews, Catholics, and Protestants. "No man [should]be expected to compromise his faith, but rather become a more worthy representative of it, adopting the attitude of a genuine comrade toward men of other faiths," stated the CIS charter.[53] By publishing an interfaith newspaper and offering interfaith souvenirs, jewelry, and other paraphernalia, the CIS sought to become a fraternal organization and convey a message of religious tolerance, cooperation, diversity, and patriotism. To accomplish these goals and expand the membership, the Comrades also established good-will interfaith teams that toured the camps. Members of the teams were to travel through the camps together. They generally included a member of the YMCA, the KofC, the JWB, and an officer representing the military. The teams were not to be "narrow or selfish" and were to go into the field "in perfect Comradeship." They were to demonstrate interfaith harmony, or as Foster put it, "spread our gospel."[54]

In Foster's opinion, the results of these team appearances "were nothing less than phenomenal." He remarked on how the troops "are not accustomed to see a K of C and Red Triangle travelling together and working on a common cause on the same platform." "Nor do they recall many instances of the Hebrew and Christian travelling and pulling together as men of a common faith." To Foster, the teams were demonstrating religious brotherhood in action, and he found that "exhilarating," noting that "it takes no prophet to foretell lasting good coming from such a campaign."[55] In fact, in the decades after the war, other organizations did take up the idea of interfaith teams and panels traveling together and giving public speeches.[56]

Not only good will teams but good will posters, slogans, and songs, as well as the jewelry, souvenirs, and biweekly newspaper mentioned earlier, all had a message of brotherhood that included men of different religions, ethnicities, occupations, and races. The newspaper printed poems and other writings composed by CIS members that spread Foster's "gospel." "Whatever their different national origins, occupations or religious beliefs, the war has made them American brothers," wrote Herbert Atkinson Jump in his poem "Comrade." It describes a "new era" and how men can now become brothers: "Out of the flame and blood of the war has come, into our language a word . . . COMRADE." It continues, "The saint must learn to say COMRADE to other saints of a breed and creed strange to him." Another poem, this one by George Alexander Kohut, called "Our Creed," focuses on the brotherhood among Protestants, Catholics and Jews who "meet at a common altar."[57]

CIS programs meant to foster male bonding helped maintain comradeship. Not only was male bonding widely practiced at the time, but Foster's own outlook and personal life favored it: to recall, he spending most of his time with other men, as an academic before the war and as a YMCA leader away from his family both before and after the conflict. And thus, male bonding, interfaith fellowship, and Progressive values shaped both Foster and CIS.[58]

Using his background in art, Foster designed various souvenirs for the Comrades that signified a fraternal organization with a manly good will message. One souvenir was a pocket piece inscribed with the words "Soldier—Citizen—Building—Fellowship" on one side and a new CIS insignia on the other side. Foster's insignia replaced the YMCA red triangle with a Star of David and a Cross against a backdrop of a shield with stars and stripes and the initials AEF. It symbolized, "in a visualized form," how CIS was "helping to bind together . . . all the forces working together in Army life for human uplift." A circular band that encompassed the star and cross comprised the words "Comrades in Service," the dates of the war, and a reference to the Old Testament book of the Prophet Nehemiah, chapter 4, verse 18, about rebuilding the walls of Jerusalem: "Let us rise up and build. So they strengthened their hands for *this* good *work*."[59]

Depicting the Star of David and quoting the words of Nehemiah, the insignia that Foster designed graphically highlighted the inclusion of Jews in the brotherhood of the Comrades. In quoting Nehemiah, Foster assumed that the troops were familiar with the Bible or, if they were not, that the insignia would pique their curiosity. Foster also designed another insignia, to denote his international goals for the Comrades. He retained the cross and the Star of David but changed the background, replacing the shield with a band to symbolize "building fellowship extending as a unifying band around the world." The insignias were used for charms, badges, medals, rings, coins, buttons, and stationery.[60]

The international scope of the war and the prospect of a League of Nations gave Foster hope that furthering camaraderie on an international scale might be a possible future mission of the Comrades. "The Allies fought side by side, not understanding . . . each other's conversations, but through the tongue of service found a growing sense of comradeship and a deeper understanding. . . . In the one world of service the nations of the earth have become comrades."[61]

Abundant expectations for the future and preparation for the homecoming of the troops led to a new design for pledge cards signed by those joining the Comrades. In contrast to the YMCA sectarian pledge cards, these new cards made no mention of religious beliefs and conveyed an expansive vision of service that introduced the words, "Liberty," "Justice," "Humanity," and "ideals of Comradeship." They were printed on postcards with a suggested "personal message" from the soldiers to the "folks at home." The name "Comrades in Service" was printed at the top, and below it, the name of a specific welfare organization. On the other side was printed a pledge to "The American People" that read in part, "I understand that in being discharged from the American Army, I am still in America's service, and must, in company with one hundred million comrades, continue to serve America, loyally and honestly, so that America may continue to serve God and Humanity." It was signed, "Four million American Soldiers." On one of the CIS cards was printed the logo of the JWB and the name of Jewish chaplain, Captain Leon Schwarz, the card's designer and an active member of the Comrades. The other CIS welfare organizations had cards with their own logos.[62]

In Foster's view, CIS, like the war itself, embodied "practical religion" because it brought men of different faiths together in service. "In creed and politics men will never unite in perfect harmony. . . . No one can ever understand the other's reasoning, but in service each understands the other. Men are much the same in the realm of actual experience . . . Service is the sign language of humanity which tongue all nations understand." He believed that service "leaps over the . . . sectarian walls to find the rose garden of God where it was thought . . . that there were only the barren deserts of other creeds."[63]

Celebrating the Comrades

After the armistice, two public events in Paris celebrated the Comrades. One of those was a mass meeting held in January 1919 at the Palais de Glace Pavilion. The second was a grand banquet held in March of the same year at the Lutetia Hotel in honor of Bishop Charles Brent, then president of the Comrades, to welcome him back to France after a visit home. While both events reflected the heady, exuberant optimism and ecstatic sense of mission associated with the end of the war, they raised questions about the future of Foster's expansive vision of interfaith fellowship.

President and Mrs. Wilson and some five thousand members of the AEF attended the January meeting. Aside from the president and his wife, numerous other luminaries were present, including Secretary of State Robert Lansing, ambassador to France William G. Sharp, and director of the US Food Administration Herbert Hoover, in charge of food relief in Europe.[64] At both events, military officers and representatives of the various welfare organizations gave speeches.

Both the January and March events conveyed a sense of idealism and American righteousness. At the January meeting, the high spirit of the moment was captured when Chaplain Jones of the Salvation Army toasted President Wilson not as "a man-elected president but a God-selected one." At that, "the vast audience rose in a spontaneous ovation."[65] Wilson made no speech or public comment about the Comrades at the meeting but was reported to have later mentioned "the real spirit and the large purpose of the movement" in a letter to Brent.[66] At the same event, Protestant chaplain Edwin F. Lee, chairman of the Comrades' executive committee, stated that American citizenship could now "be brought to the highest conception."[67] In the context of victory over Germany, it is no surprise that both events saw derogatory references to the Kaiser and slang references to the Germans, such as "Boche" and "Hun." The literature of the Comrades expressed similar sentiments.[68]

While most of the speakers at the January meeting spoke in lofty, vague terms about how the Comrades could shape a better world, only one, Chaplain

Lee, a Methodist, spoke specifically about the organization's interfaith character. He stated that the purpose of the gathering was not "entertainment" but "making history" and that CIS "proposes a union of all creeds and sects" based on the "common ground of the experience of the men who fought to make the world safe for democracy . . . to advance the best interests of civilization."[69]

It is possible that, except for Lee and Foster, the Protestants at the two gatherings were uninterested in accepting Catholics and Jews as equals in an American pluralist society and instead supported the melting pot idea, whereby Catholics and Jews would give up their respective, distinctive religions and become Protestants, if not officially by conversion then by acting and worshipping like Protestants. It is likely that many of the Protestants at the celebration viewed the American victory in the war as a nation-building event, which meant a *Protestant* nation-building event.

One of the speakers told the veterans who had escaped death they now had a chance to be of service in life.[70] Another speaker, Rabbi Hyman Enelow of the JWB, attributed the "sense of comradeship" to the "great work" of the AEF, highlighting the story of the wounded boy who wanted to get well so he could go back to the line and "help the other fellow out."[71] Observing that the war had ushered in a new order, "noble and statesmanlike . . . [as] an illustration of the idealism of American life," Rabbi Stephen S. Wise, founder of the Free Synagogue movement and founding president of the American Jewish Congress, told the thousands of AEF men gathered that "the golden years of American history lie before you and you are summoned to the highest comradeship of service in America."[72] For his part, Charles H. Brent noted that CIS was "giving an outward form, . . . to something that already exists."[73] To the speakers, they were living through the American moment, a new, almost sacred moment, a moment when it was possible to capture the wartime spirit of comradeship and service to fulfill the national destiny and shape the world. Perhaps it was felt that the presence of two Jewish speakers on the program of the January meeting, both of them rabbis, alongside Protestants E. C. Carter, and Edwin F. Lee, as well as Episcopalian Charles H. Brent, was sufficient to convey an interfaith message, without specifically developing the interfaith theme of Chaplain Lee's exhortation. E. L. Hearn, the invited Catholic speaker, was ill and did not attend.

At the March banquet, Secretary of State Lansing and Ambassador Sharp were again present. Present also were Henderson White of the Peace Commission, Samuel Gompers, president of the American Federation of Labor, Raymond B. Fosdick, chairman of the Commission on Training Camp Activities and assistant to Secretary of War Newton Baker, as well as "army men ranging in rank from generals to privates." Overall, some two hundred guests attended. Displayed in the banquet hall at the Lutetia Hotel were decorations with "patriotic colors," a reproduction of the CIS insignia, and a figure of Lady Liberty draped with the flags of the allied nations. Between courses, guests were treated to communal singing and solo selections sung by a tenor and a bass. One of the songs that was sung, entitled "Our Brotherhood," tells of "battles gory" that "bind us . . . ever." As the guests "joined together singing Comrades in Service songs . . . a pleasant feeling of fellowship" pervaded the banquet.[74]

Foster did not speak at the March event. Brent, the keynote speaker, acknowledged him in his introduction, saying that although "his name has not been met with entire approval . . . he had a vision—that it was a stroke of genius." He continued, "If merit, and not grace were to preside tonight, Dr. Foster would be in this position which I hold."[75] Three other major speakers included Edward Hearn of the KofC, Ned Carter of the YMCA, and Harry Cutler, the new president of the JWB. Interspersed between their speeches were speeches by Sergeant S. H. Carroll and Brig. Gen. Avery D. Andrews, who spoke in place of General Pershing. Captain Edwin F. Lee, chaplain, also spoke.

In his speech, Brent addressed "the aims, the ideals and the possibilities of Comrades in Service." He laid out a grand vision for the organization that echoed some of the themes of the January meeting; it included continuing, in civilian life, the sense of common sacrifice, service, and cooperation among those who served in the war but without perpetuating "military castes." "There is not a man here who was not perfectly ready at any moment to . . . make the supreme sacrifice—to lay down his life," he proclaimed. In other words, Brent felt that "the commonwealth . . . not only of our nation, but of all mankind, was of such high importance that if, by dying, he could promote the interest of the greater cause, then he must be ready to die. He indeed would be a poor man who has not had that impulse . . . if God so willed, to make a complete offer of himself." Brent went on to ask why such self-sacrifice should be confined to war service, and looking beyond the war, urged "surrendering ourselves to a great cause." He then spoke in general terms of international and national causes. On the international level he probably had in mind supporting an organization like the League of Nations, "[to] create . . . as nearly as possible a complete understanding between all nations, and prevent the possibility of any such conflict as we have been through again." On the national level, he urged building a new nation based on "justice, honor and righteousness," claiming that "the old America that we once knew has passed away and the new America is to be made by our hands." Closing the speech with a plea for carrying out "the vision of justice and honor and righteousness, in the future," Brent stated that it is a duty and responsibility "for us as citizens to go back to the United States determined to put these principles into effect, to apply them to all our national problems—the worlds of industry—the social world—aye, and the religious world." After his keynote speech Brent introduced the other speakers.[76]

Next, Edward Hearn spoke about patriotism and of the United States being "the greatest nation on the face of the earth" with a "destiny which Providence has marked out for it." He mentioned that CIS could help the returning soldiers to be leaders and to be "tolerant," but he did not elaborate.[77]

S. H. Carroll spoke of the authenticity of CIS, and how the American soldier "can smell propaganda, uplift and anything that savers of reform just as he could smell enemy gas at the front. . . . But show him a movement like this one, conceived in comradeship and . . . he will take it to his heart to cherish as he did the great movement out of which he has just come."[78]

E. C. Carter then spoke of CIS as a super society of welfare organizations which, like all welfare organizations of the time, exists to serve the soldier. He emphasized how the war, "this first-rate scrap," changed "the whole history of our land" and how in the past we lived "nationally" but now we live "internationally."[79]

General Avery D. Andrews followed. He suggested that being in the military and being in warfare had led the troops to a sense of comradeship and brotherhood. It was impossible, he continued, to estimate the future influence of CIS, but he stated with conviction that whatever the organizational structure, "comradeship" and "brotherhood" were the "cementing material" that would bind the men together.[80]

Chaplain Lee then spoke. Toward the end of his speech, he hit a note of warning. Speaking prophetically, passionately, and urgently about the need for education and idealism in the nation's future and how the Comrades might fill the need, he warned, "We cannot be . . . sure that our country will be fired by the highest type of idealism following this war." Consequently, he admonished, "Gentlemen, we may fail . . . Men! we must not fail!"[81]

The speeches at the March meeting reveal a variety of views about the future of CIS, from Brent's noble expectations to Hearn's and Carter's abstract, almost distant detachment, to Lee's urgent call for action. Only the last speaker, Harry Cutler of the JWB, dealt directly and specifically with how the war and the Comrades had the potential to further interfaith relations and the acceptance of Jews and Catholics.

Cutler, began his speech with a touch of interfaith wit. He described his placement at the end of the program and quoted from the New Testament, "the last shall be first and the first shall be last."[82] Cutler eloquently turned his attention to the recently arrived Jewish and Catholic immigrants and spoke of how they have proven their American patriotism in the war. He described the many immigrant men who were drafted by the Selective Service, how millions of them came from "monarchies where compulsory service was not only a degradation but even a persecution." Yet, in this war, he said, "these men answered the call without internal dissension or riot." They went, "across the sea" to "do their duty." He elaborated on the diverse origins, religious beliefs, and theologies of the draftees, and how "many, many of them, men who came from all quarters of the globe, men . . . whatever their accident of birth, antecedents—whatever their creed or religion . . . [they each fought for] the broadest principles of right and justice—of American ideals. The only thing that mattered was duty to the stars and stripes—duty to the call God-given."[83]

"Shall such comradeship in service go for naught?" Cutler asked, and declared, "The answer must be a decided 'No.'" He went on, "I believe we shall not forget these things; that these things will not go for naught; that we shall conserve this comradeship in service. In our national life there is no room for castes. All men are regarded as having been born equal, with a right to worship their God as their conscience dictates." Cutler then linked the Great War to equal rights and religious freedom as essential parts of American tradition, noting that patriotism inspired all Americans to take part in the fight.[84]

"When the command was given 'over the top' no officer stopped to ask of his men; 'Are you Protestant, Catholic or Jew?' The officer knew . . . if those Protestants, Catholics or Jews lived up to their ideals they answered that call [as] one hundred percent Americans," Cutler observed. "And in these days of stress we ought to bring that spirit home with us . . . you will not be true to your principles if you go back and . . . forget that fraternity which the baptism of blood and shells and gas effected in . . . the saving of civilization for our time and for the future."[85]

Distinguishing between diversity in religion and uniformity in nationalism was especially important for Jews because in much of Europe and Russia, Jews were historically seen as a separate and alien nationality, not as full, loyal, and equal citizens of the state. Even in nations considered enlightened, such as France, Jews suffered various liabilities as the Dreyfus case demonstrates. In the United States too, the revival of the Ku Klux Klan was then in full swing, attacking the Americanism of Jews and Catholics as well as of African Americans.

At the conclusion of his speech, Cutler looked to the future of CIS and linked the organization and its principles of interfaith comradeship to a rebirth of what he takes to be American (and English) traditions: "a rededication to the real American principles, the real American ideals . . . all that America has meant to us in the past . . . to us now, and all that we hope for it in the future . . . I deem a new Magna Carta based on old and true ideals,—nothing new, but such principles as live in American idealism." As for Jewish support for CIS, "I will say that three and one half million American citizens of Jewish faith stand behind you and with you on the principles of Comrades in Service . . . because we not only owe it to you, but we owe it to all our forefathers who have made our nation such as it is." He saw the potential of CIS as a vehicle of respect for religious diversity, a means of keeping alive the memory of wartime service, and a method to shore up the legitimacy of American Jews as full, equal, and worthy American citizens.[86]

Those Left Out: African American Soldiers

The military service of African Americans in the First World War brought them no comradeship with American white servicemen. Serving in racially segregated military units, many of which served with French units, they lacked the opportunities that white immigrants of European background had to develop bonds across religious and ethnic lines. On the one hand, the war helped to heal sectional rifts between white Confederate and Union veterans of the

Civil War, a fact celebrated at the banquet in March 1919. For example, "Well sonny, what part of the world do you come from?" asked General Edwards in a story he related to Brent ."'Oh, I'm a Yank,' replied the young man. "Yes . . . but what is your state?" the General asked. 'Oh . . . I'm from South Carolina.'"[87] On the other hand, the more than 370,000 African American troops who served in the European war continued to be treated according to Jim Crow racial practices that were to prevail in the military for decades to come.[88]

When the speakers at the Hotel Lutetia banquet spoke about the military service of African Americans, they mocked it. It was bad enough that E. C. Carter spoke about how, after the war, the United States would "help bear something of the white man's burden."[89] Worse, Chief of Staff General Avery Andrews, Pershing's stand-in at the banquet, related the following story: "A very well-known general staff officer was driving along up in the Second Army territory not so very long ago and came upon a body of colored troops standing around, many of them unkempt, paying no attention to military courtesy, none of them saluting the officer, and struck by their apparent lack of discipline, the officer stopped and called one of the negroes over. . . . 'What organization is this?' the officer asked. 'Organization, boss!' exclaimed the negro. 'This ain't no organization—this is just three hundred niggers!'"[90]

While the CIS did reach out to African Americans, it did so in ways that leaned into stereotypes. For example, the CIS signed up African American members in the segregated military companies and established "schools for colored illiterates," hospital centers, and "colored" Y huts in France. "A great big, husky stevedore stood at the black-board in the new barracks 'school house' . . . rubbing his wooly pate and working with all the earnestness of a beginner in the intricacies of English script," reported an article in the CIS newspaper. "Boss, Ah jest don' remember what dat letter 'D' looks like, dis monin'," the newspaper story continued. "Thought suhe Ah'd have it dis monin'." Such stereotypes and dialect appeared not only in the Comrades newspaper but also in the popular CIS minstrel shows performed by white soldiers in black face.[91]

These minstrel shows were popular with the white troops in the audience and on stage. The Comrades sponsored them as wholesome entertainments. One minstrel show written up in the Comrades' newspaper was described as a "scream." The article seems proud of how the [white] men wrote and produced their own show, made their own costumes and scenery, and got together a ten-piece orchestra. It singles out a few performers for special notice.

"The 448th quartet sang like veterans. Wetson could surely shake his feet. Cozzi and Howard had some good coon songs and Sgt. Meyer put over the ragtime."[92] The minstrel or "coon shows" remained attractive entertainments to the Comrades, reflecting the trend in American society generally. In short, racial segregation was as much the accepted practice in the Comrades as it was in the wartime American military.[93]

Those Left Out: Women in Military Service

The CIS also ignored or un-self-consciously pictured women in patronizing stereotypes. Yet American women worked as nurses and clerks for the Navy and Marine Corps and overseas. About twelve thousand worked at Amy hospitals and offices in the United States. Another sixteen thousand traveled overseas to work as nurses, ambulance and truck drivers, clerks, telephone operators, typists, canteen hostesses, clerical workers, and bacteriologists. Some of them served in uniform with the AEF and others served with the welfare organizations of the Commission on Training Camp Activities.[94]

At most, women were an afterthought at the March 2019 banquet. Near the end of his speech, Brent referred to Joan of Arc, the fifteenth-century figure undergoing a popular revival in the 1920s. He likened her going home to Domrémy after fighting on behalf of Charles VII to the return of the American troops to the United States. Speaking of the completion of her mission for the French king, Brent said, "The King was crowned, and she had finished the duty that her voices had bidden her do." Overlooking her military leadership, how she dressed as a man when she was in battle, her later imprisonment and martyrdom, Brent then quoted what he thinks Joan of Arc may have said at the moment of return: "Now I have completed my immediate task. Let me go home . . . that I may minister to those who are near and dear to me, and return to the domestic life from which I came."[95]

Cutler described a wife as being "the higher power" of her husband, neglecting her role in wartime military service and dwelling instead on her role as the mother who bravely sent her sons off to war. After briefly mentioning the father who tells his sons to go and "do your duty," Cutler spoke of "the mother who has fought every war in History," the mother who put a "piece of her heart in the kit and handkerchief she packed for you," [and] "finally when that kit was completed she wrapped it round with her soul . . . The mothers—the women in high station, the women in low . . . theirs's was a true comradeship in service."[96]

Both Brent and Cutler spoke of women primarily in their domestic roles. Neither dealt with them as actual members of CIS or said anything about the women who wore the uniform or were otherwise on active duty in the First World War. At the time, counting women as comrades or even imagining such a thing was likely outside their range of vision.[97]

CIS Versus the American Legion

When the United States entered the war the Progressive movement held sway in the country, and Foster, as a liberal Protestant academic, supported Progressive reforms aimed at efficient and good government, prohibition of alcohol, and labor protections. The Comrades also supported Progressive programs of debates, forums, and simulations such as mock trials, mock city councils, and mock peace commissions aimed at building leadership, citizenship, service, and decision-making skills.[98] When a company voted to have a forum or debate, the staff of the Comrades was right there with suggestions of topics such as "sewage systems, pure water, tenement house reforms, Sunday and weekday amusements, [and] clean politics." The Comrades thought that such topics "will afford not only interesting material . . . but invaluable suggestions for leadership at home."[99] Judging from these programs, there can be little doubt that CIS favored an agenda that was most likely of little interest to the average veteran.

Foster and others in the Comrades were men of the professional world: academics, lawyers, physicians, ministers, priests, and rabbis. The common sacrifice of the war and the elation of victory may have led them to believe that reforming American society and developing a new sense of interfaith comradeship were imminent, but keeping such goals alive among the troops proved to be a difficult task, especially once the war was over. The Comrades, like other Progressives, sought to alter American civilian society, the industrial system, the political system, and civic life, as well as to correct personal habits through prohibition of alcohol, clean living, and cultural uplift. Such changes had little to do directly with wartime experiences or veterans' benefits. Unlike the Grand Army of the Republic, which supported veterans' pensions, war memorials, reminiscing, and reenacting Civil War battles, the Comrades supported abstract, idealistic, selfless, intellectual goals. These may have put the Comrades beyond the reach of the average soldier, who by then was focused on returning home to civilian life. The question for Foster therefore was whether CIS could survive at all, after the war.

At the time of the Armistice, CIS faced some daunting problems and time pressures. Since becoming independent of the YMCA, the Comrades had expanded and trained its own staff while accommodating and working with four different organizations and four different staffs. Generally, the staffs were uncooperative. They were likely already overworked, looking forward to going home themselves, and hesitant and possibly skeptical about committing themselves to yet another organization. In the few months between December of 1918, when the independent CIS was first established, and the following spring, when most of the troops returned home, there was little time to convert wartime interfaith fellowship into peacetime camaraderie. Once the war was over, time was short for recruiting and maintaining loyal members.

The Comrades nevertheless undertook new, time-consuming tasks such as the production and distribution of more than one hundred thousand copies of a biweekly newspaper and ten thousand copies of the organization's handbook, all while raising money and organizing good will teams. Foster complained of being short-handed and needing more personnel to handle these responsibilities. In a report from March 1919, he appealed to the welfare organizations for more support and complained about their lack of cooperation: "We cannot meet most of our obligations unless these organizations rise to the occasion." He reminded their leaders of the "sacred covenant" to support the Comrades and chided them, "The time is here when we must have the backing of you men . . . both in spirit and in positive suggestions to your respective staffs. Personnel, money, sympathy and prayers are needed to meet this challenge. No man here today can shift the responsibility."[100]

In his report of April 1919, Capt. Edward F. Lee, chair of the Comrades' executive committee, likewise complained, "No agency connected with this Movement has fully lived up to its original promise, which has naturally meant a serious crippling in effort." He recommended that "each Agency be reminded . . . of the need for renewed zeal and that there be a practical delegation of authority to the Comrades in Service Office." Most likely, at this late date, Lee's and Foster's pleas went unheeded, with attention now turned to preparing for embarkation.[101]

Although the Comrades took pride in being "nonpolitical" as well as "nonsectarian," Foster was, in fact, an ardent supporter of Woodrow Wilson and what he took to be the Wilsonian principle of selfless service. Wilsonian war aims such as "peace without victory" and making "the world safe for democracy" comported with Foster's sense of selfless service. He and others in the leadership of the Comrades supported the League of Nations and the dismantling of empires they considered autocratic and corrupt. Like Woodrow Wilson, they believed that replacing those polities with smaller nations representing the aspirations of people of similar linguistic, historical, and cultural roots would allow for true self-determination. Such an obvious preference for Wilsonian policies may well have alienated potential members who disagreed.

Not surprisingly, a competing organization soon appeared, open only to those in the Army, Navy, and Marine Corps, inviting military men who were serving or had served honorably during the First World War. Welfare workers like Foster who were not in the military could not join. The idea for this organization came from Theodore Roosevelt Jr., the eldest son of Theodore Roosevelt and a lieutenant colonel in the AEF, who formed a provisional executive committee at a meeting in February 1919, in Paris, before leaving for home. One month later, in Roosevelt's absence, the still unnamed organization took shape at what came to be called the "Paris Caucus" and took the name the "American Legion." Roosevelt attended a May meeting in Saint Louis to organize the veterans now at home. At the St. Louis Caucus, the crowd cheered wildly for Roosevelt to become the permanent chairman of the Legion, but he declined. The formal founding of the American Legion took place at a convention held in Minneapolis on the first anniversary of the armistice.[102]

Meanwhile the emergence of a second organization was causing confusion and duplication of effort among the Comrades. Unless something was done to harmonize the two, it seemed that confusion would increase.[103] Bishop Brent, a major, and Leon Schwarz, a captain, both of them members of the Comrades and members in good standing of the AEF and thus eligible to join the American Legion, joined the both organizations. Brent and Schwartz, as well as Private W. E. Thompson, served on the executive committee of the Legion while continuing as officers of the Comrades. In March 1919 Brent and Schwarz reported to the other members of the executive committee of the

American Legion on the need for an understanding between the Legion and
the Comrades. In April 1919 Milton F. Foreman, chairman, and George A.
White, secretary of the executive committee of the Legion, drew up and signed
an agreement defining the relationship between the two organizations. Brent,
as president, signed it on behalf of the Comrades.[104]

The agreement provided for the Comrades to continue working among
the troops in Europe as they awaited embarkation, but to cease to exist once
they returned to the United States. The brief agreement stated that the American Legion "is concerned solely with providing the framework for the After-
the-War Association of those who served . . . It aims . . . to bring to the minds
of all concerned the fact that a spontaneous getting-together of those who so
served and which is directed and controlled by them, is desirable in their own
best interests and the best interests of the United States." The Legion made
one concession to the Comrades, however: it agreed to "perpetuate in civil life
the comradeship and associations and spirit of service for the commonwealth
developed during the war."[105]

CIS, for its part, pledged to extend its cooperation to the Legion, and,
according to the agreement, "to this end the co-operation extended by the
Comrades in Service was accepted by the American Legion it being the general
understanding that the two organizations were in no way rival organizations
and that the Comrades in Service, an organization concerned with morale and
good citizenship, would aid in every way the work of disseminating information concerning the American Legion."[106] With this document, CIS agreed
to disband once the AEF came home. Those who were members of both organizations, like Brent and Schwarz, could, perhaps, carry on the brotherly
interfaith ideals of the Comrades within the Legion, as individuals, but there
would remain no supporting organizational structure and no guarantees that
the Legion would champion such interfaith goals. It soon became clear that it
would not.[107]

An article at the time in the CIS newspaper explained Brent's position.
He believed that since "the principles of the American Legion . . . were iden-
tical with those of Comrades in Service there would be no object in effecting
a separate organization." Looking to the constitution of the Legion, he saw
that its purpose was "to perpetuate the principles of justice, freedom and
democracy . . . to cement the ties of comradeship formed in service." That

being the case, Brent looked forward "to a double organization eventually to blend in one."[108]

In the opinion of Leon Schwarz, secretary of the Executive Committee of CIS, the Comrades only had three choices: to go out of existence all together, to continue on without reference to the Legion, or to join forces with the latter. He feared that for the Comrades to continue without reference to the Legion would lead to a destructive rivalry between the two. Perhaps, like Brent, he thought that by negotiating with the American Legion and lending it support, the Comrades would have a vehicle for projecting their own Progressive agenda and interfaith goals.[109]

Foster held no such hopes for the American Legion. Looking back on this turn of events he describes how "the center of interest had shifted from service to the soldiers . . . to the formation of a permanent veterans' organization" "The soul of the Comrades was gone," and Foster's heart was "crushed."[110] He believed that those in the YMCA hierarchy who wanted to protect what he called "Y institutionalism" had contributed to the demise of the Comrades. Foster's negative experience with the YMCA at Camp Custer before shipping out for France, and his belief that the YMCA was overly ambitious, made him suspicious of its role in the end of the Comrades.[111] He did, however, distinguish between his distrust of the Y hierarchy overall and his high regard for individuals like his mentor, Henry Churchill King, who was a wartime appointee, not a member of the professional YMCA hierarchy.[112]

Despite his disappointments, Foster felt rewarded when he received a letter from General Pershing praising the Comrades and expressing an interest in seeing it continue in the regular Army after the AEF returned home. Pershing's letter thanked Foster for his part in organizing CIS: "Founded as it is, on the highest ideals of comradeship and service, it has been a large factor in helping the morale of the troops." Pershing went on to say that if the Comrades "is continued in the Regular Service . . . only the greatest good in the Army can result."[113] Pershing's military goals for the Comrades never came to pass. But Pershing channeled a gift of almost $25,000 (130,000 francs) that the *Chicago Tribune* had given him to award as he saw fit to the Comrades in appreciation of its work in the war.[114]

Foster had hoped that the war would increase acceptance of Catholic and Jewish troops as loyal Americans. He had hoped that CIS would continue after the war as a reminder of a new and broader sense of American identity. Despite his disappointed hopes for CIS it lived on in Foster's mind as a model, a "beacon," and "a precedent of commanding proportions" for his future projects. As he said, "While the Comrades as an organization died, its spirit will go on and on."[115]

CHAPTER TWO

Religious Cooperation at State Universities

I was . . . to be where camp had become campus and officers had become professors
and soldiers had become students.
—O. D. Foster, describing his projects at universities after the war

Ora D. Foster returned from the war disappointed, but not defeated. He viewed the conflict as a turning point that could further religious cooperation and transferred his efforts at building fellowship and cooperation among Protestants, Jews, and Catholics from the military theater to American civilian life. His experience in Europe convinced him that common service and common goals could bring together those of different faiths. Setting his sights on public higher education, he worked with others of like mind, some of whom he knew from the war. Together they sought to revive religious interest among students at secular state universities.

Even before the First World War, it was becoming clear that private denominational colleges were falling behind secular public state universities. From 1890 to 1920, the increase in student enrollment at private and denominational colleges was only two-thirds of those at state universities. In the decade beginning in 1910, the number of students enrolled in state universities had more than doubled.[1] This loss of religious dominance signaled a reversal of a long-standing tradition. Since the colonial period, from the founding of Harvard College in 1636 as a college to train Protestant clergymen, religion was central to American higher education. As state universities were gaining ground in the late nineteenth and early twentieth centuries, religious leaders puzzled over how best to bring religion to students at those institutions. Restrictions on teaching religion and the prominence of science at state universities and colleges troubled members of various churches, who made sporadic attempts to revive religion on campus.[2]

As discussed in the preceding chapter, America's participation in the First

World War brought new opportunities for religious cooperation. The Jewish, Catholic, and Protestant organizations in the Commission on Training Camp Activities, the tri-faith military chaplaincy, and CIS had modeled an expanded American religious identity. The common wartime sacrifice of men of all three faiths seemed to have rendered religious and denominational divisions less significant.[3]

Simultaneously, the war aggravated an apparent crisis of secularism that Foster and certain other religious leaders saw looming in higher education. "Grown men, [were] prematurely aged and scarred by the war experience . . . [and] the world-wide revolt against moral standards, religion and the church . . . was felt in this college generation," observed Clarence Shedd, a professor of religious education at Yale, religious historian, and YMCA leader. And so religious leaders like Foster and Shedd sought to find ways of reviving the faith of students at colleges and universities.[4]

Foster and others such as Presbyterian educators Richard C. Hughes and Joseph Cochran saw another related problem: the inactivity of churches in reviving religion among university students. In their view, churches needed to play a more active role and not just leave that task to the YMCA. In the course of the 1910s, increasing numbers of religious leaders took this position. In fact, some of them worried that the lack of church involvement had become so dire that state universities would become the next "great home mission field of the church."[5] Before churches could become effective on campus, however, they would need to update their teachings to keep up with science and the rigorous academic standards at universities.

The elimination of sectarian rivalry among the various competitive Protestant denominations was another issue that needed to be addressed. Promoting cooperation among churches of different denominations to invigorate religion at state universities looked like it would provide at least a partial answer to the many problems at hand. The Council of Church Boards of Education (CCBE), founded in 1912, was one of the first national Protestant interdenominational organizations dedicated to promoting religious cooperation in education. Its membership included the secretaries of the national boards of education of more than twenty Protestant denominations. When the CCBE set up a university committee—to expand its purview to include not only private denominational colleges but secular public state universities—and appointed Richard C. Hughes as chairman, he asked Foster to become the committee's secretary. Foster accepted the position and served in that capacity from 1923 to 1929.[6]

Foster's job was to promote cooperation among the denominations in an attempt to revive the religious life of the one million Protestant students at secular universities and colleges. As committee secretary, he traveled to state universities to meet Protestant campus leaders and administrators of various denominations and encouraged them to work together. Although working with the CCBE appealed to Foster's interest in advancing religious harmony among Protestants, it fell short of his interfaith goals, and he independently took steps to include Catholics and Jews in his university work.[7]

Catholic students at secular universities looked to the Newman Clubs for religious activities. The first Newman Club, named after British convert to Catholicism Cardinal John Henry Newman, was founded at Oxford University in England in 1878. Before the club proliferated in the United States, Mr. and Mrs. John Melvin of Madison, Wisconsin, hosted gatherings on Catholic heritage for state university students. The Melvin Catholic Club grew out of these meetings. When one of the early members of the Melvin Club left Wisconsin in 1893, he attended the University of Pennsylvania, where he founded the first Newman Club in the United States. Later in the 1890s, similar clubs were begun at Yale, Harvard, Cornell, and Michigan Universities. Although most of the Catholic university students at the time attended Catholic institutions, the number of Catholic students at non-Catholic campuses was growing, from about 3 percent of the total student population in 1890 to about 10 percent after the war.[8]

At first the Catholic hierarchy in the United States was largely removed from the Newman movement and focused on Catholic students at Catholic universities. In 1905, however, Pope Pius X issued an encyclical, *Acerbo Nimis*, stating that schools of religion should be set up to teach the Catholic faith and Catholic morality to students attending non-Catholic institutions. Within a few years, the Newman and other Catholic clubs expanded to various American secular universities, and in 1908, they formed an association that eventually led to the establishment of the National Federation of College Catholic Clubs. Meanwhile, the number of Catholic chaplains and Catholic students at state universities grew; Catholic students at non-Catholic institutions surpassed forty thousand after the First World War.[9]

The first major organization among Jewish students on secular campuses was the Menorah Society, founded at Harvard University in 1906. Unlike Catholic students, most Jewish students who attended universities attended secular ones. Not only did Jewish groups tend to be advocates for mainstream education, but there were few religious alternatives for them at the time. The principal Jewish institutions of higher learning, the reform Hebrew Union College in Cincinnati, the orthodox Dropsie College in Philadelphia, and the conservative Jewish Theological Seminary in New York City, primarily catered to clergy and scholars.

The Menorah Society emphasized Jewish identity through "Hebraism," that is, cultural, humanistic, and intellectual Jewish values rather than strictly doctrinal, ecclesiastical, or social activities. The society also published a bi-monthly publication, the *Menorah Journal*. In 1913, as the Menorah Society spread to some eighty American colleges and universities, it took on the name Intercollegiate Menorah Association (IMA). For a while, it dominated Jewish student life on American campuses until another organization with broader views, the Hillel Foundation, overtook it in popularity. The Hillel Foundation was first organized at the University of Illinois in 1923 and offered a wide range of Jewish activities, including religious, ritualistic, artistic, social, cultural, service, and intellectual ones. For a time, the two organizations coexisted, but over the course of the 1930s the Hillel Foundation expanded to numerous university campuses and replaced the Menorah Society entirely.[10]

The Newman Clubs, the IMA, and the Hillel Foundation shared the goal of strengthening the religious identity and loyalty respectively among Catholic and Jewish university students. The CCBE sought the same for Protestant university students of various denominations. None of these organizations had as their goal building interfaith ties among Catholic, Jewish, and Protestant university students.

Nevertheless, in September 1923, as part of his CCBE tour, Foster gave a speech at the University of Oregon in Eugene emphasizing how state universities "had a special obligation to find a way to keep the influence of religion strong among all their students. That meant to me . . . that the Catholics and Jews must be included in the plans for strengthening religious influences in a state university."[11] He spoke these words at a time when the Ku Klux Klan was on the rise in Oregon, and "the general antagonism of Protestants for Catholics was interpreted by many (generally falsely) as lining up Protestants and the K.K.K. together." Later, he would write, "It seemed to me, therefore, absolutely essential that I take the stand that I did even though I was well aware that it would be displeasing to many Protestant leaders and especially to some of the representatives of the Council of Church Boards."[12]

The Klan's Grand Kleagle of the Northwest attended Foster's speech; he was, Foster observed, "of course quite enraged." At the end of the speech Foster invited those interested in religion on campus to meet with him. Edwin V. O'Hara came forward. He was one of the few Catholic priests Foster had encountered aside from those he had met through CIS. O'Hara and Foster were roughly the same age; both were from the Midwest and had served in France during the war, O'Hara as a Roman Catholic chaplain. They became fast friends.[13] O'Hara had been at Saint Mary's Catholic Church in Eugene since 1920. He was a man of many accomplishments: a lifelong Progressive social activist, the author of the 1913 Oregon Minimum Wage Law for Women, and the former chairman of the Oregon Industrial Welfare Commission. The Wage Law had been upheld by the Oregon Supreme Court in 1914 and by the US Supreme Court in the case of Stettler v. O'Hara in 1917. In 1921 O'Hara became the director of the Catholic Rural Life Bureau, which had as an early objective helping Catholic veterans returning from the war to settle on Catholic farm colonies and developing projects to help Catholic rural residents both economically and in their religious life. That same year, O'Hara headed the Newman Club at the University of Oregon. In the 1930s he became the bishop, and later, the archbishop of Kansas City. For many years he and Foster remained allies in interfaith causes.[14]

After he left Oregon, Foster went to the University of Minnesota, where he contacted Cyrus Barnum, secretary of the campus YMCA. Barnum was an old war buddy and friend from CIS. After he complained to Foster about an uncooperative local priest, Foster took the liberty of contacting the priest to investigate. The priest recognized Foster from his work in CIS and "he all but threw his arms around me, exclaiming, 'That was the best thing in the War,'" Foster's recounted. As the two men swapped stories about mutual friends, the priest told him, "I'm not the man for you to see. You go to the top." He then arranged for Foster to meet the Most Reverend Daniel Austin Dowling, archbishop of St. Paul and episcopal chairman of the Education Department of the National Catholic Welfare Conference, the successor of the National Catholic War Council.[15]

Foster Meets the Archbishop

The next morning, a few minutes before ten, Foster climbed up the stone stairway leading to the door of the Archbishop's Palace on Summit Avenue in St. Paul. He was anxious at the prospect: "I had never met an Archbishop, and had no notion what to do, how to speak, or what not in the presence of a real flesh and blood Archbishop." Intimidated and self-conscious about his background, having been "brought up among the most humble of the humble church folk," Foster nevertheless took comfort from the "genuineness" and "sympathy" of the priest who had arranged the meeting.[16] Foster called upon the archbishop twice that day, once for a brief meeting in the morning and once again in the evening, for what turned out to be a three-hour dinner. He later recalled, "Diagonally across the great room, behind a large flat-topped desk, partly covered with letters, notes and books, sat a genial looking gentleman . . . Arising from his large chair with extended hand and inviting smile, he gave me a chair very near his." The archbishop had known of CIS and "his informed, alert mind quickly grasped the parallel of Camp and Campus." This put Foster at ease. "As I poured out what was in my heart . . . about the needs of all our youngsters in State Institutions of Higher Learning, his [the archbishop's] chair kept gently easing ever closer to mine, when occasionally his tender warm hand touched mine. It was being sensed that not only minds but hearts . . . were drawing nearer each other as well," Foster recollected. In his mind, their affection was a sign that the two men understood each other and could agree on common principles of cooperation, without compromising matters of faith. He was sure that their religious differences would not interfere with their working together in common cause.[17]

The archbishop seemed to support Foster's ideas about religious cooperation, saying they were "good for his Catholic children at state institutions." He urged Foster to address the Catholic bishops at their September meeting, soon to be held in Washington, DC. He did caution, however, that "many of our Bishops are very tepid supporters of these united activities . . . but I shall very gladly support a movement to work with you for the development of definite religious instructions and life at our Universities." He left Foster a letter to that effect, and the two men parted, "with warm handclasp over our hearts."[18]

Foster's initial discomfort with meeting the archbishop faded as this new bond of fellowship formed. Male bonding must have been an experience familiar to both men. Undoubtedly the archbishop inhabited a world in which his closest relationships were with men. Foster, too, lived in such a world. The mainspring of his social life was the company of other men. Although Foster was married and had three children, as already discussed, he had spent more than a year away from his family in the army camps during the war, and now spent months at a time traveling for the CCBE.[19]

After the meeting Foster described how the archbishop had affected him, how he "made me acquainted, not only with the best in Roman Catholicism but even with what Catholicity actually is. This illustrated why we conversed as much with our eyes and more with our hearts than with our—heads—otherwise we never would or could have come through together as we did." Taking his success with the archbishop as a providential sign, Foster marveled that "while Protestants and Catholics were regarded as antagonists everywhere we had agreed as completely . . . as any two men ever had. What was happening? Was I being taken in? No, this cooperation was surely God's will."[20]

Foster left the archbishop feeling like a new man: "I was not the same man, who with trepidation climbed those stone steps. I did not go down on stone, I went out on air; or perhaps as the old Hebrews on 'rush' or as the Greeks on 'pneuma'—both of which can as well be translated 'spirit' or 'air.'" Foster had found "a kindred spirit, such as had not been shown in my own group and who furthermore had opened the door of his great Church for me to see there were as understanding-broad gauged men in it . . . as in any other organization."[21]

Meeting the archbishop was itself a religious experience for Foster. It was "one of the many times in my life, I have felt in the grip of something so vastly bigger than myself," he would later write. "I can see him now, after these twenty-eight years, quite as vividly as when he squared himself across the table and while looking into the very recesses of my soul confided, 'My religion is my likes, my loves, my attitudes and my conscious relations with my fellow man and my God. It is not something in books, it exists only in conscious relationships between man and God; it is a godly manner of living.'" The archbishop brought Foster a level of religious connection similar to what he had experienced years before in Chicago when he had come to know Rabbi Emil G. Hirsch. Indeed, the Catholic prelate demonstrated to Foster that "a godly manner of living" could be found among Catholics as well as Jews and Protestants.[22]

Foster knew intellectually that Judaism, Catholicism, and Protestantism all shared a common Abrahamic heritage and many common teachings, but his emotional bonding with the archbishop brought this intellectual connection to life. It was another example of what he had first learned from his mentor, Henry Churchill King, at Oberlin: that true religious brotherhood could thrive if theology could be removed from the picture. "Theology . . . but leads to confusion, division and stifling of the spirit. A careful study of the life and teachings of Jesus as well as the Social Prophets of Israel leads to like concepts," wrote Foster. His bonding with Rabbi Hirsch and Archbishop Dowling confirmed his understanding of religion as something beyond Protestant theology.[23]

"Our hearts were as one," thought Foster after meeting the archbishop. He imagined himself at the camp at Gièvres, France, as a wartime commanding officer who "had to exercise the same discretion toward all." "Though I was University Secretary for Protestants, I was thinking in the terms of the Commanding Officer and of the chaplain, so far as relationships to men of all faiths were concerned. . . . I knew that it mattered not how great a percentage of the students my official relationships implied, I had to take into account . . . the opinions, rights and interests of all regardless of ecclesiastical heritages."[24]

When Foster returned to the CCBE in New York, he spoke of his plan to include Catholics and Jews in his university outreach activities. In doing so, he ran into a firestorm of ridicule led by Frank Lincoln Kelly, the council's executive secretary. Foster addressed a plenary session of the CCBE, telling the story about his visit with Archbishop Dowling, and his invitation to address the meeting of Catholic bishops gathered in Washington, DC. "Scarcely had I finished, when Dr. Kelly began burlesquing the whole fantastic idea; stating in most positive language before all that during all his years of effort to get Catholic cooperation, 'they would do nothing unless they could dominate everything to their own ends. They . . . are simply making a fool of Foster, who had been taken in by them during a war emergency.'" But Congregationalist Frank M. Sheldon, who had replaced Richard C. Hughes as chair of the university committee, came to Foster's defense and decided that Foster should go to Washington to meet with the bishops.[25]

When Foster arrived in Washington, at the headquarters of the National Catholic Welfare Conference (NCWC), he was ushered in to see James H. Ryan, "a gentleman, a scholar, and a cooperator." Ryan, the NCWC executive secretary of the Bureau of Education, received Foster "most cordially." "At the very outset, we were quite as much as one as had the archbishop and I been before him," Foster remarked. The archbishop had briefed Ryan and the bishops on Foster's ideas about interfaith outreach and cooperation at state universities. At their meeting the previous day, the bishops had carried a motion to cooperate with the CCBE. "You as secretary for all the great Protestant Boards of Education and I as secretary of our Board with the Bishops behind me, seem to be in rather a responsible—unique position," Ryan commented.[26]

Ryan and Foster worked together in Ryan's private office uninterrupted, stopping only to lunch with John J. Burke, a Paulist priest and general secretary of the Executive Department of the NCWC. For the rest of the day Foster and Ryan put their heads together envisioning what Foster called an "imaginary organization." They sketched out a tentative organizational structure and a list of possible prospective members of what would eventually take shape as the American Association on Religion in Colleges and Universities.[27]

The day with Ryan stood out in Foster's mind as "an illustration of how two men representing so much and of such different backgrounds and connections could go through an entire day at first acquaintance without the suggestion of difference. No finer example of cooperative spirit . . . could be found between old friends of long years of acquaintance within the same fraternity."[28] All these signs that a Catholic and a Protestant could cooperate to achieve an apparently common vision convinced Foster that interfaith cooperation in civilian life could be within his grasp. The [interfaith] objective to me was worth all it might cost, if it could just be done. To me it was the greatest single need in State Education and basic for a philosophy of education, adequate for the time . . . for cultivating a democratic society worth the name," he later wrote.[29]

Next, he approached Hyman Enelow, a reform rabbi at Temple Emanu-El in Manhattan, the leader of the Jewish Welfare Board, and member of CIS during the war. He suggested to Foster a network of respected rabbis, scholars, and public figures. From this network, and the Protestant and Catholic contacts of Foster and Ryan, a group of leaders from the three faiths was formed. Together they founded the American Association on Religion in State Colleges and Universities.

The American Association on Religion in
State Colleges and Universities

From its beginnings in 1923, the American Association on Religion in State Colleges and Universities (AAR) brought together a group of prominent Jewish, Catholic, and Protestant, academic, community, and religious leaders. All of the AAR members were men, well connected and well regarded. In that respect, the AAR was an elite association, more like a board of directors or an honorary society than a grass roots organization. Although membership changed during its five year history, keeping a balance of Protestants, Catholics, and Jews remained a priority.[30] For Foster, one of the organization's central goals included cultivating religious brotherhood among these men. His past experiences of reaching out to men who thought deeply about religion inclined him to favor an organization that would provide similar experiences.

Oblivious at times to restrictions against Jews and Catholics in clubs, housing, and universities, Foster's focus was on the life of the mind more than on practical matters, although of course he opposed such restrictions. No doubt the secularism of public universities, the inability of the churches to attract capable young men, and the bigotry and violence of the Ku Klux Klan also motivated Foster to take the lead in organizing the AAR. So did the tri-faith bonding he had experienced in the war. But the religious dimension of tri-faith equality and camaraderie seem more important to Foster than the utilitarian goals that likely interested many of the other members of the AAR.

An AAR pamphlet showcases its anti-secular goals: "Hundreds of thousands of America's best young people attend annually our great State and independent institutions of higher learning, where character is being formed without the same religious facilities that can be provided in denominational institutions." Although a few state universities had established schools of religion, they were denominational in origin, usually located off campus, and generally paid for by the denominations, not the university. None of them were based on tri-faith cooperation.[31] The University of Iowa had once offered a program of religious studies, but that program had a short life and was discontinued more than a decade before the AAR was founded. Nevertheless, interest in restoring a religious program was revived at Iowa in the early 1920s, likely leading the AAR to choose it for the first project, namely, helping establish a school of religion, this time a tri-faith one.[32]

The goals AAR were to build "a consciousness of brotherhood . . . to nurture good will and confidence" and to develop "a common approach to university authorities and students" in matters of religious belief and life that "could only be effectively attained if all religions worked in unison."[33] Other goals included gaining the same recognition from university administrators as other branches of knowledge, promoting a common approach to "university authorities" and "students' organizations," advancing the "religious welfare" of the students, and serving "as a clearing house" and "information bureau" for "religious work at colleges and universities." The AAR was to act as a deliberative, roundtable, policy-forming body, and also to provide publicity, raise funds, conduct surveys, and hold national conferences to promote interfaith projects. While it fell short of some of these goals, the AAR achieved the major goal of gathering together Protestant, Jewish, and Catholic leaders to help found long-lived interfaith educational institutions at state universities.[34] Although the ISR and the URC were the only two such institutions actually founded, the AAR had made contacts with several other state universities before having to abandon these plans, thanks in part, to the economic dislocations of the 1930s.

Jewish and Catholic Voices in the AAR

As a small religious minority in American society, Jewish Americans stood to benefit from cooperation with and favorable exposure to American Catholics and Protestants. Such exposure was thought to build tolerance.[35] Reform rabbi David Philipson, the best known of the AAR Jewish contingent, had been participating in interfaith projects for more than two decades before he joined the AAR. In 1903 he spoke at the Episcopal cathedral in Cincinnati and soon thereafter cooperated with the local Episcopal priest to form the Cosmic Club, "to foster interreligious discourse" among Catholic, Jewish, and Protestant ministers.[36] Other reform rabbis involved with the AAR and the founding of the ISR and the URC had similarly embraced interfaith projects. Nevertheless, the AAR Jewish contingent voiced several concerns. One was to avoid domination by Catholic and Protestant interests that might pressure Jewish university students to convert. Another concern was maintaining strict separation of church and state. A third was maintaining Jewish independence and autonomy while being outnumbered by Catholics and Protestants in the university population. Frank discussions at the AAR meetings give us details of these concerns.

On the question of domination, Philipson clarified that he was "not contemplate[ing] a union of religious groups along lines of doctrine." "It is purely a practical movement," he stated. "[No] religious group wants to proselytize amongst university students. The sole purpose should be to try to impress upon them the religious viewpoint."[37] The "sole aim" of the founding group was to "promote and develop, under the auspices of their respective religious leaders, religious faith and ideals already professed by each student, and thus to preserve for our American life what has always been recognized as the best and highest principles of action."[38] In response, Episcopal bishop Charles H. Brent reiterated a point made earlier by Foster that "there is no idea of trying to obtain a unity of belief. All that is desired is . . . coordination."[39]

To recall, the issue of separation of church and state was central to the Jewish contingent of the AAR. "One great objection must be overcome before any progress could be made," Philipson declared. "A clear statement ought to be made on the question of separation of church and state" to prevent "interference on the part of the churches in the working of our state universities."[40] Rabbis Simon and Zepin raised similar concerns.[41]

"No interference was contemplated," Foster responded.[42] For his part, Brent spoke of the success of the tri-faith chaplaincy in the First World War, adding that "the same policy could work in our public universities."[43]

Philipson, concerned about an overbearing presence of Protestant and Catholic buildings and symbols on campus, asked whether the universities would allow the different religious groups to have their own buildings for religious instruction. This concern appears to have been more worrisome to the Jewish contingent than secularism.

Religious groups would not need to use campus facilities to do their work, Foster replied. Protestant AAR member Matthew Willard Lampe agreed that religious work could be done in buildings off campus.[44]

Unlike the Jewish AAR contingent, the Catholic contingent seemed unworried about the separation of church and state and more concerned about gaining a voice on campus for Catholic teachings. They were less inclined than Jews to join the AAR, and their representation in the organization was spotty, as we shall see. Nevertheless, some Catholics could see an advantage in serving the religious needs of the increasing number of Catholic students at secular state universities. Moreover, the Catholic contingent seemed interested in having a Catholic point of view heard at these institutions, to refute what some members of the contingent regarded as offensive attacks by scientific, atheistic professors. In their view, the very presence of science and the secular orientation of state universities threatened Catholic teachings, although departments of religious studies that might have countered Catholic teachings with specific Protestant ones had not yet been introduced. One way to combat this would be to offer religious instruction to Catholic students.

In this vein, AAR Catholic member John Eliot Ross brought up the question of whether universities could give credit for religious instruction. Replying that the state could not give religious instruction, Brent asked whether it would be unconstitutional if perhaps instead the state "saw to it that religious instruction was given."[45]

Priest Vincent O'Hara from Oregon suggested adding to the draft a statement on the importance of teaching religion at universities, "purely and simply on its own merits." He proposed that, since "practical difficulties" will not allow religion to be offered as a part of the ordinary curriculum at state universities, "the American university . . . make it possible for the different religious groups to function, in providing for the religious needs of their communicants." Such religious instruction should meet the "generally accepted academic standards for university work," O'Hara added and further suggested that a possible way for the different religious groups to meet the academic standards would be to pool their resources and cooperatively found a house at each university that they would share. The house would contain a general library, an auditorium, and separate class rooms that each religious group could use.[46]

The meeting discussions on these concerns of Jewish and Catholic AAR members reveal a sympathy and willingness on the part of the AAR to address them, but whether and how they were actually addressed will come into view when we discuss the founding of the Iowa School of Religion and the founding and progress of the URC.

Catholic Reversal

In 1925 the Catholic bishops began to exhibit reservations about official membership in the AAR, as archbishop Dowling had hinted two years earlier that they might. The following year the bishops officially rescinded their support for the Catholic hierarchy to join the AAR. While we are "most cordially in sympathy with the plans and hopes you have for the religious life of students at our state universities, still so far we have no mandate to speak for everybody but ourselves as individuals," Dowling wrote to Foster, continuing that "we feel also . . . it would be nothing short of deception if we accepted your flattering invitation to enter as representatives of the Catholic body into the permanent and formal organization of the plan."[47] A few days later Foster heard from James H. Ryan about Dowling's decision, "The circumstances being what they are the archbishop could not decide a course different to the one he has taken." Ryan went on to say, "The decision of the archbishop affects profoundly my own position in the work . . . It is needless for me to say how painful all this is." He concluded, "My personal advice would be to go right along with the organization, omitting all mention of *official* Catholic participation, yet enlisting the services of Catholics who do not represent us officially."[48] Foster followed Ryan's advice and enlisted the support of lay Catholics as individuals, like John Agar, but not as official representatives of the church.

The loss of official Catholic participation notwithstanding, the AAR set to work on two interfaith projects: launching what it called "Project Number One," helping to establish a School of Religion at the University of Iowa, and launching what it called "Project Number Two," helping to establish a School of Religion at the University of California at Los Angeles.

In the 1920s, schools of religion generally fell into two types: university-centered and church-centered. At the university-centered schools, the university faculty and administration had responsibility for teaching the courses and determining their content, curriculum, calendar, and funding. Often located off campus, the church-centered schools had responsibility for offering courses, generally non-credit, supplying the faculty, facilities, and funding, and setting the calendar. Foster thought that religion and the church needed to be at the heart of these schools, but he objected to what he considered the amateurish standards of the church-centered schools, especially as contrasted with the higher academic standards of universities. Moreover, he worried about the inability of church-centered schools to attract university students and doubted that such schools could even revive the students' early religious ties.[49] Nevertheless, he supported schools that emphasized teaching religion from a sympathetic, churchly perspective rather than from an abstract, academic one, even while he wanted these churchly schools to be rigorous, professional, and based firmly upon tri-faith cooperation.

The states varied in how strictly the separation of church and state was practiced. The California Board of Regents was the strictest in the country in terms of maintaining the separation of religion from the state university. The state of Iowa was less strict. Taxpayer money could be used for a university-centered school of religion, provided that no one religion was favored over another, that no proselytizing took place, that there was no compulsion for students to enroll in religion courses, and that no tax dollars were used to fund the participation of the churches, clerical faculty, or clerical administration. Those costs were to be paid by the churches or denominations.[50]

Founding the Iowa School of Religion

The Iowa School of Religion at the University of Iowa opened its doors in 1927. As Project Number One of the American Association on Religion, it was the first tri-faith school of religion at a state university in the United States. To mark the launching of the Iowa School and to showcase its tri-faith character, O. D. Foster and Rufus Fitzgerald, director of the student union and YMCA at the University of Iowa, organized a conference in January 1928. The theme of the conference was "Working Together for a Common Goal: Promoting Interfaith Cooperation to Save America's Youth at Secular State Universities." Fitzgerald hoped that the new Iowa School would lead to "divine ties which shall bind together men of different faiths in common cause." The conference's approximately twenty-five attendees included roughly equal numbers of Catholic, Protestant, and Jewish religious leaders, from the University of Iowa and other state universities, as well as from the Hillel Foundation and Newman Hall. They had each had first-hand experience in working with religious groups and "the frankness and open-mindedness essential . . . to cooperate . . . in the spirit of sons of a common Father," wrote Foster. They came "all the way from New York to California and from Wisconsin to Texas" to "share ideas" and further interfaith cooperation and fellowship.[51]

William Bergen, a Catholic priest affiliated with the Columbus Society of the University of Illinois, described the gathering as an opportunity to "refresh our minds and our hearts by communion with high-minded and no-ble-hearted men." Other attendees also praised the conference and the tri-faith spirit that animated the founding of the Iowa school. "All our work is re-ally a common one for life ideals. . . . No less than inspiring, I shall cherish that visit [to the Iowa School of Religion] as one of the outstanding experiences of my life," stated rabbi Solomon Landman of the Hillel Foundation at the Uni-versity of Wisconsin. "We must cure undue denominationalism," commented R. M. Hughes, president of the Iowa State College at Ames. "Great strength will come through mass action of the churches." According to Methodist pastor E. W. Blakeman, from Berkeley, California, "We need to unify our-selves . . . to free our educational activities from organizational competition or differences." For his part, Congregational pastor Robert J. Locke, from the University of Illinois and superintendent of the Congregational conference of Illinois, remarked, "There is a common area of idealism, which belongs to all of us; our fundamental needs are the same"; he added that the conference "was one of the most outstanding things in recent times although no horns were blown or a great noise made about it."[52]

The University of Iowa had experimented with a school of religion be-tween 1908 and 1911, but an exploratory committee was formed to investigate its feasibility only about ten years later.[53] One of the first people the committee sought to interview was Charles Foster Kent, professor of biblical literature at Yale and a popular author of numerous books on the Old Testament.[54] Like Foster, Kent was concerned about what he saw as the lack of religion at state universities. To address this problem, Kent founded the National Coun-cil of Schools of Religion (NCSR), with the major goal of bringing religion to "the ninety tax supported state and municipal universities and colleges in the United States, with over a quarter of a million students."[55] The membership of the NCSR included "the outstanding leaders in the religious, educational, professional and commercial activities of each state." Among them were col-lege presidents like W.H.P. Faunce of Brown University, Henry Suzzallo of the University of Washington, Charles Eliot, former president of Harvard Univer-sity, and Walter Jessup, president of the University of Iowa.[56]

Foster and Kent knew each other well. Kent used Foster's office in Chicago as his western headquarters and paid part of the rent. The two men undoubt-edly shared ideas.[57] Foster described Kent as a "Christian gentleman," "a rov-ing high-brow evangelist," and a popularizer who "wrote for the thousands and spoke to the masses." He went on tours "with the enthusiasm of an evangelist—not the Billy Sunday type, but . . . [one] who reached better poised educators" and "big capitalists." So effective a speaker was Kent that he "swept" his listeners "off their feet" and made them "ready to jump in with him" on his proposals. He had managed to raise significant funds from various bankers; eventually the NCSR recruited a membership numbering more than one hundred.[58]

While the religious education plans of Kent and Foster shared certain similarities, there were significant differences. Kent's plan proposed several courses on Christianity, but only one, a one-semester course, "Great Non-Christian Religions," that included all the others. Similar to the "freshman universal history course . . . being introduced into many of the secular eastern colleges at the time," Kent's course was to cover "Confucius, Zoraster, Guatama, Buddha, Socrates, Plato, the great Stoics, Muhammed, the Hebrew prophets and the founders of Judaism."[59]

Foster, on the other hand, was adamant that his plan would provide for separate and equal courses covering Judaism, Catholicism, and Protestantism. Foster's plan was to offer courses in religion that would reconnect students to their religious roots and revive their prior interest in religion. He also wanted to promote tolerance by teaching courses about the religions of their fellow students. Rather than giving them Kent's wide coverage of what he considered exotic religions, Foster wanted to include courses on the three major faiths then current in American society. They also differed in their views about teaching religion. Kent wrote that teaching religion was like teaching "history or economics or any other university subject."[60] While Foster agreed that religion was compatible with science and other academic subjects, he maintained that there was more to religion than academics and that clergy were needed to teach their own religion in its full magnitude and significance. The emotional power of religion set it apart from "history or economics or any other university subjects," in his view.

Kent wanted to "promote research and investigation in the history, science and practice of religion." This approach resembled views held by Edwin Starbuck on the Iowa University committee and probably by other committee members as well.[61] Academic faculty could of course teach religion from an abstract perspective, thought Foster, but he insisted that clergy faculty teach what he called sectarian religion from a personal and moral perspective. He

was disdainful of Kent's plan of "ignoring ecclesiastics and teaching youngsters religion 'scientifically and without bias.'"[62]

In fall 1923, almost a year after Jessup had invited Kent, the university
committee invited Foster to come to Iowa City to meet with them and "think
through the problems and possibilities" of establishing a school of religion.
At the time, Foster was traveling to universities for the CCBE and organizing
the AAR. Compared to Kent, Foster must indeed have seemed like a poor
cousin. He had no current academic connection and his Yale affiliation was
more than a decade old. He was not a popular author and speaker. His most
respected organizational association was with the CCBE, an organization of
Protestant church administrators, not of academics. It had no "inducement of
great funds." Nor did the nascent American Association on Religion.[63]

Psychology Professor Edwin Starbuck met Foster's early morning train
and shepherded him around campus during his two day visit. He spent the
first day "until late at night" meeting with Seashore, Kay, and the other committee members as well as with Rufus Fitzgerald, the head of YMCA and the
student union at Iowa.[64] Observing that none of the committee members
"showed enthusiasm," Foster was nervous about how the meeting scheduled
for the next day would go. "I was keenly conscious of the fact that Professor
Kent had the committee . . . behind him—his philosophy of teaching religion
in State Schools and the inducement of great funds and a colossal organization
as well."[65]

Nevertheless, his experience in building an interfaith organization like CIS
and setting up the interfaith AAR gave him experience unmatched by Kent.
That strengthened Foster's resolve. His experience became his "foundation
rock," and upon it he built his plan for the School of Religion. "It [the plan]
didn't come here from thin air with but a wild-eyed enthusiast proposing it."[66]
Such thoughts seemed to have given Foster enough confidence for presenting
a persuasive case before the committee.

And so, Foster met with the committee the next afternoon and left feeling
confident of its support. A few days later he received a letter from Starbuck
stating that "all are committed now to the notion that the School in name
shall be one in fact" but suggesting that it be "correlated" with the School
of Commerce and the College of Education.[67] A few days later another letter
arrived. It read, "We propose now to establish . . . the school as a department
in the University." To deal with the problem of funding, the letter suggested

that "the churches . . . turn over their means to the treasury of the University and specify that the university will be held entirely responsible for the control of the school." Such an arrangement "would settle the institutional aspect of the case. Would the churches . . . be willing to play the game under those circumstances?" Starbuck ended the letter wondering "whether the work of the School of Religion can enjoy the same dignity and command the same respect as can the work of other departments and colleges?"[68]

"In strengthening the case for the University, you weaken it . . . for the Boards of the churches," Foster responded, continuing, "I do not believe you can even get a start with them on this basis. This is frank . . . but there is no use in following leads that will soon bring us to grief." He emphasized that "some official connection must be maintained with the Churches or we cannot hope to carry them along with us."[69] A few days later Foster leaned on similar points in a letter to university committee chair George F. Kay. "Whatever is done we must carry these Church officials with us. . . . It may mean tardy action but when they have acted it will be foundation stones upon which we may safely build."[70]

The CCBE played less of a role than the AAR in helping to establish the Iowa project. Specifically, while the AAR approved of Foster spending as much time as needed to launch the Iowa project, the CCBE did not. As for the issue of funding, it seems that neither the CCBE nor the AAR were in a position to help, but Foster expressed hope that through the Iowa religious denominations "we may be able to raise sufficient endowment for the school of religion to "get the highest grade of instructors."[71]

Meanwhile, the university committee's plan stated, "We have found invariable evidence of a spirit of active sympathy and goodwill on the part of religious bodies and . . . the founding of such a School is as practicable as it is desirable." The plan contained goals, sentiments, and language that Foster himself could have written. Among other things, the plan recognized that "religion has a vital relation to education in a democracy" and "every effort . . . should be made to develop and foster the religious growth of our future citizens."[72]

The objectives of the plan must also have pleased Foster. One of them was to offer credit granting graduate and undergraduate courses "that will help students gain a wholesome view of religion and to create an interest . . . in religious activities." Another was "to serve the State in all its religious

interests by training religious leaders and teachers." Other objectives, perhaps proposed by Starbuck, a proponent of scientific study, were to promote
"thoughtful insight into the nature and meaning of religion and lay a scientific
foundation for religious education." Still others were that the school "enable
the University to respond . . . to the 85 percent of students who come from
church homes" and provide "proper training for the more practical lines of
humanitarian and religious work." Finally, the school was to stimulate "a vital
religion, functioning in all departments of life," by "unit[ing] the Churches
and University in a common task and responsibility."[73]

The committee proposed a sharing of power between the state university and the private religious bodies of Iowa, resembling the structure of CIS,
which, to recall, involved a sharing of power between the military and four
private religious organizations. Both the university and the religious groups
in Iowa were to carry equal weight in selecting a body of electors, who in turn
would choose the school's governing board. The board would have responsibility for funding the part of the school not covered by the state, determining
school policy, and employing the director and staff of the school "with the
approval of the Administration of the University."[74]

The plan of the Iowa committee left much of the final shape of the school
to the director, who would enjoy the status analogous to directors of other
schools in the university, such as the schools of music and commerce. Among
the director's specified duties were providing "academic guidance and spiritual leadership in the University, Churches and State," enlisting the cooperation and participation of university departments in the school of religion, and
developing ways of making the school available "to the Churches of the State
and to the people of the commonwealth generally."[75]

The university faculty committee sent the plan to the university's president
Walter Jessup in April 1924. It was accompanied by a letter signed by the committee members, by pastors who were members of the Iowa City Ministerial
Union, by the local religious workers of Iowa City, and by the student pastors
on campus. Jessup was "heartily in favor of the plan," Kay wrote to Foster a
few weeks later, telling him that Jessup would be presenting the plan to the
State Board of Education "at an opportune time." Jessup was "anxious" for
the state board "to pass on it favorably," as was Kay. But both agreed that tact
and good judgement were required and that it was "better to take our first
steps deliberately."[76]

"I have never been so hopeful of getting something on the map here," wrote Foster to the AAR and the CCBE's university committee. He reported that the plan had received the university's endorsement. Yet, urging patience, he pleaded with the CCBE committee "not [to] grow impatient" and exclaimed, "We *must* make this go. It is our *chance*." Soon thereafter, Jessup presented the plan to the state board and judged that it "would not meet with opposition"; however, "in accordance with well-established policy," the matter was "laid over for consideration" until the next meeting.[77]

Three weeks later Kay again wrote to Foster telling him that the State Board of Education had approved the plan. Now it could be publicized in the state to garner support. It nevertheless took three years after state approval for the school to take shape and begin operation. Foster continued to play an important role: during that time, Kay looked upon him as the "most influential" person capable of bringing the churches along.

Finding Support from Iowa Religious Groups

Kay turned to Foster to put the plan into effect, asking him, "What do you think step number 1 should be?"[78] Foster responded that "electors were needed to elect the Board of Trustees of the Iowa School of Religion."[79] The electors were to be chosen by the various religious groups in Iowa.[80] He took on that job, and over the next several months, contacted the Iowa church leaders of various denominations and religions to urge the "proper religious authorities" to put their "machinery in motion to appoint their electors." Through CIS contacts and those he had made through the CCBE and the AAR, Foster found many of the Iowa religious leaders needed.[81]

James H. Ryan and Archbishop August Dowling, both sympathetic to the AAR, helped enlist the support of the bishop of Davenport Edward D. Howard, who in turn smoothed the way for the participation of William Shannahan, monsignor at St. Patrick's Church in Iowa City.[82] Shannahan had previously served with Edwin Starbuck and Rufus Fitzgerald on an earlier exploratory committee and in other campus religious activities. Shannahan went on to serve as an elector and later as a board member of the school.

Through AAR member Rabbi David Philipson, Foster found a willing and steadfast Jewish participant, Eugene M. Mannheimer, rabbi of the reform

Temple B'nai Jeshurun in Des Moines. Philipson had been Mannheimer's teacher. "From the day [Mannheimer] knew that Philipson supported the project, he was wholeheartedly with us," Foster recalled. Both Mannheimer and Philipson remained loyal supporters of interfaith activities.[83]

Foster's next task was getting the different religious groups to participate in an interfaith project. Not only was interfaith cooperation an unusual practice at the time but it ran counter to the nativism and religious intolerance prevalent in certain Protestant churches in many sections of the country and espoused by the revived Ku Klux Klan. Overall, Catholics and Jews stood to gain by being recognized and accepted as legitimate members of American society, whereas Protestants were already part of the majority. Some of them feared that acceptance of Catholics and Jews would threaten their dominant status. Foster had long complained about the stubborn, divisive, and fractured character of Protestant sectarianism and that his biggest problems "practically always came with the divers and sundry types of Protestants with their respective fears and "sub-rosa Klanism."[84] "Not all, of course," he quickly added, singling out pastor Archibald Cardle of the First Presbyterian Church of Burlington, Iowa, calling him "'the Nestor' of the Protestants of the State," referring to Homer's *Iliad* and presumably meaning that he could act as a peacemaker.[85] Foster generally kept such negative observations about his fellow Protestants to himself.[86] In this case, he wanted to avoid discouraging Kay and keep him from being "so frightened [that] he would throw up the sponge." Instead, Foster wrote that "churches move slowly" and that it "required patients [*sic*] to do any cooperative work.[87]

Eventually nine Iowa religious groups chose electors. These included one Catholic, one Jewish, and seven Protestant representatives: Baptist, Congregational, Disciples of Christ, Episcopal, Lutheran, Methodist and Presbyterian.[88] Particularly daunting was Foster's plan to have weighted representation for Jews and Catholics. He recalled how he "struggled to get more Catholic and Jewish representation on the [Iowa] Board than one each" and that "both Catholics and Jews generally look upon Protestants as a block and thus an overwhelming majority."[89] Arguing against proportional representation, he used the Methodists as an example. They alone would have "many times the representation of the Jews" and "leave the Catholics in an indefensible minority." He commented that this issue led to the "sharpest thrusts."[90] Foster envisioned the Iowa school as a tri-faith ideal of American society in which

Catholics, Jews, and Protestants would carry equal weight regardless of their numbers.

Another cause for concern was that the university academic departments would be teaching courses about religion, such as the history, literature, psychology, and philosophy of religion, and that those academic courses might be taught from an abstract, unsympathetic, scientific perspective, despite the fact that a separate faculty of Jewish, Catholic, and Protestant clerics would each teach his own religion from an emotional, interpretive, and moral point of view. These tri-faith, clerical faculty members would be specially appointed and funded by their respective churches, synagogues or religious groups.[91]

Nevertheless, Foster worried that there would be confusion, and that certain Jews, Protestants, and Catholics would be "sensitive" about outsiders teaching their religion. "If we give . . . the impression that the University Faculty will *interpret* Religion they will oppose us," Foster wrote in a letter to Rufus Fitzgerald. He suggested that "we . . . constantly guard our statements" and keep clarifying that the academic professor does not interpret religion but rather shows the contribution of his academic discipline to the "moral and religious life of the Nation."[92]

Overcoming the objections of the various religious groups took time and good will. The common desire of various religious leaders to improve religious education at state universities and Foster's persistence and persuasiveness helped carry the day. Good humor seems to have helped, too. Foster recalled a meeting of the Iowa religious groups when "the storm [about weighted board representation] was at its height." Monsignor William A. Shannahan from St. Patrick's Church, "full of Irish" and "irenic spirit," called out in his "droll voice" [to Eugene Mannheimer, reform rabbi], "I hear that the K.K.K. has gotten [so] successful that the Jews are going to take it over." "When there are any good investments in sight, some of us are likely to be nosing about," Mannheimer replied, adding that "I heard the other day that since the Klan has been so successful in resolidifying [*sic*] the Catholic Church that the Jesuits started it." "Nothing less than an avalanche . . . of laughter followed, shaking the Old Capital building to its very foundations," Foster observed, commenting on how "the good natured repartee between Shannahan and Mannheimer had shown their human side and lightened the mood of the meeting in contrast to the previously grim disposition of the others" and that the "minority groups had saved us from disaster by the majority."[93]

The first board of the ISR included eleven Protestant members, two Catholic members, and two Jewish members. Although short of Foster's goal of equal, weighted religious representation, the numbers roughly reflected their proportion in the Iowa population at the time.[94] Moreover, that first year E. D. Adler (Jewish) served as the second vice president of the board and Thomas Farrell (Catholic) served as treasurer, and both served on the executive committee. Foster's commitment to building tri-faith fellowship took shape, and project number one of the AAR helped transfer his concept of tri-faith cooperation from the wartime military to American civilian life. One major hurdle remained, however: finding a director for the Iowa School.[95]

The first director to be chosen (serving from 1927 to 1953) was Foster's good friend Matthew Willard Lampe. He had served as a Presbyterian student pastor at the University of Pennsylvania and generally as a religious leader of university students. As the secretary for university work of the Presbyterian Church on the Council of Church Boards of Education, Lampe "greatly admired" both Robert E. Speer, secretary of the Presbyterian board of foreign missions, and Yale professor Henry B. Wright. Wright had written *The Will of God and a Man's Life Work*, a book that Lampe "treasured almost as much as the Bible." "Cradled and reared in a family of strong missionary spirit," Lampe was captivated by Wright's statement that "state universities are the greatest missionary field in the world." The rapid growth of secular, public higher education had led Lampe as well to see state universities as a fertile field for what Wright called missionary work. But Lampe's friendship with Foster had radically changed his understanding of "missionary work." Rather than viewing it as spreading Christianity he now understood it to mean spreading tri-faith fellowship. He claimed that Foster taught him "to suffer with one another's defeats, and rejoice in one another's victories, as much as" [if they came] "to one's own group."[96] With this in mind, Lampe devoted his career at Iowa to teaching university students religious cooperation, fellowship, and respect for religious diversity.

Project Number Two: The University Religious Conference

Once Project Number One at Iowa was underway, O. D. Foster boarded a train from New York City to Los Angeles to begin work on Project Number

Two, a school of religion at the Southern Branch of the University of California, soon to be known as the University of California at Los Angeles (UCLA). Foster arrived in spring 1926, when the Southern Branch was seven years old. Located on the campus of what had been the California Normal School, on Vermont Street in Hollywood, within a few years UCLA would be moving to a new campus in Westwood, a suburb then being developed about ten miles to the west.

Foster stayed in Los Angeles for a month, returning several times for later visits. He came to Los Angeles as part of a national program of the CCBE to build Protestant cooperation at secular state universities.[97] The CCBE sent Foster to work with the interdenominational District Superintendents' Council of the Protestant Churches of Southern California (DSC). Although together they were meant to set up a Protestant program at the Southern Branch, Foster instead wanted to lay the foundation for an interfaith school of religion, a goal supported by the AAR.[98]

Meeting the members of the DSC was Foster's first step. He was pleased to discover that two of them were open to working with non-Protestant groups. Specifically, George F. Kengott and Guy W. Wadsworth seemed sympathetic to Foster's plan of devising a multireligious outreach program for the students at the Southern Branch and to join the committee that Foster was hoping to organize. Kengott, a Congregationalist, was president of the DSC and "knew something beyond ecclesiastical horizons," in Foster's view. Wadsworth, a member of the Church Federation of Los Angeles, was a leader in the Presbyterian USA Church in Southern California and struck Foster as "an unusually understanding man."[99]

Foster then turned his attention to the university. The most influential leader at the Southern Branch was E. C. Moore and so Foster called on him. It turned out that the two men had much in common. Both were born in the 1870s and raised in the Midwest. Both had graduated from technical colleges before receiving more advanced degrees and ultimately PhDs from highly respected universities. Both had spent years in Chicago and held favorable views of Hull House, among the most prominent of the Chicago settlement houses. Moore had volunteered there, as mentioned earlier.[100] Academics both, Foster a biblical linguist and an educator, Moore a classicist, a teacher, and professor of education and philosophy, the two men were equally seekers and innovators. Their paths had briefly crossed at Yale, shortly before the war, while

Moore was there as a professor of education and Foster as a doctoral candidate and teacher of Greek. The Yale connection "brought us to a good start," recalled Foster.[101]

Foster and Moore saw university education as a vehicle for advancing ideals of civility and tolerance. This came naturally to Moore, who had served on the faculty of the University of California at Berkeley in his early days, then as the superintendent of the Los Angeles public school system, and thereafter as a professor at Yale. After that Moore became a professor at Harvard, then the president of the California State Normal School at Los Angeles, and finally a principal founder, director, and provost of UCLA. Perhaps their most important similarity involved a lesson both men had learned from the First World War, namely, the urgency of working for their idealistic goals: Foster as a leader for interfaith fellowship and Moore as a crusader for liberal teacher training. Moore's goal was to turn the California Normal School into a teachers' college, "a great school of education for the Pacific west comparable to Teachers College at Columbia University and the School of Education at the University of Chicago." At the end of the war, Moore's crowning achievement was helping to establish the Southern Branch as a university to educate teachers in the humanities so they could teach each of their pupils "to use his own mind in comprehending the process of human living."[102]

Ultimately, Moore's postwar visionary goal may have inclined him to listen sympathetically to Foster explain his vision of expanding religious brotherhood among students. It seemed that the First World War had once again played a crucial role for Foster, in that the connection with Moore would lead to transforming tri-faith idealism into a future reality at UCLA. At their meeting Moore introduced Foster to Earl Miller, the UCLA Dean of Men, and Helen Matthewson Laughlin, the UCLA Dean of Women. Laughlin, like Kengott and Wadsworth, seemed willing to join the committee for university student religious outreach that Foster was working to assemble. At the same time, Moore also appointed a university committee to study the issue of religious and moral life on campus.[103]

Continuing on, Foster turned to the Catholic leaders in southern California. His connection to Archbishop Dowling smoothed his way when he called on John Joseph Cantwell, Catholic bishop of Los Angeles and San Diego. Cantwell knew of Dowling's support for religious cooperation a few years earlier at the bishops' meeting in Washington, DC, and his own mentor, Archbishop

Edward Joseph Hanna of San Francisco, also favored religious cooperation.[104] Cantwell became a "devoted cooperator," Foster reported, suggesting Thomas K. Gorman for Foster's aborning committee. Gorman was the editor of the *Tidings*, the oldest continuously published Catholic weekly on the West Coast, first published in 1895. It served the Los Angeles-San Diego diocese and the Monterey-Fresno diocese. He would later be appointed as the first bishop of Reno.[105]

For the Jewish representative, Foster approached Edgar Magnin, rabbi of the reform Wilshire Temple. Foster had heard that Magnin was "generally accepted as the leader of Los Angeles Judaism." Several Hollywood figures such as Louis Mayer and the Warner brothers were members of Magnin's congregation. It was Foster's connection with supporters of the AAR that helped open the door to Magnin as it had to Cantwell. Magnin knew David Philipson. It was Philipson's name on the AAR letterhead that persuaded Magnin to consider serving on the committee that Foster was organizing, "so long as it does not conflict with some of the ideas which I believe are fundamental. I am still opposed at heart, to the erecting of any buildings on the campus for religious purposes."[106] Soon thereafter the California Board of Regents took a similar position, and plans for locating a structure for religious worship on campus were discontinued.[107] Subsequently Magnin became a dedicated supporter of religious cooperation at UCLA and, over the decades, remained an active participant in the URC. Several Hollywood figures, such as Cecil B. DeMille, the Warner brothers, and Louis B. Mayer, also became active participants and contributors to the URC, likely because of Magnin.[108]

In less than a month Foster had assembled his "cabinet," or the "four cornerstones" upon which he had hoped "to erect a state-interfaith structure." From these beginnings, Foster organized the Provisional Committee of Religious Cooperation (PCRC). The committee members included Helen Laughlin, Gorman, Kengott, Wadsworth, Magnin, as well as Foster himself.[109]

Foster took the lead in proposing the PCRC's basic goals. After some discussion, Gorman moved and Laughlin seconded a motion that Foster's proposals be adopted. Most of these resembled principles of religious cooperation that had shaped CIS and the ISR: "To cultivate good will and confidence between religious groups at the University" and "to promote, through helpful co-operation and sympathetic understanding, the vital interests of each group without sacrifice or compromise of principle or practice." Other goals were to provide "high grade religious instruction," to consider "the views of the different groups," and to "foster comprehensive, co-operative religious activities in the university community."[110]

The following year the university committee that Moore had appointed made its report, which recommended that the university be sympathetic to what it called a University Religious Council and cooperate with the churches "in the gradual attainment of religious and moral objectives." The report commented on the "almost unprecedented measure of religious concord among the Jewish, Catholic and Protestant faiths" in the Los Angeles area and predicted that "a different situation" will obtain "at Westwood than normally exists."[111]

All except Magnin attended the first two meetings, the first held on May 7, 1926, at the Hotel Alexandria, the next one scheduled soon thereafter at the Ladies' Dining Room of the University Club. Foster later found out that the University Club was closed to Jews. Upon finding out about these restrictions, he admitted his "thoughtlessness" and scheduled future meetings elsewhere. His obliviousness suggests how out of touch he, and the university committee appointed by Moore, must have been regarding the practical daily exclusions imposed upon Jews in American and Los Angeles society in the 1920s.[112] As suggested earlier, Foster's interest in furthering interfaith relations seems to have stemmed more from a desire for expanding religious dialogue and cooperation than from personal knowledge of specific exclusions.

The new university campus in Westwood, a suburb then being developed by the Janss Investment Company on some four hundred acres of open barley fields, had few houses of worship nearby.[113] This scarcity likely strengthened the determination of the URC founders to work together to provide their own facilities. They agreed to construct a building cooperatively, located near the campus, where representatives or student pastors of various faiths could meet with students of their flock, offer pastoral care, and afford opportunities for Jewish, Catholic, and Protestant students to cooperate with each other in extracurricular religious activities. The building was to give each of the denominational and religious leaders equal office space next to one another in the hope of fostering ongoing ties among them.[114]

The goals laid out by the PCRC during Foster's first month in Los Angeles were more in line with his own interfaith values and those of the AAR than with the Protestant agenda of the CCBE. In fact, the committee agreed "to maintain a close relationship with the American Association on Religion." Nothing was said about the CCBE.[115]

During the coming months, the PCRC met several times. In October, when Foster returned to Los Angeles, there were some replacements on the committee, which by then had enlarged its membership and taken on a new name, the Central University Religious Council (CURC). The DSC had replaced Kengott with Edwin P. Ryland, a supporter of liberal Protestant ecumenism, member of the DSC, and secretary of the Federation of Churches of California and of Los Angeles. He had been the pastor of the First Methodist Church of Hollywood before being expelled for his pacifism during the First World War. He then became the pastor of the Mt. Hollywood Congregational Church. The DSC also appointed conservative J. D. Fox of the Baptist Mission, and a good friend of Frank Padelford of the CCBE.[116]

The larger membership of CURC included new Catholic and Jewish members. Charles C. Conaty, later chaplain of the Los Angeles City College Newman Club, became the second Catholic member. Mayer Winkler, Conservative rabbi of Temple Sinai in Los Angeles, joined Magnin as the second Jewish representative. Foster recalled how, when he first called on Winkler, an immigrant from Vienna, he was "frigidly received and we were getting nowhere." Then they began discussing their academic interests. Winkler's scholarship had been on patristics. Foster's doctoral dissertation had been on the ancient languages of the Old Testament. Foster commented, "How curious! You, a Jew, took your degree in a Christian field while I, a Christian took mine in a Semitic field." After that Foster claimed that he had "few warmer friends in Los Angeles."[117]

An at-large category with a slot for two members was added and set aside for the Board of Regents, but the regents left the slot unfilled. Instead, the CURC filled one of the slots with Foster to represent the AAR and Bertram Stevens, Episcopalian bishop of Los Angeles, to represent a "middle ground position between Catholic and Protestant groups." Stevens also served as a liaison between the CURC, university students, and the general public. Foster described Stevens as "nearest in spirit to Bishop Brent, Episcopal Chief of Army Chaplains of the American Expeditionary Force in World War One, former president of Comrades in Service and of the AAR."[118]

The URC Takes Shape

Surprisingly, helping to found the URC turned out to be easier for Foster than helping to found the Iowa School. The Southern Branch was a new school with little religious infrastructure to dilute Foster's influence. He had only to deal with religious leaders from Los Angeles, not from across the state. Ironically, the stringent California restrictions against promoting religion at state universities left the way open for Foster. He got in on the ground floor and was able to line up support among the local groups outside the university and from the academic and administrative leaders at the Southern Branch as well. Most of the Los Angeles religious, community, and educational leaders he dealt with seemed amenable to his interfaith plans and open to cooperating on building a headquarters for the URC off campus. In fact, the building of the off-campus URC headquarters turned out to be a cooperative Catholic, Jewish, and Protestant project.[119]

Over the next two years, the CURC was renamed the University Religious Conference, and Foster continued to make occasional visits to Los Angeles to oversee its progress. Changes in the membership and organizational structure took place, and the URC became a multifaith institution, bringing together not only Catholics, Jews, and Protestants but Mormons and eventually Greek Orthodox members. Student pastors of these faiths ministered to students at UCLA in the URC building. Unlike the Iowa School, the URC offered no university credit courses and paid no university faculty. It had no funding from or formal affiliation with UCLA or with any tax supported public university in California.[120]

The URC was less academic than the ISR. The ISR hired a tri-faith clerical faculty to teach credit-granting courses on campus to the university students. To recall, this faculty's salaries were paid for by the religious groups in the state. Eventually the ISR developed a program for student involvement in community activities, but clerical faculty directed the community program and the central focus of the ISR remained academic course work.

As for the URC, aside from the student pastors of the different faiths and denominations who offered pastoral care for the students, the organization's central focus came to be student social action in the community. Although there were various religious activities such as lectures, religious clubs, and events celebrating religious holidays, the most popular URC programs were community social action programs.

Looking back on the Jewish and Catholic concerns of the AAR members, it seems some of them were met. In the case of the ISR, he Jewish concern about separation of church and state was addressed in part. Although the state of Iowa approved of teaching religion on the Iowa campus, it did not pay for the clerical faculty and no openly religious buildings were allowed on the campus except for the YMCA building. The ISR board of trustees did not have the weighted representation that Foster wanted, but the two Jewish representatives on the board overrepresented the Jewish population in Iowa. As for the URC, it satisfied the Jewish requirements. Separation of church and state was observed, and no religious buildings were built on campus, largely thanks to the strict requirements of the California Board of Regents. As for the Catholic requirement that Catholic doctrine be taught, the ISR had a Catholic faculty member who taught courses from a Catholic perspective, but the Catholic faculty slot often was unfilled. The URC lacked a Catholic faculty member but had provision for a Catholic religious figure to offer student pastoral care, just as other student pastors did for their coreligionists.

While the Iowa model more closely resembled Foster's plan, he had reservations about the URC. As a man of religion, an academic ill at ease with conspicuous displays, he looked down on the glitz, celebrity, and wealth of nearby Hollywood and what he believed was the undue influence of the Janss Investment Company. He thought that the latter had pulled strings with the Board of Regents for private gain, in order to have the Westwood site selected for the university. He called the Westwood site the "Janss-Banker-Regents site." Foster preferred the Palos Verde site, which had also been considered. "One was inspired by a generous and noble vision, the other by tempting dividends and opportunities. One looked across the seas to the Orient, up the coast to Alaska, down the coast to Chile . . . in an atmosphere of tranquility conducive to study. . . . The other had the pull, glamour, distraction, moral shaking . . . of Movie-Stardom and real estate manipulations," Foster wrote.[121] He failed to anticipate what a positive force the figures of the movie world would be for URC funding and publicity.

Foster also failed to anticipate how the URC would influence other universities and colleges in California. He failed to foresee the prestige and notice that the URC would bring to the new California university, a humble institution in the 1920s. Nor did he predict its impact on the larger community, as branches of the URC opened at other schools and universities in the city and the state.[122]

Moore, of course, was aware of the potential influence of the aborning URC on the prestige of UCLA. The favorable publicity and new status that the URC brought to the university seems to have vindicated him. He recalled the early days of the Southern Branch, when "contempt . . . was poured upon our efforts to provide adequate training for elementary school teachers." It was "a thing of humble beginnings . . . not socially capitalized . . . not a country club. That is its strength. Students come to it for work, not because it is the thing to do to go there." He added, "Those who want to go to a country club go elsewhere." Perhaps Moore was thinking of the University of Southern California (USC), which then drew its students primarily from the elite. It must have gratified him when, a few years after the URC was established, USC became a member and set up a branch on its own campus.[123]

Finding the right leader was key to making the URC successful. The hiring committee chose Thomas St. Clair Evans as executive secretary, a post he held from 1928 until he retired in 1945. Frank Padelford and Frank Lincoln Kelly, both Protestant ecumenists from the CCBE and opponents of Foster on interfaith outreach, supported Evans. Foster's views about him at the time were tentative. A Presbyterian then at the interdenominational Protestant International Council of Religious Education in New York City, Evans had spent his career working with Protestant students and the YMCA, at Princeton, at the University of Michigan, and at the University of Pennsylvania, where he had devised the Pennsylvania Plan, which included the campus YMCA and the local churches, all working cooperatively with the Protestant students at the university. During the First World War Evans had been on the staff of the War Work Council of the YMCA, working with men in war industries. Although not an academic with an advanced degree, Evans turned out to be a good choice to lead the URC. He had had experience combining religious outreach and social action. He and his wife had lived at a settlement house in Philadelphia and had directed a camp for underprivileged children when he was at the University of Pennsylvania.

Foster thought that perhaps Evans "had learned enough lessons both in successes and failures to profit by experience and that if he rose to the idea [of the URC] as a real challenge [it would] . . . bring out the best that is in him." But Foster was still undecided and wanted to consult with Lampe. If Lampe approved, Foster would recommend Evans for the position. Lampe and Foster "had long talks over it." Lampe, who had worked with Evans at the University of Pennsylvania, thought Evans could rise to the interfaith challenge.[124]

Evans met with the hiring committee of the URC in Los Angeles, and in Foster's words, he was "quickly taken to their arms." Soon after Evans was hired, Foster paid a two-month visit to Los Angeles to observe him and the progress of the URC. In a confidential report to the AAR, Foster commented on how "patiently, tactfully and successfully" Evans was in handling his new position. "During this time I discovered in him no favoritism of any group . . . He is the embodiment of the spirit of fairness and is trusted and respected by all." "It was indeed gratifying to see how much progress has been made" and how "there has evolved a working corporation with standing committees and an active staff," the report continued. Foster praised not only Evans but also Adaline Guenther, "his efficient and indefatigable secretary," whom Evans had worked with in New York City before following him to Los Angeles. "They are feeling their way in a prophetic pioneering enterprise. . . . [and] must work without precedent."[125]

Foster's report also commended some fifteen Catholic, Protestant, and Jewish leaders and supporters of the URC. "Here Catholic, Jew and Protestant are working together to a common end arraying their forces along-side of instead of against each other." Furthermore, "A new era of good-will, mutual understanding, and cooperation has dawned. The leaders of all groups have learned to know each other . . . the higher motive of each other, and of the real desire for fair play on the part of all. In fact, the influence already of the U.R.C. will reach to the very ends of the earth."[126]

The hiring of Evans and Guenther took place as the URC opened its doors in 1928. "After nearly two years of discussion and consideration by representatives of all religious interests in Southern California, there has been formed the Conference whose inception has been hailed by clergy and laity alike with approbation," wrote Catholic chaplain of the URC Newman Club Charles Conaty to E. C. Moore. Commenting on the spirit of religious cooperation, Conaty's letter continues, "We are working together with this common end in view, the Youth in our universities shall have that which is its right and due—an education in religion commensurate with its education in secular knowledge, an opportunity to know God and His creation as well as man and his works."[127]

The interfaith character of the URC especially pleased Moore. It "has brought all the groups together and made them know each other and talk together of their common interest without at all encouraging them to aloofness and separateness." He noted that such "respect" and "helpfulness" are "the finest thing in our civilization" and "an antidote to war. Wars have been fought about religious differences. It is time to make an end of them by learning to live in cordial regard and amity."[128]

To be sure, not just idealism but practical considerations helped create the opportunity for interfaith cooperation at the URC, as they had with CIS. Such considerations were an important starting point and sharing space in a building within blocks of the UCLA campus was a tempting lure. It gave the participating religious groups access to the students and the possibility of offering them pastoral care.[129] As a newly developing suburb, not only did Westwood have few places of worship nearby but the cost of having an office at the URC for each religious group was less than building a separate house of worship in the area.

There were other apparent benefits, as well. "Not the least among the notable accomplishments of this movement [the URC] has been a realization that the groups could work together without infringing upon or attacking the doctrinal positions of participating churches. This phase of the effort alone has resulted in a better mutual understanding," Catholic URC leader Thomas K. Gorman declared, observing that the "greatest cordiality has existed between the various groups which presages well for future mutual understandings."[130] Foster too thought that the URC was building religious understanding in higher education by addressing religious prejudice and the "blind competition in religion," which he called "suicidal." He saw the URC as providing an alternative framework for religious cooperation.[131]

Catholics played an important role in housing the original URC. Before the URC moved to Westwood, its first home was Newman Hall, a club house on Willowbrook Avenue, just north of the old California Normal School campus. The Newman Club was located in Newman Hall, which was now open to all university students. It had a lounge, library, and lunch room, and housed the offices of the Baptist, Catholic, Disciples of Christ, Episcopalian, Jewish, Lutheran, Methodist, and Presbyterian student pastors.[132]

The principle of interfaith cooperation governed the composition of the URC officers and the board of directors. The first URC president was

Baptist James B. Fox. Catholics and Jews also held positions of leadership with Thomas K. Gorman as first vice president and Edgar F. Magnin as second vice president. In addition, URC officers rotated positions annually among Jewish, Catholic, and Protestant members. The presence of Catholic and Jewish leaders alongside Protestants demonstrated that at the URC those of all three religions were accepted as legitimate members of society and deserving of respect.[133] Such legitimacy and respect were not to be taken for granted in the 1920s in the face of widespread religious intolerance and nativism.

Foster left the scene after Lampe and Evans assumed their respective positions. With these two institutions, he had achieved his goal of transferring to civilian life the spirit of interfaith fellowship that he had experienced in the First World War.[134]

CHAPTER THREE

Building Community at the
University Religious Conference

It is a spirit of light in an age of darkness, a ray of hope in a world of gloom, in which
death and catastrophe are . . . close to our shoulders . . . The Conference deals with
the intangible and the imponderables . . . that count in this world. They decide
whether men shall be human beings or beasts.
—*Rabbi Edgar F. Magnin, speaking of the University Religious Conference, May 1938*

The University Religious Conference emerged in the 1930s, amid economic
and political turmoil that included not only the Great Depression at home
and abroad but the rise of Nazism. At the time, Nazi organizations in Southern California were hatching plots to hang Louis Mayer, Samuel Goldwyn,
and some twenty other Hollywood figures and to machine gun thousands of
Jews living in Boyle Heights, a Los Angeles neighborhood near downtown.[1]
Hollywood was in the sights of German and American Nazis because of its
importance as a propaganda center and the large number of Jews involved in
the movie industry.

Dozens of donors and leaders at the URC were marked as victims of these
Nazi plots or were involved in foiling them. As established in the previous
chapter, Rabbi Edgar Magnin was one the major religious leaders active in the
URC. Louis Mayer and Sol Lesser were among the many URC Jewish donors.
It is unlikely that Thomas Evans and Adaline Guenther knew the specifics
of the Nazi plots, but they clearly envisioned the URC as an institution that
would stand in opposition to the master race ideology and the Christian nationalism of the day. They sought to teach university students and the public
about religious pluralism and equality through the URC example.

While UCLA was in the process of moving from its former campus in Hollywood to the developing suburb of Westwood, the URC was looking for its
own Westwood site to construct a building near the campus. Raising the funds
to purchase the site and constructing the building turned out to be a major

84

cooperative religious venture in itself. A URC building committee of members from Jewish, Catholic, and Episcopalian backgrounds was formed. It comprised Edgar Magnin, rabbi of the reform Wilshire Temple; John J. Cawley, Catholic monsignor and vicar general of Los Angeles; and Cecil B. De Mille, Hollywood producer and director. De Mille, who chaired the committee, came from a family of both Jewish and Episcopalian heritage. He contributed major financial backing, as did Mrs. Seeley Mudd and the Catholic E. L. Doheny family. In 1930 the Dohenys donated $30,000 to purchase the land for the building. The following year construction was completed, and the URC moved in. Located at 10845 Le Conte, just blocks from the UCLA campus, it was constructed of brick, in the Italian neo-Romanesque style, echoing the architecture of the campus but far more modest.[2]

The very architecture of the new URC building communicated equality and cooperation among those of different religions. The windows of the adjacent offices of the student pastors, sometimes called religious advisers—all of whom were of different faiths—looked out upon a common courtyard, symbolizing their equal status, cooperative spirit, and common purpose to provide pastoral care for the UCLA students.[3] URC founders and staff also hoped that the design would encourage the religious advisers to work with one another on interfaith projects and encourage the student visitors to get to know one another and work together on their own interfaith initiatives.[4] In fact, the religious advisers, who often worked part-time, rarely engaged in interfaith projects themselves. Engaging the students in working together on interfaith projects became a major responsibility of URC executive secretary Thomas Evans and his assistant Adaline Guenther.

John Joseph Cantwell, the Catholic bishop of Los Angeles-San Diego, J. D. Fox, of the Baptist Mission in Los Angeles, and Edgar Magnin all took part in the dedication of the new URC building in 1931. The building inscription read, "To our common faith in God, For the development of keener appreciation of the values inherent in our religious faiths and culture, To the creation of harmony and friendly understanding between peoples of varying religious faiths."[5] The first religious groups to be involved in the URC included Baptist, Episcopal, Church of Jesus Christ of Latter-Day Saints, Jewish, Lutheran, Methodist, Presbyterian, and Roman Catholic. The membership changed over time, but most of the original religious groups remained with the URC for more than fifty years. Groups that joined later included the Congregationalists, Disciples of Christ, the Eastern Orthodox Church, the Society of Friends, the Unitarians, and the nondenominational YMCA.[6]

One year after the dedication, Mrs. Lyman Farwell, Mrs. O. P. Clark, and Mrs. Milo Bekins donated money for the addition of a small dormitory wing for URC students in need. Most of the URC students commuted from home, except for the few who lived at fraternity and sorority houses. Four years later, another wing was added for guests, thanks to gifts from the Church of Jesus Christ of Latter-Day Saints, Louis B. Mayer, and Presbyterian Alphonso Bell.[7] The URC building was the "only structure in the world," later wrote the *Los Angeles Times*, "paid for with money raised by religious groups for the purpose of carrying on other religions than their own."[8]

URC Executive Secretary Thomas Evans favored the expansion of the URC to other nearby colleges and universities through the formation of extension branches on their campuses.[9] Within the first few years of operation, the URC expanded its local footprint to include two other campuses, the Los Angeles Junior College (later called the Los Angeles City College [LACC]) and the University of Southern California (USC). Soon after UCLA vacated its original Hollywood campus on Vermont Avenue, the LACC was founded and occupied that campus. The LACC opened its doors in 1930 and soon thereafter established a URC extension branch that lasted for decades. In 1933 USC opened an extension URC branch on its campus that lasted about seven years.[10] Both branches were included in the URC budget; the URC provided both of them with an organizational and programmatic model and, when needed, assisted with their administration.[11] Students at each of the three schools participated in several URC student programs and developed similar ones on their own.

The three schools differed from one another. USC was founded in 1880 as a private university with Methodist affiliation, not subject to the same rigorous religious restrictions that the California Board of Regents had placed upon UCLA. As a private university, USC could and did pay faculty and staff for religious instruction on campus. Although a public institution, LACC was under a different jurisdiction than the California Board of Regents. As a two-year college, it had fewer religious restrictions than UCLA, but more than USC. Occasionally the LACC held student assemblies on campus that dealt with religious issues and offered a course or two on religion for limited credit. Despite their differences, all three schools found the URC student projects, religious programs, and clerical connections to be of value for their respective student bodies and communities.[12]

The expansion of the URC was a promising sign that it was gaining ground and increasing its influence in Los Angeles. Other URC branches were set up in the 1940s, at East Los Angeles City and Harbor City Colleges, both junior colleges; in the 1950s, a branch of the URC was established at UC Riverside and an independent institution modeled on the original URC was set up at the University of California at Santa Barbara soon after its foundation in the 1940s.[13]

New Student Board

Mindful of the surrounding bigotry, Evans and Guenther sought to teach university students and the public about religious pluralism and equality through the URC example. The organization's main goal became to encourage students of different backgrounds to work together across religious lines. In search of programs to engage student interest and cooperation, Evans and Guenther turned to student-centered service projects, beyond institutional religion, as vehicles to stimulate interfaith fellowship. Overseeing the URC Student Board at UCLA was Guenther's job. Disappointed with the previous student board, which had been made up of student representatives of the URC extracurricular religious clubs such as the Menorah, Newman, and Wesley Clubs, Guenther came up with a plan for a more dynamic board that would appeal to students and expose them to diversity.

In order to change both the membership and purpose of the board, Guenther sought to replace the old membership with popular students of various religions or of none. The selection criteria included their popularity and leadership ability. The board members' job would be to develop, staff, recruit, and generate enthusiasm for extracurricular projects that would attract diverse students and get them to cooperate. Whereas the purpose of the old student board had been to plan and organize student religious activities that emphasized identification with a particular religious tradition or institution, the new board would work outside the bounds of conventional religion to plan and organize projects with wide appeal to a cross section of UCLA students. These student-centered projects would become the heart of the URC, in contrast to the academic approach of the tri-faith ISR.

No doubt the prohibition of the California Board of Regents against granting university credit for courses on religion and other campus-based conventional religious activities made it all the more imperative for the URC to focus on projects that would attract students to its off-campus location. Although other tax-supported state universities (like the University of Iowa) had worked out various stratagems for conducting robust religious programs on campus, such stratagems did not work in California, considered to be the strictest of all the states when it came to the separation of church and state.[14] Fortuitously, these restrictions played into the strengths of Evans and Guenther. Both the decades that Evans had spent as YMCA student religious leader on university campuses and Guenther's practical Methodist bent prepared them well to experiment with social action projects. As a result, not only was their mission of expanding religious inclusion undeterred by the California restrictions but the latter propelled the pair to keep experimenting with novel projects that would appeal to students. Guenther in particular was always on the lookout for promising new student projects.

"Adaline Guenther always said you have to have one project that you're completing, one project in process, and one project that you're getting underway," URC graduate Bill Burke commented, adding that "she always had three projects."[15] "In the early days . . . the URC student activities were participated in only by a small group of students," said former URC student Bill Gray. "Those of us who were in the various [religious] clubs felt they were worthwhile . . . But we had a hard time convincing the campus at large. And then in 1934, Miss G. asked me for a list of the twenty most important people on the campus. Quite easily I put down the ASUC president, the head of Pan Hel, the football team's best lineman. Then she said: 'Now invite them to make up the membership of a Student Religious Board. I have an idea they will accept.'" He went on to say, "I had no such idea—but as others have learned, Miss G. is a hard woman to say no to—and I did, and they did."[16] All at once Guenther replaced the denominational students with student leaders who had a sphere of influence. As it happened, they also had good looks, charisma, and lively minds.[17]

After the new board took shape, two distinct and separate groups emerged at the URC, each with different goals: the denominational clubs, for the propagation of institutional religion, and the new student board, for promoting cooperation among those of all faiths. The new board's other goals included arousing curiosity among students on campus, stirring up their interest in joining the URC, and making participation in the URC a mark of status on campus and in the community. As a result, proportionality among Catholics, Protestants and Jews—while still an important URC principle—took a back seat to choosing the right students for the board: those who could meet Guenther's standards for popularity and leadership potential.[18] The students on the new board became her favorites.[19] Guenther had an eye for students best able to attract others, and she used her shrewd salesmanship to bring them in and lead the URC with energy, verve and flair. She handpicked them year after year and worked closely with them.

For Guenther, an important attribute of the board members, perhaps *the* most important attribute, was leadership potential, certainly more so than religious commitment. Unsurprisingly, some of the new members told fellow URC Board Member Jean Burke that they didn't know why Guenther had invited them since they were not religious and did not go to church. Her "whole philosophy was we pick out the leaders and then we give them religion," Burke explained. "You can't take leadership out of somebody's body, but you can rarely ever make a leader out of somebody who isn't already a born leader, so we'll take the leaders and we'll get them religion and get them respect for each other."[20]

And so, the URC Student Board came to be comprised of attractive and popular university leaders who got the nod from Guenther, "an avowed elitist who had a knack for making the Board a mark of status," observed former URC Student Board members Robert and Shirley Hine. "Guenther soon transformed it into her own elite student governing body, her politburo, her working cabinet."[21] "Everybody wanted to be a part of the student board. It just got to be the thing," declared another member, Irving Goldring. "If you were invited to be on the student board, you were in and fraternity leaders, everybody would come. I mean, she really had influence, and I think we were all in awe of her."[22] A "real manipulator," exclaimed another URC Student Board member, Bill Burke, relating how Guenther had picked Bill Gray to head the board over Al Chamie because she thought Gray had more drive than Chamie, who she saw as too much of a negotiator. She "didn't want people looking at both sides of things. She wanted them to be pretty much committed to what her program was."[23]

Guenther had an innate attraction to charismatic people and understood how to enter their circle and to make them part of her own. She was well-suited to work her spell over college students who were a bit insecure, conscious of status, and wanted to be part of an "in group." Born on the cusp of the twentieth century, she was about fifteen to twenty years older than the students who graduated in the 1930s, young enough to understand their world, yet old enough to exert cultural authority and savoir faire. As a woman in a position of authority, she took on the persona of a grandmother, although for the first decade of her career she was obviously too young for that moniker. But it gave her authority, brought her affection, and made her seem safe and approachable.

Guenther's charisma came with a manipulative streak. Knowing that religion by itself was insufficient to draw the attention of most college students, she combined it with status, glamor, and popularity to make it exciting and attractive, and with service to make it fulfilling and the basis for camaraderie. She turned the student projects into a shared experience of cooperation, which was in her mind akin to a form of religious cooperation. Guenther's age and authority set her above the students and made it a mark of prestige to be in her good graces.

Members of the new board numbered about twenty. They were campus athletes, editors, debaters, campus politicians, members of different fraternities and sororities, independents, a few Catholics, a few Jews, Protestants of various sects, an African American or two, and about equal numbers of male and female students, each with a spark, "an outreaching spirit and mind."[24] "Most of us, even the most sophisticated," said former URC student Bill Gray, "have a deep-seated hunger for religion, and a desire to participate in the things for which the URC stands."[25] That said, Guenther would nevertheless dredge up "a lonely atheist . . . from the bowels of the library if he had the spark which would ignite others," noted Robert and Shirley Hine.[26] "You know, more new ideas come out of the religious conference," UCLA History faculty member Paige Smith told his friend Luke Fishburn, "than come out of the university."[27] The new board was "so composed that the sparks would spring whenever it gathered."[28]

"The Student Board opened my mind and made me think for myself," board member Don Hitchcock said, describing how the board became "a training ground for its members, who . . . discover the tremendous thrill which the recognition of a stranger-as-a-brother can give."[29] "My experience as a member and chairman of the Student Board," wrote Frank Wilkinson, "has meant more to me than anything else I have encountered during my four years in the university. . . . The greatest work of the Student Board is . . . experiencing absolute religious understanding among . . . fellow student leaders of the university."[30] These bright, charismatic student leaders, whether religious or not, defined the new board. Guenther looked to them to undertake large service projects that would carry students "beyond home, classroom, fraternity or playing field."[31] In these circumstances, the board came to be the most dynamic part of the URC, giving it shape and direction. It became the core of the URC, its intellectual center and its heart, indispensable to its identity. Valuing spirited debate on moral, philosophical, and religious questions, Guenther saw the board as a means to bridge the gap between religion and the academy, linking "the transcendent search" and "intellectual pursuit" at a time when students found churches "ineffectually irrelevant" and "universities isolated, amoral and abstracted from everyday life."[32]

Every other Sunday evening Thomas Evans and his wife Edith would invite members of the student board to their small, plain house on Missouri Avenue in Sawtelle, a poor neighborhood west of the UCLA campus, populated mostly by those of Mexican American and Japanese American background. At their simple house, in line with their simple tastes, the Evanses would host a group of the students on the board for discussions and socializing. Later Adaline Guenther took over hosting similar Sunday night salon-like get-togethers at her house on Elwood Street in Westwood. There she would serve up light refreshments and religious, political, and philosophical topics to "draw everybody out," said Jean Burke who described how Guenther would stimulate discussions by asking a question like, "What's your theory about the afterlife?" Explaining that these discussions would take place "so often" and "month after month and year after year" so that the students "became really good friends," Burke concluded, "this is what . . . cemented everything together." Guenther was determined to "get these leaders to be friends or else."[33]

"Students would sit on the floor by the fireplace," wrote Robert Hine. "The Jew would sit in the same circle with the Christian fundamentalist . . . If there were a Marxist, fine . . . And then all must talk, oh, how we all talked! Hours and hours that flew like jet planes over tiny states, with the thoughts and impressions shaping . . . the geography below. Always there was Adaline Guenther, looking up from her knitting with a sharp eye to throw in a word or a question . . . Like the food and drink which would appear unobtrusively, her ideas were the constant sustenance of the discussion." Guenther believed that university life was the platform for dialogue, "bull sessions" changing your mind, and the dialectical method to explore personal views and measure them against other views and science.[34]

Persuasively cultivating the persona of a grandmother, Guenther not only knitted but wore spectacles and tied her hair back in a tight bun. The students affectionately called her "Gramma" or "Gram." The names stuck, and generations of students continued doing the same. Never having married, Guenther took on these students as her family, and the URC became her life. Likely taking on this persona allowed her to carve out the role of matriarch within her circle of men and women students and form close relationships with them.[35]

Guenther's emphasis on student leaders with a spark, status, and good looks seemed to be right out of a Hollywood playbook and a departure from O. D. Foster's emphasis on bringing together those of earnest religious affiliation. It is likely that Foster would have disapproved of Guenther's scouting around for just the right student leaders without strict regard for their religious engagement. Different as the approach of Guenther may seem from that of O. D. Foster, however, both of them viewed service, rather than denominational affiliation, as a means to create bonds of fellowship.

In fact, Guenther and Evans were following in Foster's footsteps. The pattern Foster had established in his work with the recruits in the Army camps during the First World War when he and others developed CIS relied less on conventional religious activities than upon cooperative service in the military and in recreational and educational programs. Ten years before the URC began, Foster had looked to CIS to engage military personnel outside the bounds of their church membership.

To achieve wartime inclusiveness among the diverse American and immigrant recruits, Foster had helped expand CIS from what was originally a YMCA program into an interfaith organization with military backing. Achieving solidarity among disparate military recruits seemed to require that bonds of fellowship be strengthened and maintained through education and recreation. Comrades in Service had responded by developing activities that sought to create a sense of patriotic purpose and fellowship akin to a variety of religion. In the postwar era Foster wanted to replicate this sense of fellowship at state university campuses. Years after Foster, Guenther and Evans also sought to achieve a similar sense of fellowship. They turned to service activities and cooperation that would engage university students outside their academic studies and their individual membership in a church, synagogue, or denominational club.

Evans was the idea man for such student service projects. As a longtime YMCA leader at universities, he easily came up with project ideas. Guenther claimed that out of every one hundred ideas that Evans suggested, only one was practical, and she was the one who decided which idea made the grade. In addition, once she had recruited the popular campus leaders to the newly constituted student board, she persuaded them that the idea proposed by Evans and vetted by her was really their idea and got them to think of ways to implement it. Together, Evans, Guenther, and the board built student service projects into a quasi-religion, as we shall see.

University Camp Begins

With the new student board in place, new student programs followed. The first large-scale service project was a ten-day summer camp for underprivileged children called Uni-camp, begun in the summer of 1935, a year after the new board was established. Guenther attributed the idea to the board despite the fact that Evans had headed up a similar camp at the University of Pennsylvania, in 1908.[36] Members of the student board comprised the camp staff and did much of the preliminary work to get it started. The camp was successful. "Nothing wins the attention of the campus, or the friendship of it, for the Conference as thoroughly as University Camp," stated the URC Student Board Report of 1940.[37] The camp lasted as a URC project for more than forty years and was later taken over by UCLA. The camp still functions today as a UCLA project, staffed by UCLA students.[38]

From the start, Guenther chose the head counsellor of Uni-Camp; the latter helped select the other counsellors, all volunteers, primarily UCLA students, although students from USC and LACC also served at times.[39] Student board members were often counsellors, fundraisers and camp maintenance crew, from time to time going up to camp for a few days in the off season to prepare the facilities for the next summer, such as repairing the plumbing system, the outhouses, and the tents.[40] In the 1950s a separate student camp board was organized; it met every other week to look after the building and maintenance needs of the camp.[41]

The first camp was at the Big Pines Recreational Center, located in a rural part of Los Angeles County and administered by the Los Angeles County Department of Playgrounds. The site was described as a "a truly beautiful one" in a pamphlet about Uni-Camp. In addition to the tall pine trees, the site had "rugged mountain slopes, winding trails, and a quiet lake. . . . [It] afford[ed] a splendid opportunity for rest and relaxation as well as physical development." Big Pines also had a swimming pool, a commissary, and two cooks; it offered first aid and the services of doctors and nurses.[42]

At first there were two ten-day sessions at Big Pines, one for boys and one for girls. Camp activities included hiking, swimming, archery, volleyball competitions, horseback riding, Ping-Pong, pole ball, horseshoes, boxing, baseball, wrestling, and other sports, music and dramatics as well as nature study and handicrafts for the girls. Evening entertainments included a forty-five-minute camp fire with "Fireside lore," plays, singing, and readings. Each tent group was expected to perform a stunt on a given night, and counselors put on stunts on other nights.[43]

Campers were to bring heavy shoes, tennis shoes, three changes of underwear, handkerchiefs, a bathing suit, towels, soap, comb, toothbrush and paste, pencil, and writing material.[44] The cost of a ten-day session was eight dollars, and parents paid on a sliding scale.[45] The Community Chest and later the State Relief Administration (SRA) assisted the URC in selecting the campers, who, at that time, had to live in the West Los Angeles district and be from thirteen to eighteen years of age (the age range and residence requirements later varied).[46]

The first summer there were some fifty-four campers and about a dozen counselors. The counselors were "chosen from the leading university students," described as top UCLA athletes and student leaders: a boxing champion, a member of the wrestling team, a captain of the track team, a member of the football team, the vice president of the URC Student Board, the vice president of the UCLA women students, a member of the glee club, and an editor of the student handbook. Other university students visited on weekends to get "to know and play with the campers."[47]

The student board helped raise about four hundred dollars that first summer, an amount matched by Mrs. E. L. Doheny.[48] By 1938 the fundraising goal had increased to three thousand dollars. Raising funds became a major

student board activity. Every spring the board would hold a camp fundraising drive. At first it was held off campus, but eventually moved to the UCLA
campus as well as the LACC and USC campuses and later at other schools with
URC branches.[49] Individual contributors included Hollywood figures Shirley
Temple, who donated some five hundred dollars for camp equipment, and
Joe E. Brown to honor his son, Captain Donald Brown, who had died while
serving in the Army during the Second World War. Donald Brown had been a
much beloved head counselors at Uni-Camp in the 1930s.[50]

At one of the camp sessions in 1938 that accommodated twenty-five
younger boys, more than one-third were classified as Mexican; the rest were
listed as white, except for four Jewish boys, listed as being from Boyle Heights
without specific reference to race or ethnicity. There were five other campers,
one identified as half Mexican, one as Negro, two as Japanese, and one as
half Japanese. During that session, the camp gave out awards for the two best
campers; one was given to an African American camper, the other to a Mexican American boy. Since many of the campers were of Mexican descent and
assumed to be Catholic, the URC got the Catholic chancery to send a priest to
camp to conduct Sunday morning mass. Sometimes the camp staff would also
organize a fifteen minute "nonsectarian" Protestant service under the trees,
later in the morning. All the campers were required to attend, Catholics and
non-Catholics alike.[51]

Although there were class as well as racial differences between the university student counselors and the campers, not all the university students at the
URC came from comfortable economic backgrounds. These students rarely
had the means to serve as camp volunteers. For example, student board members Tom Bradley, an African American, and John Krumm, a white Episcopalian, had little money and lacked the resources to volunteer at camp. While
the camp counselors were rarely well-to-do, the students who did volunteer
as counselors needed to have sufficient financial support to forgo a job while
at camp. In the 1930s, both Bradley and Krumm lived in the small URC dormitory for needy students in exchange for doing chores. Even if Bradley could
have paid for lodging, he could not have found it in Westwood because housing restrictions there excluded African Americans. Since UCLA was primarily
a commuter school, much of the housing available on campus was provided
by sororities and fraternities, which were not open to African Americans, and
the 125 or so African American UCLA students that decade were commuters.[52]

This pattern lasted for many of the African American students for decades thereafter.

There were few health problems at camp except for ringworm (past the contagious stage), an infected finger on a camper who had to be sent home, and a "bad toothache . . . the result of a filling that had come out some six months before," as well as three cases of homesickness and "a few cases of nausea due mainly to over-eating."[53] "These kids were hungry when they came there . . . Sometimes they had stomach pain . . . and it would turn out just to be from overeating," reported former counselor and URC student Jean Burke.[54] The campers were not accustomed to the sheer quantity of food offered at camp. "Several were . . . dumbfounded. The first night many of the boys were impressed by the amount of food they had to eat and how good it was." Describing how amazed some of the campers were "at getting seconds and also getting desert," a camp report noted, "one little fellow . . . in Johnny Anderson's tent didn't even know what desert was, and Johnny spent the whole camp period trying to explain it." To some campers the kind of food served was strange and overwhelming, including meatloaf and Swiss steak. . One camper recognized only oatmeal, beans, and potatoes, as real food but little else.[55] The variety of vegetables and fruits and meats served at camp so confused one of the campers that he stopped eating for two whole days. After that, Guenther recalled, the counsellors decided to offer beans, tortillas, and frijoles.[56]

Counselors tried modeling good manners at the camp dining hall. "I would always stand at the entrance . . . and say, 'Good evening or good afternoon,'" counselor Jean Burke related, though at first, they'd be "really, really startled . . . and then they'd say, 'good evening' or 'good afternoon.'"[57] Campers would "come and take things, and they'd hide it under their coats and take it out. You're going to have another meal," Counselor Bill Burke tried to reassure them.[58]

In 1939 Uni-Camp moved to an abandoned Civilian Conservation Corps camp in the Castaic hills, north of Los Angeles. There the URC experimented with running a camp jointly with the SRA. The SRA bore much of the expense for this venture and helped train the counselors. The number of UCLA and LACC staff increased four-fold, to serve close to six hundred campers who attended camp that summer. About two hundred of the campers were from Sawtelle; the others were children from families on state relief and came from all over the city, most of them from south Los Angeles. Those campers were primarily African American, Native American, and Mexican American.[59] "I remember going all over the city in big buses picking up State Relief Administration (SRA) children. It was hot and we were all moist and smudgy but bubbling with excitement," counselor June Breck recalled. "Then Castaic, ghastly, barren barracks on top of a hot hill—117 in the shade."[60]

URC Buys Its Own Campground

A committee of university students raised enough money in 1940 to purchase grounds for the URC to have a camp of its own. The site was located on twelve acres near Barton Flats, about thirty miles east of Redlands, in the mountains of the San Bernardino National Forest, at an altitude of over six thousand feet. It was shaded by cedars, willows, cottonwoods, and big pine trees. The site, formerly used as a camp by the Glendale Boy Scouts, was obtained from the National Forest Service and sat on a stream that flowed into the Santa Ana River. It could accommodate about fifty campers and eight counselors per ten-day session and had a dining hall (later be named Tom Evans Hall), a recreational stone lodge (later named Don Brown Memorial Lodge, in memory of the much beloved counselor), and a small dispensary that served as the camp infirmary, all of them paid for by donations from camp supporters. There was a swimming pool, showers, and twelve concrete tent bases. Usually, the tents stored personal belongings and luggage, and the campers slept outdoors on cots in good weather.[61]

At this new Uni-Camp site the URC worked with some especially needy campers who lived beyond the Sawtelle area, many of them of Mexican American background. After the Los Angeles Zoot Suit riots of 1943, a series of clashes that took place between Euro American servicemen and Mexican American youth, some of the campers came with their parole officers, who took charge of them while the URC counsellors ran the overall camp. Commenting on how fascinated some of the campers were with the sunburn marks on her body, Jean Burke surmised that many had never seen anything like that on their own bodies and noted how they "got hilarious and they all came over to look at my leg where it was white and then it was dark."[62]

In addition to holding their own camp sessions for underprivileged children, the URC opened the site to other groups for camp sessions, which those

groups staffed and ran for themselves. One such camp, called Uni-Betic, served
diabetic campers sponsored by an organization that helped those diabetic children who could not attend a standard summer camp. Another was for blind
campers. Yet another was for problem adolescents. During the Second World
War, other such camps were held for the children of aircraft workers to help
decrease absenteeism among their parents and for the children of hospitalized
servicemen.[63] In 1943 there were two camp sessions for probationary boys,
staffed by the Catholic Big Brothers.[64] The camp also had specific sessions for
children chosen by local welfare agencies from the First and Temple Street
area, a poor neighborhood located near downtown. Those sessions were partly
staffed by LACC students.[65] After the Second World War, the camp housed
sessions for the children of veterans.[66] Later on, students from UC Riverside
and other URC campuses also served as camp counselors.[67] By the 1960s, the
URC camp program had expanded to two sites, one called Uni-Camp, the
other College camp.[68]

Little is known about what most of the campers thought about camp,
although a few of the comments attributed to them have survived. For example, camper Louis Ramos Jr. told his counselor, "My parents were very
happy and proud of the great improvement I had, being stronger and gaining
four pounds," adding that "on my way home while I was on the bus I felt
sad and gloomy because of leaving one of the happiest places I have been."[69]
Another camper, Pansy, an African American whose father had died, was one
of thirteen children. She had gone to camp for three summers. "You bet, I'm
going to college—I'm going to make something of myself," Pansy told Adaline Guenther, adding that "my Councillors [sic] say you can work your way
through if you want to hard enough, and I'm going to."[70] After the summer,
counselor June Breck recollected that she had received a letter from a camper
saying that "she'd beaten up the kids in her neighborhood who thought going
to Uni-Camp was 'sissy.'"[71]

An esprit de corps grew up among the counselors as they shared common
experiences, like "moments of dread when fires or wild donkeys or endless
days of rain taxed their inner resources."[72] The bonds among them remained
strong. One member of the camp staff later remarked that many of his friend-
ships were made at Uni-Camp.[73] Years later others still had vivid memories
and spoke fondly of counselor Donald Brown.[74]

The counselors also seem to have loved going to camp, working together and spending time with the campers." Some recalled, "Losing oneself in some large project was to court the possibility of abandoning those unexpressed divisions which plague our society. So we would take off to the mountains, cramped in buses with little kids from Sawtelle, teach swimming together, eat horrible pudding, plan campfire stunts."[75]

Donald Brown had suggested that the URC utilize the best campers as junior counselors and possible future counsellors to "build leadership among underprivileged children."[76] Guenther never seems to have warmed to this suggestion. She felt that the main purpose of the camp went beyond serving underprivileged campers. Its mission was not only to teach university students what it meant to love someone outside their orbit but also to open themselves up to what she and Evans regarded as an inner religious sense through service and building bonds of fellowship with the other counsellors via common experience and cooperation.

Moreover, paternalistic views about democracy might also have influenced Guenther's preference for university students over former campers as counselors. She seems to have assumed that campers needed to be led to an understanding of tolerance and democracy, and that such understanding was more important than developing their leadership skills. In districts "where there is ignorance and poverty," Guenther wrote, "there is a need for constructive work which will lead people to feel that they too have a stake in democracy and what it can do for them."[77] This constructive work needed to be done by university students, she likely thought.

Like the residents of settlement houses in the late nineteenth century, camp counselors had a sense of noblesse oblige and saw themselves in a missionary role: to convert campers to having faith in American democracy, education, fair play, tolerance, and overall middle-class values.[78] The camp operated on the assumption that middle-class students had a responsibility to guide disadvantaged campers, usually darker skinned, to a better life and an understanding of American ways. Camp did, in fact, provide the campers with American food, training in American sports, American student mentors, and experience with American songs, ideas, and entertainments. It was an experiment in acculturation.

The camp's mission also included modeling "brotherhood in action"; as such, counselors were instructed not to preach but "to show each child a good picture of brotherhood."[79] Guenther seemed to be developing a larger sense of brotherhood herself, one that included race and ethnicity in addition to religion. Her close relationship with Tom Bradley, begun in the 1930s, appears to have awakened in her a deep sense of connection across racial lines. Bradley recalled that Guenther wanted to find out all about him and his culture, how Blacks saw themselves, what goals and dreams they had. The two of them had frequent, probing talks, and he came away with the feeling that she really cared about him.[80]

By the time the Second World War broke out, Guenther had become a committed advocate for civil rights and her sense of religious inclusion had evolved to embrace racial inclusion.[81] Perhaps her work with many African American youngsters at Uni-Camp as well as her relationship with Bradley had led her to see that racial inclusion was a necessary part of religion.[82] She understood that modeling brotherhood of any type was a tall order that took practice and required "learning by doing." She believed that Uni-Camp could provide the practice needed. "Lest you think that this is just another camp, let me remind you that the Conference must find pegs on which to hang its idea of people learning to work together," she reported. "Nobody was ever made either tolerant or religious by sitting in a chair and listening to speeches . . . living for ten days under crude camp conditions with other students of all faiths and sharing with them the responsibility for children of assorted backgrounds and needs, demands religion and builds tolerance like nobody's business."[83] Guenther understood that at bottom, camp was about building inclusion as an expression of religion, and that most of all, it was aimed at the counselors, so that they could experience religion by reaching out to campers different from themselves. "Nothing was more fundamental to her [Guenther] . . . than that people will . . . understand differences more clearly when they have worked together."[84]

At camp, the counselors got to know Evans and Guenther more deeply than before. "None of us knew him [Evans] as well as those who knew him at camp," counselor Robert Hine recalled. "Those who played baseball with him as he stood at the plate in his battered straw hat, or those who worked with him . . . coaxing a stubborn pump-motor into action."[85] Neither Evans nor Guenther was really the outdoor type, but each tried to participate in camp life. Evans and his wife Edith stayed at the camp for both sessions at times and occasionally visited the camps thereafter. It was difficult for Guenther to stay for a full camp session. She "honestly hat[ed] the roughhouse, [was] troubled by sleepless nights on the cots, but sticking it out . . . [she would keep] the questions flying and the ideals never far away."[86]

Evans saw camp as an opportunity to expand the counselors' sense of religion through fellowship in service more so than church or synagogue activities, understanding the Uni-Camp experience as overcoming religious differences. In his view, religion in action leads to common service, which brings people together rather than setting them apart. "Losing oneself in some large project," noted Robert Hine, "was to court the possibility of abandoning those prejudices and unexpressed divisions which plague our society." At camp, Hine recalled, "We could see so clearly what Mr. Evans so often says, that it is the personal contact of men knowing one another intimately and living together which spreads the good and the progressive in the world, and that speeches and laws are only incidentals."[87] "It was at camp," declared URC counselor Jim Taylor, "that I learned how human beings could come to understand each other—and it was the experience of living together, the experience of sharing food, clothing, shelter, opinions, excitements and fears. Once we had this experience . . . speeches had meaning and reality, as never before."[88]

Camp was about developing a spirit of love toward the campers and fellow counselors by living and working side by side. For former counselor Luke Fishburn, who later became URC's successor to Guenther, it was about "what it really meant to get outside of yourself and to love somebody else."[89] "How I learned and grew," counselor June Breck said gratefully about working at camp, "how I realized that summer how fortunate we are to have an opportunity to serve humanity."[90]

For Guenther, reared as a practical Methodist, one function of the camp was to give the student counselors opportunities to feed the hungry, to clothe the naked, to heal the sick, as it says in the Gospel.[91] Camp also gave opportunities to "teach students . . . what poverty was all about." Although "the counselors only came for one session, ten days," said Fishburn, "they were with the children twenty-four hours a day for those ten. We really immersed them in it."[92] "Uni-Camp opened my eyes to social problems and made me run elbows with reality," recalled counselor Don Hitchcock.[93] Such practical experience could teach the counselors about life and about poverty and to channel their religious feelings into seemingly secular service, similar to the experience that O. D. Foster had while at Camp Custer when he said that he felt more religious mailing a letter of a Custer trainee than he did on his knees in church.

Above all, camp was for the counselors. "The thing about the camp that people who were not close to it didn't grasp," Fishburn explained, "is we didn't run the camp for kids. We ran the camp for the students and the experience that that gave to them . . . how to run an organization, how to raise money, how to deal with children, how to relate to various racial and ethnic groups." Dealing with the campers was "not too hard," he elaborated. "They have fun no matter what we do. We can hardly go wrong."[94] Camp did good work in helping the underprivileged children in material ways, but most important, its purpose was to provide an experience in brotherhood for the counselors. "University Camp was significant . . . in what it did for underprivileged children," but even more important to Guenther and to Robert and Shirly Hine it "was a vehicle . . . [to experience] the brotherhood of mankind."[95]

URC After Camp Social Service and Cultural Outreach

The service ethic of Uni-Camp and the experience of working with the staff of welfare agencies led students to experiment further with other social service projects. Most of these had to do with continuing contact with the campers, but some involved serving youngsters who never went to camp and needed help. For instance, at Los Angeles City College, the student board undertook a service project at Dayton Heights Elementary School in 1939. Dayton Heights had three classes in what were called "welfare rooms," rooms for boys who had failed in school mainly for disciplinary reasons. Most of them had come from broken homes and were "extreme cases of poor social adjustment." The LACC Student Board arranged for one college student to be assigned to each boy and carry out the "big brother" ideal.[96]

As early as 1938 a few clubs for former campers were organized to continue the work begun at Uni-Camp. Two years later the URC hired a part-time co-ordinator, but as the camp grew, more follow up was needed.[97] "It was clear to everyone who worked at Uni-Camp that in Sawtelle there was room for more work with the children than the ten days during the summer allow," counsellor Bob Jaffee explained. "So some of us began meeting our camp kids after school and on weekends, and the first thing we knew we had a full fledge club program going."[98]

One question "that all camp counselors ask at the end of the summer," wrote student board chair Hanford Files in the 1942 URC annual report. "'Can't we do something for these children after we bring them back to the city from camp?' This year we did."[99] The student board organized a community committee, which pioneered various projects for the Sawtelle children, among them a playground baseball league with four teams, daily breakfasts for forty children, two Easter vacation camps, six personality development teas for girls, one championship football team, organized and coached by the UCLA students, and seven weekly clubs. In addition, the students on the URC committee sponsored a toy loan drive and a canned food drive to raise funds for the relief of Japanese evacuees, perhaps in response to the wartime mistreatment of those they considered their Issei and Nisei neighbors from Sawtelle. For the Sawtelle families, the committee also sponsored plays and Christmas parties for children, hosted by UCLA fraternities and sororities.[100]

Although the URC staff worked mostly with students on religious and educational goals, the staff, as well as volunteer committees, frequently also had to engage in fundraising in the broader community. While some of the funding came from the various URC constituent religious groups, some from the URC Businessman's Committee and other conference committees, some of it also came from individual and community support from those outside the URC. Those donor contributions at times included funds to pay the respective salaries for Guenther and Evans and other staff members, to supplement the denominational funding for the URC religious advisers who ministered to the students, to pay for subsidizing Uni-Camp activities, for supporting other student programs, and for sponsoring URC social functions. As the program of student after-camp activities increased, the URC again looked to the community for increased financial support and backup from adult volunteers. Both were needed to help the students carry out the growing afterschool neighborhood programs.

In response, the Social Service Department (SSD), funded largely by the newly founded Social Service Advisory Council, a council of adult community volunteers, was set up expressly to raise money for student social service activities as part of the URC budget in 1943. It replaced the earlier URC Community Committee with a larger and better-funded organization. Meanwhile, a long-standing URC auxiliary group of adult women volunteers, the Junior Hostesses, also raised money to help the neighborhood children's afterschool clubs. The hostesses furnished and decorated what they called the "University

Club Room," a place for children to gather on the days when their club did not meet. Two student URC counselors staffed the room, which was supplied with games and a lending library.[101]

Through the SSD the university students—both former camp counselors and a cross section of other URC and LACC students—could embark on an ambitious afterschool and vacation program to keep up contact with the former campers and other neighborhood children. The program for the younger children, ages five to fourteen, consisted of sports, day camps, and clubs.[102] The latter became a mainstay of the afterschool program, their number growing to fifteen. Most of them were year-round clubs that met weekly. Each had about fifteen to twenty-five members and two student counselors. They offered hiking, sports, dramatics, dancing, story-telling, and handicrafts. The URC also set up a program whereby each child could bank ten to fifteen cents per week with the counselors to contribute toward a session at Uni-Camp.[103]

For the older children there was the Teen Age Club, with a membership of about thirty "Anglo-Americans." It met one evening per week for sports, parties, and dances. The "Anglo-American" designation undoubtedly aimed to acknowledge the geographic and cultural divide between those of Anglo and those of Mexican background, although at Uni-Camp there was no such separation.[104] There were also clubs for those of Mexican background. In addition, there was a Sports League of six teams that held year-round competitions. The West LA Playground Department cooperated with the URC Junior Hostesses to furnish and supply the playground, some of the club rooms, the playing fields, and an auditorium where many of the activities were held. While the West Los Angeles schools conducted a survey about the children in the clubs, the URC staff used the survey for future planning.[105]

As part of URC outreach to Mexican youth in the wake of the Zoot Suit Riots, the SSD helped found the Vagabond Club in July of 1943. The club comprised about forty Mexican American young adults, directed by two volunteer UCLA students.[106] The club held weekly meetings and dances, special holiday and seasonal events, and assisted in setting up and running East Side clubs. The SSD also expanded afterschool programs to three East Side neighborhoods: Rosehill, Alpine, and Happy Valley where many of the children were of Mexican background. These clubs were for young adults, ranging in age from fourteen to twenty. They met twice per week for recreation and discussion, and some of them participated in a program called Hi-House, designed especially for high school students.[107] The East Side clubs were run jointly by four UCLA students and four Vagabond Club members who cooperated with the County Probation Department, the Coordinating Council for Latin-American Youth, and School and Housing Officials.[108]

"The Religious Conference station wagon would go around, two nights a week," URC volunteer Bob Jaffee recalled, "picking up [UCLA] students . . . and delivering them downtown in Happy Valley, Alpine . . . to run clubs like those we had originally set up for our camp kids."[109] These university student volunteers were being ferried to the East Side neighborhoods to run clubs while other clubs were formed that ferried East Side neighborhood children to UCLA football games and dinners given by the sororities and fraternities.[110] These exchanges brought benefits to the student volunteers. "When we found out how the kids in those [East Side] districts acted, we wanted to know why, and what we could do—and a whole process of education started for some of us," Jaffee recalled.[111]

The clubs cooperated with one another to produce a mimeographed newspaper every two weeks with UCLA students as advisors. The leaders and student counselors of the clubs got together for a meeting once a month. The afterschool program grew to a staff of more than fifty, primarily URC students, who served some seven hundred youths each week as counselors and support staff. The counselors held their own training sessions every two weeks.[112] These afterschool activities provided channels of service for the UCLA students, as well as those from other nearby colleges. They also helped expand the URC presence on campus and in the community.

Borrowing a service idea from the turn-of-the-century settlement house movement, the URC began staging cultural events for Mexican American and African American youth. In addition to the clubs for young Mexican Americans, the URC organized a "Latin American Fiesta" in 1944. The fiesta was designed to "awaken the pride of the Mexican-American children" in their cultural heritage.[113] It was a success, and other URC cultural events followed, among them two ambitious art exhibitions. Both were displayed in the URC auditorium on Le Conte Avenue. The first one, held the same year as the fiesta, showcased Mexican art and culture and included paintings by such prominent Mexican painters as Jose Clemente Orozco and Diego Rivera.[114]

The URC obtained the works of art by writing to museums all over the country. Once the exhibit was installed, the URC "brought in these busloads of Mexican kids" from the inner city to see the exhibit free of charge. "The kids," Jean Burke explained, "could not believe that these paintings and art works were done by Mexicans. They would ask over and over again, 'Are you sure that was done by Mexicans?' And then, they said, 'why are all these [non-Mexican] people coming?'" The kids were puzzled that non-Mexicans were paying "a lot of money" (ten dollars) and Burke was impressed by how she thought the attitude of the kids had changed. They were "so thrilled." They had come in "being kind of pushy and resentful" and went out "with their heads held high."[115]

Two years later the URC mounted another exhibition in the auditorium, titled "Panorama of the American Negro in the Fine Arts." It was an extensive show that featured paintings, sculptures, ceramics, and music by such African American painters as Romare Bearden, Thelma Johnson Streat (the first African American woman to exhibit her paintings at the New York Museum of Modern Art), sculptor Sargent Johnson, and pianist, composer, band leader, and assistant musical director at MGM Studios Calvin Jackson, who performed with Lena Horne. Horne also gave a talk on the "Negro Contribution to Fine Arts."[116] "Various movie people came," Jean Burke recalled, noting that "there had never been a Mexican Art and Culture or a Negro Art and Culture" exhibition in the URC area before."[117]

These cultural outreach programs followed a path begun by the Hull House Labor Museum, founded by Hull House in 1900, about a decade after Hull House itself was opened. Located in a Chicago neighborhood populated with thousands of immigrants from Southern and Eastern Europe, as well as migrants from elsewhere in the United States (including Native Americans), the museum showcased the handiwork of these Hull House neighbors with exhibits of their traditional crafts. On display were looms, spinning wheels, grinding stones, and similar tools of immigrants and Native Americans, who demonstrated them through such activities as sewing and weaving textiles and preparing foods. Those who put together these exhibits at the Labor Museum hoped they would help heal the alienation between members of an older generation from traditional cultures and their Americanized children and would indicate that all of them were welcome and appreciated in America.[118] This direct, hands-on approach was typical of both the URC and the settlement house movement.

Indeed, the settlement house movement and the URC had much in common; the URC was the movement's successor in developing outreach programs undergirded by religious sentiment. Both worked with young professionals or university students who volunteered in community service programs. Both sought to aid their neighbors in times of dislocation, transition, and strife. Both sought to learn about and understand those in their respective communities through building bonds of mutual trust and cooperation. To Evans and Guenther, outreach, service, understanding, trust, and cooperation were foundational to religion, as they had been to Foster, decades earlier. URC's Uni-Camp, social service, and cultural outreach programs sought to further religious fellowship among those of different faiths and engage students in the wider world. Secular as they may seem to some, these activities were intended to stir religious feelings, and I dare say that many in the settlement house movement would likely have agreed with this motivation.

CHAPTER FOUR

Partnership with the NCCJ

The current rise of ugly prejudices and selfish and cruel exclusions challenges both
education and religion to find a solution. . . . We believe that we are on our way,
largely through sincere and devoted youth and . . . [we] are finding . . . a genuine ray
of hope in an otherwise dark and oppressive atmosphere of sinister and dangerous
forces.
—*Thomas Evans, June 1939*

It was autumn of 1934 when handsome, athletic John Burnside, UCLA student body president and Baptist member of the University Religious Conference, set to graduate in the spring, was threatened by some of his fellow students. The threats came from vigilantes who wanted to purge the university of Burnside and others protesting the administration's cancellation of a campus speaking engagement by California Democratic gubernatorial candidate, socialist, writer, and muckraker Upton Sinclair. To add insult to injury, UCLA provost E. C. Moore suspended Burnside and the other protesters on the grounds that they were communist sympathizers. Thanks in part to the intervention of attorney J. Wiseman Mac Donald, a Catholic URC supporter, who called president of the University of California Robert G. Sproul, the charges were dropped and Burnside returned to campus.[1] He finished his senior year at UCLA. After graduation he returned to the URC and became a staff member, as we shall see in this chapter.

Meanwhile, Evans and Guenther had been eying the National Conference of Jews and Christians (NCCJ), an organization that seemed a promising source of programs and a vehicle for furthering student cooperation across religious lines. The "journey of a priest, a minister and a rabbi across the continent . . . [has] created tremendous interest," wrote Adaline Guenther in 1934. "There is no livelier group than the National Conference of Jews and Christians."[2] That same year the two organizations joined forces, coordinating their activities and combining resources in Southern California. For more than a decade the URC served as the NCCJ's local branch, while the NCCJ's national director became an honorary member of the URC Board of Trustees. This arrangement helped eliminate duplication and competition, especially for fundraising in Hollywood.[3]

The two organizations seemed to be a good fit. Neither the NCCJ nor the URC was affiliated with a particular church or synagogue. The NCCJ was founded in 1927, on the initiative of Protestant Everett Ross Clinchy, who had served in the First World War; both organizations sought to further interfaith understanding as Clinchy, like O. D. Foster, organized projects promoting interfaith cooperation and fellowship in the postwar era.

Both organizations saw benefits in the cooperative arrangement. The NCCJ introduced programs to the URC and enlarged the URC footprint in California and nationally. It served as a model for URC public presentations and demonstrated how to perform them. It inspired the students and helped the URC gain name recognition, build audiences for its presentations, and expand its national connections. The NCCJ benefited from this cooperative arrangement too, by gaining access to California college and university campuses and to the URC interfaith infrastructure, funding, staff, and students. Both organizations raised their voices for religious cooperation and tolerance in the face of the increasing violence and bigotry in American society, first against the Ku Klux Klan during the 1920s, then against Naziism in 1930s.

Despite their similarities, there were major differences between the NCCJ and the URC. The NCCJ gave presentations demonstrating tri-faith fellowship, usually among a trio of professional clergy, a priest, rabbi, and minister. The presentations were meant to influence the audience to become more tolerant and understanding of all three religions, especially those religions other than one's own. The NCCJ also gave workshops on interpersonal relations, held institutes with noted lecturers, usually scholars of religion, and presented roundtables at which Protestant, Jewish, and Catholic speakers, often civic leaders, gave talks on their own religion, again with the aim of increasing audience understanding and acceptance. These programs attracted much media attention, favorable publicity, and wide audiences.

Unlike the NCCJ, the URC was not originally performative. It dealt with building religious fellowship akin to religion among university students of different religions or of none. To accomplish this, the URC relied on daily experiences that brought students together on an ongoing basis; as seen from the preceding chapter, the most successful of these initiatives involved the URC summer camp and student board. Being in the audience at an NCCJ brotherhood trio performance, or attending an institute, roundtable, or workshop were useful of course, but by themselves would fall short of building the deep and lasting connections central to the URC programs. Undoubtedly the NCCJ brought useful program ideas to the URC. The true benefits, however, came from the opportunities it offered the URC students to adapt NCCJ programs to their own lives, to their relationships, and ultimately to their education.

NCCJ Programs Appeal to URC Students

The NCCJ had developed several programs that appealed to URC students. Among them were the traveling trio of a minister, priest, and rabbi. Others included brotherhood events to mark American tri-faith pluralism, civic round tables that engaged communities in interfaith discussion of public issues, the Williamstown Summer Institutes that attracted students and prominent religious leaders nationwide, and radio broadcasts on religion. The NCCJ introduced all these programs to the URC, and the students participated in them and adapted them to their own use.

Soon after the two organizations joined forces, Everett Clinchy visited Los Angeles as part of a trio panel to speak at Loyola University. The other panelists were Father Michael J. Ahern, S.J., and reform rabbi Morris S. Lazaron. They spoke about prospective educational work in the field of human relations. They also presented a three-day priest-rabbi-minister workshop at the Ambassador Hotel. The trio used the occasion to speak to teachers, professors, and the general public about the status of group relations in the United States and the methods and value of interfaith cooperation.[4] This NCCJ panel was similar in format to the traveling tri-faith panels that O. D. Foster had helped organize in Europe to address the troops as part of Comrades in Service, at the end of the First World War.

Begun and sponsored by the NCCJ in 1934, Brotherhood Days included an annual series of community events in California and in different parts of the nation. The goals included furthering tri-faith tolerance and celebrating a spirit of fellowship among American Protestants, Catholics, and Jews. In 1936 governor of California Frank Merriam and Los Angeles mayor Frank L. Shaw issued proclamations designating a week in late February as Brotherhood Week. The following year President Franklin D. Roosevelt declared Brotherhood Day an official national observance, expanding it to Brotherhood Week in 1939.[5]

In 1936, two years after the NCCJ and URC joined forces, the URC established an extension council and appointed board of trustees member Judge Marshall McComb as its chair. The goal of the council was to organize joint community projects between URC students and the NCCJ. As chair, Mc Comb was to oversee these projects and report on them to the URC board; the projects sought, in his words, "to perform in the community much the same 'small miracles' as the University Religious Centers are doing on local college and university campuses. . . . [and create] an atmosphere in which the spirit of real religion may thrive."[6] That same year, 196 URC students spoke throughout Los Angeles, both at Friday night synagogue services and Sunday morning church services, about the cooperative work of the URC and the NCCJ.[7]

Later that year John Burnside was chosen as the secretary of the URC extension council. He was by then a graduate of UCLA and a staff member of the URC, hired despite his temporary suspension and support for socialist Upton Sinclair. This is noteworthy, since movie mogul Louis Mayer, a major donor to the URC, apparently saw Sinclair as an existential threat.[8]

Burnside's new job was to act as a liaison between the URC and the NCCJ, to coordinate and publicize joint programs. A special grant by URC supporter and Hollywood producer Sol Lesser paid Burnside a salary of one hundred and fifty dollars a month.[9] With Burnside as council secretary, URC students and recent graduates presented NCCJ programs in new community and campus settings.[10] Burnside made personal trips to many of these events and oversaw the dissemination of information about them through the mail, newspapers, magazines, and radio.[11]

During Burnside's tenure, the URC further extended the territory covered by its students. According to the 1938 annual report, some two hundred URC students from UCLA, USC, and LACC spoke at churches and synagogues all over the city of Los Angeles and in the surrounding communities of San Bernardino, Redlands, Colton, Riverside, Laguna, Long Beach, Redondo, and Whittier, as well as in "other localities from Tehachapi to San Diego." The report added that "students inform[ed] the community of the inter-faith cooperation as it is being developed in the universities and at the junior college pointing to the ideal and to its practical application."[12]

More than two hundred free radio spot announcements and twelve fifteen-minute programs were broadcast on the local stations, accompanied by "a quantity of newspaper publicity which surprised even the most optimistic."[13] URC and NCCJ Brotherhood activities extended to "all towns in southern California from Fresno to San Diego." Personal visits were made in Bakersfield, Visalia, Tulare, Hanford, and Fresno. In each town cooperation of the minister and lay groups was highlighted in the promotion of this work.[14] The wide recognition of the NCCJ and Burnside's publicity helped attract new audiences to these events.

To commemorate brotherhood celebrations of fellowship, in 1936 the NCCJ visited Los Angeles, Long Beach, and Pasadena and cooperated with a local sponsoring committee of one hundred clerical and lay community leaders and a central committee of six members. The central committee included representatives from the KofC, the B'nai B'rith Lodge, the Wilshire Methodist Church, the Los Angeles Chamber of Commerce, radio station KFI, and the *Los Angeles Evening Herald*. That year the NCCJ also launched a major brotherhood campaign on the radio, in the newspapers, and in the churches and synagogues.[15]

The prominent NCCJ religious speakers who drew community leaders to these cosponsored public interfaith events included Father T. Lawrence Riggs, a Catholic priest, chaplain, and head of the Newman Club at Yale. He visited Los Angeles to lead a discussion with members of various denominational groups and with civic and business leaders.[16] In addition to speaking before the Pasadena Round Table Committee at the Athenaeum, Riggs appeared at USC, where he spoke with students at a special breakfast. A citywide breakfast and an exchange of pulpits took place in Long Beach, while the Long Beach Board of Adult Education held classes to instruct Sunday school teachers in methods of teaching intergroup relations. The following year, in Los Angeles proper, some one hundred civic and religious leaders again participated in brotherhood activities. Not only did audiences in Los Angeles, Long Beach, and Pasadena attend brotherhood events as in the previous year, but so did audiences at campuses in Santa Barbara and San Diego, where special meetings were arranged.[17]

Clinchy, the best known of all the NCCJ speakers, made return visits to

Los Angeles, sometimes on his own, sometimes as part of a trio panel. In 1937 he spoke before the URC Women's Division, a fundraising group, at the invitation of its president, Clara Reynolds.[18] Protestant, Jewish, and Catholic women "were all eager to bring about a spirit of understanding and friendliness," wrote Reynolds, "realizing that the trouble with the world today is hatred and intolerance; and that people, like religion, were better appreciated as they became better acquainted."[19] Clinchy attracted more than 350 Protestant, Jewish, and Catholic women from Los Angeles and neighboring cities to the luncheon meeting held at the URC building. Reynolds wrote in her report that year that his talk was so "inspirational and enlightening" that the women followed up by organizing interfaith forums.[20]

Soon thereafter close to one thousand women assembled at Bovard Auditorium at USC to hear another speaker, Mrs. Jesse Bader, women's secretary of the NCCJ. The event was followed by two teas given for the women faculty members at UCLA and USC, one featuring Monsignor John Cawley, then president of the URC, accompanied by Clinchy and his wife and Rabbi Morris Lazaron. A second tea, this one just for the women faculty at USC, featured Mrs. Von Klein Smid, wife of the president of USC, and Mrs. Bader. "We realize that at these crucial times . . . [it is] the common responsibility to extend to women in Southern California, the chance to be associated with this interfaith work. . . . [and] share the privilege of being part of this great American movement," wrote Reynolds in 1937.[21] Her comment is revealing, indicating that the NCCJ and the URC had limited most of their interfaith work to men, even though women were enthusiastic about it and eager to join the movement.

In 1938 another NCCJ trio of speakers came to Los Angeles to speak to UCLA students at Royce Hall and to the URC Clergy Council, which brought together prominent Los Angeles clergy.[22] At LACC the trio spoke before a special faculty-student dinner and a group of Jewish students. They then met with communities in Long Beach and Fresno and were honored at a tea given by URC supporter Mrs. Samuel Berch. The trio then traveled north to UC Berkeley, staying at the International House and appearing before a large convocation of students. Afterward they went to Reno, Salt Lake City, Denver, and Phoenix.[23] William Randolph Hearst expressed an interest in these brotherhood programs and had a representative contact Thomas Evans to set up a meeting to discuss publicity and possibly have the *Examiner* conduct a civic program in conjunction with the URC.[24]

Hollywood had ties to the URC and to the NCCJ. Roger W. Strauss, one of the founders and Jewish cochair of the NCCJ, came to Los Angeles in 1938, and Louis Mayer hosted him at the executive bungalow of Metro-Goldwyn-Mayer. There Strauss outlined the aims and organization of the NCCJ. Thomas Evans and URC supporters Sol Lesser, Alphonso Bell, and H. G. Johansing were also present to welcome Strauss. Hollywood was helpful in giving donations to the URC and providing their programs with "star talent." Such Hollywood regulars as George M. Cohan, Andre Kostelanetz, and Basil Rathbone participated in brotherhood observances. On at least one occasion, Rathbone read a speech prepared by Rupert Hughes, a Hollywood script writer.[25] They were among the many Hollywood figures who made their talents and connections available for URC publicity, fundraising, and programs.

Louis Mayer and the Warner brothers were among the Hollywood figures who were both donors to the URC and members of the Wilshire Temple, the reform congregation of rabbi Edgar Magnin. Magnin, a devoted officer of the URC, was also a devoted follower of reform rabbi David Philipson (as discussed in an earlier chapter). Magnin, like Philipson, was an advocate for interfaith causes and for Jewish assimilation into American life.

Other Hollywood figures were also active in URC fundraising. Sol Lesser, was a frequent URC donor. Prominent Hollywood attorney Mendel Silberberg, who chaired the anti-Nazi Community Committee, was a member of the Businessmen's Committee, a fundraising arm of the URC. Louis B. Mayer, in addition to his previous donations that went toward the URC building, gave twenty thousand dollars in memory of his parents, in the late 1930s. Mary Pickford "offered her whole-hearted support" to the URC, but it was unclear whether or not she ever gave donations.[26]

URC Students Develop NCCJ Programs for Themselves

By the middle of the 1930s, students and staff at the URC were boldly showcasing religious cooperation by adopting programs begun by the NCCJ and adapting them to their own talents and purposes. One such NCCJ program was the annual Williamstown Summer Institute of Human Relations, held in Williamstown, Massachusetts. It was a national program that attracted students and religious leaders, and sponsored tri-faith forums, lectures, and seminars. In 1936 Thomas Evans, John Burnside, and URC Student Board chairman-elect Gilbert Harrison attended the institute and helped arrange the sessions. Rabbi Edgar Magnin also took part in the Williamstown program that summer.[27] Three years later, seven men and one woman served as delegates to Williamstown from Southern California, "the largest delegation west of Chicago" and "one of the most active." The delegates "were in every forum and meeting and attended every lecture in order to bring back to Los Angeles the best information and techniques available."[28]

The Williamstown Institute put the URC name forward in national religious circles and provided material for URC students to publicize when they got back to Los Angeles, as Harrison did when he gave a talk about the institute to an assembly of LACC students and faculty.[29] One of the Williamstown Institute programs, Religion and Contemporary Civilization, was later replicated by the URC. It consisted of a series of lectures given by prominent scholars of religion over a period of several days, held on the UCLA campus. Speakers included William Ernest Hocking, Arthur Compton, Alfred Noyes, Ellsworth Faris, and Ch'en You Shi.[30]

The Student Round Table was another URC program developed first at the Williamstown Summer Institute. There Everett Clinchy had asked Gilbert Harrison to help set it up. After that, Harrison helped URC students set up round table discussions on their own. Modeled on the NCCJ adult round table discussions by community civic and religious leaders of different faiths, the Student Round Table was adapted to the URC and designed to open up communication among Protestant, Catholic, and Jewish students as they faced one another around a table placed in front of an audience. Each student speaker answered questions about his or her religion. The goals were to learn about those of other faiths, dispel friction, mistrust and confusion amongst them, and promote understanding and good tri-faith relations.[31]

The program spread from Williamstown to campuses and other localities in California, and the URC Extension Council helped plan, staff, and carry it out. "In Fresno with enthusiastic reception from . . . the student officials of Fresno State College, a permanent Round Table has been set up. Bakersfield and other valley towns are following this lead," stated McComb's report of 1936 to 1937.[32] Closer to home, the UCLA Student Board picked up the idea and "undertook the promotion of Round Table discussion groups"; as a result, a "continuing group of Protestant Catholic and Jewish students met throughout the year," Harrison wrote. They gathered to consider such subjects as "What's Wrong with the Jews, and the Catholics, and the Protestants?"[33] Round tables "got out into the open the things they did not understand about each other or the things they did not like, and . . . the most severe critic of any group . . . [was] always to be found within that group itself," stated Adaline Guenther.[34]

The Student Round Table Program grew "to such proportions" that the UCLA Student Board divided the program into beginning and advanced sections.[35] At USC, round tables "aroused thoughtful students" who "wished to know more of their classmates' beliefs." About twenty students would get together for a "discussion of the history, doctrine, and practices of various faiths."[36]

At UCLA, still other NCCJ programs were taken up by the URC students. One was the annual commemorations of brotherhood observances. These commemorations called attention to the tri-faith nature of American society through a variety of venues, from lectures, discussions, joint worship services, to dialogues among various religious leaders. It was celebrated in February to connect the idea of American religious pluralism with George Washington, Abraham Lincoln, and American patriotism.[37]

On the lighter side, brotherhood cartoons were put up at the URC, as well as on "billboards up and down the boulevards, posters in the windows." There was also the selection of Miss Brotherhood, a publicity stunt and riff on the Miss America beauty contest. The winner of the contest was "the first photogenic student to come into the building after the idea struck," quipped Guenther.[38] Miss Brotherhood was one of several activities that engaged women students. Overall, URC women had been active primarily on the student board and at Uni-Camp, as well as in the after camp social service programs.

Although she makes a joke of it, Guenther's participation in the Miss Brotherhood contest reveals her willingness to take advantage of the gendered image of glamour, youth, and beauty of the Miss America contest to gain publicity. It reflects her paradoxical willingness to deploy a highly gendered image of women to support a highly gendered male concept of brotherhood. She would also later use a similarly gendered stereotype of women to attract attention to the concept of Americanism, as we shall see in discussing the Panel of Americans.

Using radio broadcasts as a vehicle for publicizing brotherhood programs was another NCCJ project that attracted URC students and recent graduates.

Political leaders and clergy of all stripes had been using radio to broadcast their message, from President Franklin D. Roosevelt with his Fireside Chats, to the Canadian priest Father Charles Coughlin with his anti-Jewish rants, to the "Boston radio priest" Michael J. Ahern, S. J., a popular speaker on the NCCJ traveling trio circuit. The NCCJ also used radio to broadcast a variety of brotherhood programs on both local stations and the major radio networks. Some of them featured such popular figures as singer Kate Smith.[39]

In 1938 Gilbert Harrison, by then a graduate and member of the URC part-time staff, and Al Chamie, a member of the URC Businessmen's Committee, worked with the NCCJ on brotherhood programs and formed a local commit-tee of volunteer radio experts from the off-campus community. It included Tom McAvity, Albert Lasker Jr., Don Gilman, and Bob Redd.[40] That year local radio stations publicized brotherhood events, primarily through public ser-vice announcements and occasionally by broadcasting brotherhood programs presented by students and faculty.[41]

Soon thereafter Harrison organized a URC radio division to expand and professionalize radio coverage at the URC. The radio division easily became "the most exciting thing" to have "happened this year," Guenther reported. "The radio up to a year ago was something over which the Conference oc-casionally had a speech read. Perhaps three speeches, if the occasion was re-ally important. Now, with the radio division in place all this has changed," she continued.[42] Alongside the NCCJ, the URC began using more national networks to broadcast brotherhood programs and local stations to introduce student productions.

After the URC radio division was formed, the Radio Committee added new volunteers: chairman Norman Morrell, head of the Hollywood office of the Lord and Thomas Advertising Agency, and members Donald Thornberg of the Columbia Broadcasting System (CBS); Louis Frost and Walter Bunker of the National Broadcasting System (NBC), Lewis Allen Weiss of the Mutual Broadcasting System (MBC); and Joseph Stauffer of the Young and Rubicam Advertising Agency. The committee made the decision "to cultivate consci-entiously radio as an outlet for the [URC] . . . message of amity, justice and cooperation among Protestants, Catholics and Jews," commented Harrison, describing how the decision yielded "amazing radio coverage."[43]

In 1941 the URC Radio Committee arranged brotherhood broadcasts using more Hollywood figures than before, among them, Bette Davis, Pat O'Brien,

David Selznick, and author Hartzell Spence. The four of them conducted a round table discussion on the meaning and importance of religious understanding. Some fifty transcriptions of this discussion were made and distributed nationally to the various area secretaries of the NCCJ.[44] On occasion an entire show was devoted to a brotherhood theme, such as Edward G. Robinson's *Big Town*, or to personal statements by popular radio personalities such as Fletcher Wiley or on programs like Art Baker's *Notebook*, or Arch Obler's *Everyman's Theater*.

Although brotherhood radio programs differed from one another, the committee generally agreed that, when possible, the brotherhood material should be woven into large commercial shows, like the one hosted by Kate Smith, whose show already had a large audience. "This technique enabled us to reach millions of listeners who could not have been reached by a single, sustaining program since it has been proven that large audiences cannot be built up except over long periods of time." Under the guidance of Morrell and the committee, the URC radio division that year reached more than sixty-nine million listeners across the nation.[45]

The Russian actress Alla Nazimova, a Hollywood star, made the following personal statement on the radio: "This night marks the end of Brotherhood Week, that time set aside to renew our national unity of mind and heart. We affirm the inherent worth of every human being of whatever blood or creed. And, beyond all the divisions of our imperfect society, we assert the brotherhood of man. The defense of America begins in the hearts of our countrymen." The brotherhood theme that year was "One Nation Indivisible with Liberty and Justice for All."[46]

Echoing Roosevelt's 1939 State of the Union address, Nazimova connects brotherhood with uniting America for the defense of democracy in the face of German and Italian fascism, as well as against Japanese imperialism. Here, the religious concept of brotherhood is used to define American nationalism as internationalism, and American pluralism as essential to democracy. Religion, internationalism, and democracy became central to Roosevelt's vision of the United States in the war ahead.[47]

During the first several months of Harrison's tenure the radio division presented approximately one thousand experimental radio programs apart from the special broadcasts to mark brotherhood observances. Some of these were interfaith programs presented by clergy and academics in the local community.

One of the first was "West Coast Church of the Air," a thirty-minute program broadcasted Sunday mornings on CBS. It featured priests and rabbis as well as various representatives of the Protestant, Mormon, and Episcopal faiths who shared the microphone. Others were "The Pastor's Study," a series in which a specific Jewish, Catholic or Protestant member of the clergy spoke about his faith, and "To Keep Our Freedom," a series of discussions by professors and clergymen.[48]

In addition to the networks, individual local stations in Los Angeles, Long Beach, and San Diego expanded their broadcasts of radio programs during brotherhood week. All of this radio work was accomplished by the URC radio division with an expenditure of eighty-five dollars. Networks and stations donated air time and writers, actors, radio producers, and executives donated their talents "because of their enthusiasm for the . . . inter-faith movement."[49]

Students and other young people in the local community also presented radio programs. "Youth Demands an Answer" was a thirty-minute roundtable discussion among four young men, not enrolled in college, who represented different religions. Their aim was to "honestly examine" their "agreements and differences" and share their views on "common problems." The program was broadcasted for ten months over KFWB.[50] Other programs included "The Book of Books," readings from the Old and New Testaments by students accompanied by background selections of classical music sometimes sung by Marian Anderson and the Monks of Solesmes Abbey. It was broadcasted every Sunday morning over KFI or KECA and continued for several years.[51] "Well—You're Wrong," a program with swing music background that attempted to correct current misconceptions about various religious faiths with factual evidence, was broadcasted over Los Angeles station KMPC. It went so well that "it has been copied in Chicago and points east with talk of a national hookup," reported Adaline Guenther.[52] Single broadcasts were also aired. One was broadcasted from Royce Hall auditorium at UCLA and another, featuring the music of the San Francisco Theological Seminary Choir, was broadcasted from Long Beach, both of them by NBC.[53]

The URC Radio division also sought to clear the air of radio programs in the Los Angeles area that attacked ecumenism and the interfaith movement. It did so by listing those programs that the division believed were using radio for stirring up religious and racial hatred and giving the list to the chair of the Southern California Broadcasters' Association.[54]

The NCCJ offered Gilbert Harrison a job at their headquarters in New York City to set up a radio division similar to the one at the URC so that the two coasts could "coordinate efforts in developing an even more effective radio coverage."[55] "This entire inter-faith radio development is unique in America, and the results of this pioneer endeavor should be spread to other sections," declared Marshall McComb."[56] The URC radio division had already been using material prepared in New York City. Among that material was a program based on news compiled by the Religious News Service that the URC had broadcasted in Los Angeles on KMPC. It carried the information on the religious work being done among the various denominations.[57] Accepting the NCCJ offer, Harrison spent about six months in New York City before returning to Los Angeles, where he rejoined the URC staff and participated in various projects.

The URC radio division lasted for several more years, continuing during the Second World War. The NCCJ and the URC carried on during the war, with the radio divisions sponsoring some 450 broadcasts in 1942. Most of them, like the West Coast Church of the Air and the Book of Books, were produced and transmitted locally.[58] During Brotherhood Week, however, Hollywood figures such as Norman Shearer, Robert Young, Sherilan Gibney, and David Selznick produced radio programs that were broadcasted and transcribed for distribution to forty-one stations across the nation.[59]

The URC Trialogue on Campus and in Community

Another URC student project adapted from an NCCJ program was the so-called trialogue, an analogue of the traveling trio of priest, rabbi, and minister. A trio of UCLA men, composed of students and recent graduates, gave live presentations to audiences at houses of worship, schools, social clubs, and fraternal organizations.[60] "The assumption here was that what people need more than anything else is changing their emotions, how they feel about one another, not through their minds but through their . . . hearts . . . [by] talking together, enjoying themselves, enjoying life and . . . [showing that] these are people who can get together and live together and enjoy one another," recalled URC Protestant trialogue speaker Robert Hine.[61]

All three of the URC trialogue speakers were men; all were handsome, and all were articulate. The image that these speakers projected was a highly favorable one. Each of them looked like a typical well-educated member of mainstream American society and not like a stereotypical ethnic type. They wore coat and tie and were neatly barbered and shaved. In many ways they were indistinguishable from each other. They were not stereotypes of their religious group. Their goal was not to serve as archetypes but to appeal to the audience in the broadest possible way. Even before they began speaking, the trialogue presenters were primed to make a good impression. Indeed, the first impression was important, especially when some of the audience may never have actually met or even knowingly seen someone from outside their own group. Moreover, unlike the clerical trio that generally presented at NCCJ events, the student trialogue speakers were not professional clerics. They were just college students or recent graduates.

The URC trialogue program gave the Catholic, Jewish, and Protestant student and graduate speakers an opportunity to speak in public, not only about their respective religions but also about their personal beliefs, values, and circumstances. They were to show their human side, and to demonstrate that although the they belonged to different religious groups, all of them were good Americans, good friends with good values, who cared about their religion. Each speaker gave a five-minute presentation and at the end of their talks, each would answer audience questions.

A significant message of the trialogue speaker program was similar to those of Alla Nazimova and Roosevelt in his 1939 State of the Union address referred to earlier: that although American society is diverse in religious affiliation and belief, we are all one nation of good, loyal Americans who can (and often do) get along.

After one of the first presentations in 1936, at Rabbi Magnin's Wilshire Temple, URC trios visited other houses of worship, schools, social clubs, fraternity and sorority houses, college and university assemblies, business groups, and Hollywood gatherings. In format both the trialogue and NCCJ trio programs resembled the tri-faith speaker programs of Comrades in Service that had toured the American army camps and that Foster had helped develop at the end of the First World War.

"The question always used to come up . . . how can these various groups be participating with each other," said Catholic speaker Bill Burke, "So, our speeches at this time . . . [were about] what it meant to be an American from

various religious backgrounds and what was the motivation in your background for being able to live as a good citizen and cooperate with other citizens?" "Particularly at this time" Jews wanted to show that they were good
citizens "because you had Hitler who was out there telling everybody . . . that
the Jews were a racial group," and therefore would always remain alien. The
Catholics "were more interested in some sort of recognition on the campus
level because they were highly critical of . . . pragmatist [professors] who simply told . . . philosophy classes that belief in God or a deity is . . . a bunch of
idiocy." The Catholics wanted "some access to the university . . . to get some
balance," he explained.[62]

Although most of the trialogue teams featured Jewish, Catholic, and Protestant speakers, Episcopalians and Latter-Day Saints, both active, long-standing URC members, would at times replace the Protestant speaker.[63] One of the
first trialogue teams consisted of John Krumm (Episcopalian), Gilbert Harrison (Jewish), and Stuart Ratliff (Catholic). Like the teams that followed, they
were handsome, articulate, and well-dressed, which was not surprising, since
appearance was important to Guenther, "a very shrewd woman [who] knew
what she was doing." She would "always" choose the "top notch students,
good looking" and "make sure they wore the right things . . . no going out
in shorts or anything. We didn't dress up, but we looked nice," Robert Hine
reported.[64]

According to Hine's contemporary, URC member Marian Hargrave, the
trialogue men were "very articulate, very charming, very substantial." They
were "good . . . box office" [and] "that was . . . smart. I mean, this was part
of the whole strategy to have Catholic, Protestant and Jew . . . win attention
from audiences." Talking about religion might otherwise "be a big bore." In
addition, each would "involve people and get them . . . excited about their
own backgrounds and other people's backgrounds . . . and have an interesting
discussion and questions afterward."[65]

The trios were entertaining and exuded a relaxed demeanor. Harrison said
that he, Ratliff, and Krumm were close friends beyond their trialogue presentations, and they often shared ideas. In their presentations each could tell jokes
about himself and his religion with ease and good humor.[66] Like the other
trialogue speakers, each of them spoke concisely and with emphasis on human
interest stories both in their speeches and in answering audience questions.

Hine tells how the trialogue speakers would practice answering questions beforehand by questioning one another.[67] Harrison relates how most audience members were Protestant, and that most of the questions were directed to the Jewish and Catholic panelists.[68] Questions often asked included: Why don't Jews eat pork or do you really believe that the body of Christ is in the bread?" Another was "do you really think I'm going to hell?" Burke recalls how he would answer this question with "Do you want a theological opinion or what I really believe?"[69]

Some of the presentations addressed fraternal groups. Others aimed at groups with an interest in education: American Legion Posts, Parent-Teacher Associations (PTAs), schools and teachers' organizations. All of these organizations furnished audiences for the trialogue presentations. The audiences evinced great interest in the speakers and listened carefully. They asked good questions that revealed how much more work still remained to be done in the field of interfaith relations. All this was mostly a rewarding experience for the speakers. The trialogue speakers were often heartened by the apparent good will, intentions, and innocence of the audience questions, despite the misinformation they evinced, Harrison noted.[70]

Some thirteen hundred UCLA students gathered on a Sunday afternoon at a Youth Understanding Meet at Royce Hall, to hear a trialogue presentation given as part of brotherhood observances in February 1936. After a speech by presiding UCLA provost Ernest Carroll Moore and the playing of "Ave Maria," "Eli Eli," and "Ein Feste Burg," William Hensey (a UCLA Catholic graduate), Gilbert Harrison (UCLA Jewish student), and Frank Wilkinson (UCLA Protestant student), each spoke.[71] "The three of them were standing on the same platform, each describing "what his particular religion means to him. . . . This modern world may say that it should not be unique that three students stand on the same platform but history will bear me out that it is a unique thing. . . . The students were demonstrating to the community that it could be done, and the community responded with a wave of appreciation for their doing," reported Marshall McComb.[72] The event was "the most civilizing influence ever exerted on that platform," E. C. Moore was reported to have said.[73] Soon thereafter, Moore wrote a letter to Hensey, saying that the meet gave him "pride and confidence" and that the Religious Conference "may be breaking ground for the nation."[74]

The following year audiences at the junior colleges heard similar trialogues. Representatives from the various southern California junior colleges gathered at Newman Hall at LACC for a conference where they heard from Catholic, Protestant, and Jewish university students. Such trios spoke at other junior college and college assemblies, including those at Whittier, Redlands, and Pomona colleges.[75] "So you see that last year what was considered unique was now done over and over again and never once branded as unique," reported McComb.[76]

UCLA trialogues went beyond the February brotherhood observances in 1938. Like the Student Round Tables, they were given throughout the year. According to Harrison, trialogues were popular both on the luncheon club circuit and at nighttime gatherings, which often involved travel in and around Los Angeles.[77] They also spoke to civic clubs and service organizations in various parts of southern California. Some of these three-student teams gave talks nearby as well, at local Los Angeles social clubs, churches and synagogues, universities, and junior colleges. Audiences at the Elks, Masons, B'nai B'rith Lodge, the Knights of Columbus, the Ebell Club, the Wilshire Optimists, the Sisterhood of Temple Sinai, the Hollywood Rotary, the Beverly Hills and Westwood Kiwanis, the Lynwood Exchange Club, as well as at Citrus, Santa Ana and Fullerton suburban junior colleges, and the more distant Kern County Taft campus all heard trialogues given by university students and graduates and saw them modeling brotherhood.[78]

"It was the sending [of] speakers in teams to all sorts of gatherings that made the Conference really famous this past year. The word 'trialogue' as meaning the conversation of three people seems to be practically a household word in Southern California, at least among program chairmen," Adaline Guenther reported the following year. She wrote that the "community office has a list of 75 young men and women, of whom only a small percentage are still in college, who are willing to spend evenings being trained, get their own endorsements from their religious advisers, take time off from their work to go to meetings, and buy their own gasoline to get there. They go in [groups of] three or four and they talk about the necessity of individual religious convictions and how men of different faiths may live together in justice and amity. . . . They have covered Southern California towns and villages and crossed through service clubs and women's clubs and schools and churches. They were rated 4 Star by Rotary. They provided the program at the Chamber of Commerce Christmas luncheon. They got an ovation. . . . from the Los Angeles Breakfast Club. They were the most outstanding and stimulating program in years at the Friday Morning Club."[79] Rave reviews also poured in for a trialogue program at an advertising club in San Diego: "When we got through, the chairman gets up and he says, 'What these young men have been talking about . . . is good Americanism,'" related Bill Burke. "'It's not only what they stand for . . . it's what this club stands for.'"[80]

During the 1939 to 1940 academic year, trialogue teams reached a total audience of twenty-five thousand speaking to 130 separate organizations in twenty-three California towns, John Burnside estimated in his annual report.[81] That same year, according to Guenther, the trialogue program "moved the idea of the Religious Conference, which is religious groups united to do a job, away from the campus and into the community. Many thousands who never came near a college campus are now familiar with what the Religious Conference stands for."[82]

High schools were another venue for trialogue presentations. John Burnside, Gilbert Harrison, and Stuart Ratliff attended regular meeting of the senior high school principals of the Los Angeles City high school system, where they arranged to give trialogues at student assemblies. The first one was at Hollywood High School. Others were arranged at Lincoln High School, University High School, and Polytechnic High School. The presentations probably helped principals and teachers in their efforts to promote religious tolerance. "Principals, directors and presidents of educational institutions are constantly urged to . . . promote religious education and understanding," Burnside reported in 1940.[83] He gave the trialogue program wide coverage in the high schools of Los Angeles County beyond the city as well. Thanks to him, trialogue programs were scheduled at some high schools further afield, for example in El Segundo, Redondo, Alhambra, and Gardena.[84]

"Every high school in Los Angeles County with three exceptions, has had, or will have within the next week, one, two, or more [trialogue] assemblies, attended by all the students," Guenther predicted.[85] That year student assemblies reached an estimated sixty-two thousand students, and, close to what Guenther had expected, trialogues were given at thirty-six of the forty high schools in the city.[86] Trialogue programs averaged about one per day during the 1940 to 1941 academic year, as URC graduate George Hill, a Baptist, joined the roster of speakers. Guenther remarked how Hill and Krumm, by that time both members of the clergy, "stole time from their jobs . . . to face from 400 to 2000 wiggling . . . adolescents."[87] More engagements followed, mostly at mandatory student assemblies. The extension division also arranged two assemblies at Pasadena Junior College, as well as another at the annual interfaith banquet at San Diego State College.[88]

According to Ivan Olson, chair of the LACC Student Board, fifteen hundred students heard the trialogue team of Burnside, Ratliff, and Harrison at an assembly in Los Angeles City College.[89] The trialogue program had "developed really to the limit" in the fraternity and sorority houses "on meeting nights when the members are obliged to be present," Jim Stewart, chair of the UCLA Student Board.[90] Requests for trialogue programs continued the following year, with Burnside making most of the arrangements.

The year from May of 1940 to 1941, "an irregular year of world strife and conflict and much chance for anti-something feeling," became "one of the greatest trialogue years the Conference has ever had. More persons were reached . . . than ever before and every one was received with terrific enthusiasm," wrote John Hessel, UCLA Student Board chair. He described an outstanding trialogue given to the whole [UCLA] student body at Royce Hall, chaired by Gordon Sproul, the president of the University of California, and broadcasted over thirty-three radio stations. The URC trialogue was then invited to UC Berkeley to address the student body there. The trialogue team also visited Arizona and spoke at several gatherings in and around Phoenix. "Some of the groups have asked that the teams return and give the trialogues over again."[91] The trialogue was also presented at Davis. That same year during Brotherhood Week, "any day . . . which did not see the major trialogue team speaking five times was almost a failure," wrote Guenther.[92]

Prominent Hollywood figures such as Louis Mayer and Dore Schary especially liked the trialogue program. Schary even supervised the making of a movie short of it.[93] Both of them liked the program because they appreciated a performance and the fact that it seemed to lessen anti-Semitism, speculated Gilbert Harrison.[94] As trialogue speakers at the Hillcrest Country Club, a popular spot with movie executives, Harrison and Krumm spoke to an audience of about one thousand people. At the time there were a number of films featuring a Jewish cantor or a Catholic priest. Krumm turned to the movie executives present and asked them why they didn't do something to make the Protestants look interesting. At Krumm's question, the Country Club roared into fits of laughter, recalled Harrison.[95]

The URC Trialogue Tours California Military Bases
and College Campuses

The staff of the URC reached out to the military on the eve of the Second World War. Just before the United States entered the conflict, John Burnside negotiated with military leadership and arranged for trialogue teams to give presentations at training camps, including at the recently opened Roberts Training Camp in the Salinas Valley. Bill Burke, who spoke at Roberts, recalled that the process would start by contacting the chaplains or commanding officers at the camps and volunteering to help solve problems of morale or religion.[96] Other camps visited were the Marine Training station in San Diego, where two thousand marines heard trialogues, as well as Fort McArthur in San Pedro, Camp Callan at Torrey Pines and Camp Hahn at Riverside. At the request of the chaplains, programs were also scheduled at Ft. Ord and Fort San Luis.[97]

The military trialogues typically had a rough script to guide the speakers. It began with ground rules. One was that when the speakers could not agree, they "agree to disagree agreeably." Another was if you "want to know something about a Jew . . . don't ask . . . [a] Catholic, but . . . ask a Jew. . . . We believe in letting everyone speak for himself." While there was an audience question period at the end of the overall presentation, at times when one speaker finished his presentation, he would ask the next speaker a question to get him started and set a conversational tone.[98]

The Protestant speaker was frequently asked, "Why don't Protestants get together more?" A typical answer would be, "If you could get religion like a Methodist, experience it like a Baptist, propagate it like an Adventist, pay for it like an Episcopalian and be proud of it like a Presbyterian, that would be some religion." The Protestant speaker further explained that "the inevitable result of the Protestant premise of individual interpretation will be a multiplication of denominations." He would then usually add that at present there is "increased cooperation among Protestant groups" and might mention the Federal Council of Churches of Christ, the International Council of Religious Education (where Thomas Evans and Adaline Guenther had worked together during much of the 1920s), and the University Religious Conference.[99]

The perpetual question for the Catholic speaker was, "Do Catholics really believe that all non-Catholics will go to hell?" A typical answer would be,

"We know that the religious label we bear is not a sure sign of our going to heaven or to hell. In fact we're pretty sure that all of the good Jews and good Protestants will have a fighting chance along with good Catholics of getting to heaven.[100]

An ongoing question addressed to the Jewish speaker was, "How do you define a Jew?" A typical reply was, "There is an old saying that the only thing two Jews can agree upon is what the third should give to charity—so you can be sure that there is no agreement." The speaker would then say he "define[s] a Jew in terms of what he is not: He is not a member of a Jewish race. There is no such thing. . . . with the exception of Hitler's scientists [all] are agreed upon that." He continued by saying, "There are black Jews, yellow Jews, brown Jews, Jews who look like Arabs, Spaniards and Englishmen." "The Jews are not a nation. They are nationals of every country, just as the Catholics or Protestants are citizens of the country in which they live." He would elaborate by saying "Jews, to me, are people who believe in a certain religion . . . Judaism," explaining that "it is the religion of the Prophets of the Old Testament. . . . A Jew is one who belongs to the group which believe in Judaism. When he ceases to believe in Judaism and joins another church, he is no longer a Jew."[101]

It is interesting to note that the Jewish trialogue speaker considered Judaism a belief system rather than a racial, cultural, or national grouping. In this respect Judaism resembled American Protestantism, a system in which the member of a particular denomination could give it up or change membership to another denomination to reflect a member's preferred belief system or other preference. Unlike European Jews who were generally considered by their countrymen as members of a separate nation or an alien racial group, often one that was unassimilable and unalterable even despite conversion, Gilbert Harrison, the principal Jewish trialogue speaker at the time, considered American Judaism a choice. Perhaps this was in response to the rise of Hitler's theories of Ayrian racial superiority, as Bill Burke suggested. It seems likely that Harrison was influenced by the liberal religious beliefs of certain American reform Jews at the time, such as anti-Zionist rabbis David Philipson and Morris Lazaron, both of whom were supporters of interfaith projects like the URC.[102]

When asked about intermarriage, all three of the trialogue speakers agreed that it was not a good idea and should be discouraged. "The couple should agree upon as many fundamentals as possible. . . . If there is serious disagreement the marriage stands a good chance of breaking up." This agreement led one of the speakers to say that "this marriage question is only one of the many things we agree upon."[103] On the question of intermarriage, the trialogue speakers seem to have agreed that it was best to refrain from endorsing it. It is likely that doing would have crossed a line that most members of the audience would not have accepted at the time and would have alienated the good will the program sought to achieve. Gilbert Harrison later did intermarry, as did several others in the URC.

The trialogue programs given far from home were often delivered by URC graduates. Thomas Evans praised this development and reported that the URC had received calls from San Francisco, Pittsburgh, Pennsylvania, the NCCJ in New York City, and from "colleges and universities [in] the entire country" because of "the richness of experience of our graduates." Sending URC graduates to these distant places was like a religious mission to him. He reported how the URC "is destined to go far beyond its original purpose at the campus" and that "young leaders who have caught the vision at the campus are now the creative agents for religion . . . far and wide."[104]

In the fall of 1941, the NCCJ and the URC cooperated to send Gilbert Harrison, Bill Burke, and George Hill on a two-month national tour of colleges and universities. The local directors of the NCCJ arranged the agenda, scheduled the trialogues, and accompanied the trio. "We were the ones that Adaline instructed, told us each to write our own speech, get ready," Burke recalled.[105] While on tour they presented a trialogue almost every day.[106]

Among the campuses listed on the itinerary were several public state universities, including Colorado, Connecticut, Cornell, Louisiana, Michigan, Minnesota, Missouri, Ohio State, Texas, and Wyoming. Also listed were Milwaukee State Teachers College, Denver City University, and private colleges and universities; the latter included Amherst College, Brown University, Carlton College, Carnegie Tech, Catholic University, Georgetown, Macalester College, Mundelein University, New York University, Northwestern University, Purdue University, Princeton University, Smith College, Stevens College, Washington University, Wesleyan College in Connecticut, Williams College and Yale University.[107]

When the three speakers were at the University of Denver, Burke reported that they took over a class on "Religions in America," after speaking to an "enthusiastic assembly of 600 students."[108] While the trio was at Carlton College,

Harrison received a telegram written on behalf of Eleanor Roosevelt. She requested that he go to Washington, DC, to direct the newly established National Youth Division of the Office of Civilian Defense (OCD). His job was to design educational programs to build morale among young people and encourage them to take part in civilian defense activities. After checking with Evans and receiving his approval, Harrison left the trialogue for the OCD; he was replaced by Bernard "Bud" Desenberg, a Jewish Stanford graduate who had attended the Williamstown Institute and was a staff member of the URC.[109]

On the trialogue tour the questions asked of the speakers were "the same questions they had been asked a hundred times in California."[110] As in California, most of the questions were addressed to the Jewish speaker. While the Catholic student still received many questions, those addressed to the Protestant were few. This is not surprising since most in the audience were Protestant and fewest were Jewish. "Is it not true that much of the anti-Semitism in the country is purely imaginary?" "Do you think it American for Father Coughlin to have been put off the air?" "When a Jewish boy joins a non-Jewish fraternity, do you think it helps or hurts his cause?" These were some of the questions addressed to the Jewish speaker. Typical questions for the Catholic student included, "How can an intolerant belief create tolerant people?" "Why do Catholics say that the Jews killed Christ?" "Are Catholics Fascists?" The Protestant speaker was often asked, "What would you suggest to improve the institutionalized church?" "Do not the numerous divisions within the Protestant church tend to weaken the structure of [a] particular church?"[111]

"We did a good job," Bernard Desenberg reported. At Yale the trialogue drew the "largest [chapel] attendance that year." "They came to be skeptical and went away amazed at our frankness."[112] Judging from a letter written by student body president, Donald M. Brieland, the trialogue went well at Carlton College. He commented that "to develop spontaneous enthusiasm in a college group is one of the most difficult things which can face a speaker or group." He continued, "As a student at Carlton, I have never seen questioning work as it did today. The floor seemed eager and interested. The student apathy, which so frequently accompanies chapel assemblies, has been replaced with a sincere desire to participate." He concluded that "probably in no other way can the Conference better impress upon the college minds throughout America the importance of cooperation and 'unity of spirit.'"[113]

As part of the tour, the speakers stopped in New York City, where they talked with a youth group at Riverside Church and met with its liberal pastor, Harry Emerson Fosdick. They also met with entertainer Eddie Cantor, a long time URC supporter, and had tea with Eleanor Roosevelt. She "seemed much interested in their work and asked many questions about their tour which she mentioned in her column, 'My Day.'"[114] The national trialogue tour ended in the fall of 1941. Within weeks of the trialogue's return, the Japanese bombed Pearl Harbor and the United States declared war on Japan. Soon thereafter Germany declared war on the United States.

CHAPTER FIVE

The University Religious Conference in the Second World War

The University Religious Conference stands for the interfaith cooperative idea. . . .
our first question always is where and how we may promote this brotherhood among
the various people of our democracy.
—Glenn W. Moore, Presbyterian, URC religious leader, in a letter of April 2, 1942

When the United States entered the Second World War, it assumed the role of defender of democracy, as it had in the First World War. But this time things were different. Hitler's German master race ideology, Mussolini's glorification of Italian fascism, and Japan's vision of racial superiority in establishing hegemony in the Pacific made it imperative for the United States to define its democratic national values as those of diverse inclusion in contrast to its adversaries. Having accommodated some fifteen million immigrants in the decades before the First World War, American society was in a position during the subsequent conflict to demonstrate values of diverse inclusion. Indeed, the American population was more diverse than that of its adversaries, but could it demonstrate aspiration to common national values?[1]

From its founding in 1928, the URC had sought to practice multifaith inclusion. With the coming of the war, the URC expanded its programs beyond religion to racial and ethnic inclusion as well. Despite the wartime problems of staffing and turnover, as students and alumni left to serve in the military, the URC deployed its ongoing interfaith experience to develop new, broader programs highlighting diverse inclusion as national values, aspirational and ambivalent thought they were in the context of American society in the 1940s.

URC Programs During the War

In January of 1942, soon after the founding of the United Services Organization (USO), its board director Lyman Johnson, wrote to Episcopalian bishop
and URC religious leader W. Bertram Stevens, on behalf of USO chairman
A. H. Giannini. Johnson suggested several ways the URC could cooperate with
the USO. These included selecting, training and posting URC volunteers or
staff members to USO local hospitality centers to disseminate information on
church and community activities that were "providing suitable recreational
and social activities" and stimulating "interest in this phase of our program."
To accommodate the increasing number of troops in Los Angeles, he suggested decentralizing the USO hospitality centers and possibly opening up a
center at the URC. "There is a definite need for such a center in the West Los
Angeles and Sawtelle area."[2] Days later Charles Posner, administrative secretary of the USO, wrote a letter introducing Adaline Guenther to Los Angeles
military personnel as a "representative" and requesting that "any courtesy" be
extended to her.[3]

The URC seemed well suited to serving the needs of the diverse USO
membership which, like Comrades in Service and the Commission on Training Camp Activities during the First World War, included the YMCA, the
Salvation Army, the JWB, and the YWCA, as well as the National Catholic
Community Service and the Travelers Aid Association. In fact, the USO was
a successor of CIS in its broadly diverse membership, if not in its context or
all of its goals.

"What can be done in the way of promoting an inter-faith brotherhood so
far as the army and navy personnel is concerned?" asked Glenn W. Moore, as
he looked for opportunities beyond the USO.[4] Moore was a prominent Presbyterian and head of the URC Clergy Division, which brought together distinguished religious leaders well known in the community. He urged the URC
to take advantage of opportunities to aid the American war effort by drawing
on its years of experience with religious fellowship and cooperation. Such an
opportunity arose working with the Chaplains' Aid, later renamed the Chaplains' Service Corps (CSC).[5]

The CSC was a civilian organization of volunteers who helped military
chaplains during the Second World War. At the request of Chief Chaplain Earl
D. Weed of the Western Defense Command, the URC Women's Division and

Women Associates (adult community women volunteers who supported various URC projects) took responsibility for chairing, staffing, and fundraising for the Los Angeles CSC, a responsibility that continued through the Korean War.[6] For much of that time, it was chaired by Louise K. Sims, a member of the Church of Latter-Day Saints and a long time URC volunteer and trustee.

The CSC sought to supplement the resources available to chaplains of all faiths by providing such material things as altar equipment. This included linen, crosses, draperies, candlesticks and vases. Other equipment needed was athletic gear such as punching bags, Ping-Pong tables, fishing tackle, volley balls, baseball mitts, and balls. Christmas paraphernalia like Santa Claus suits, Christmas cards, gifts and calendars were also needed, and the URC donated those items. The URC also donated musical instruments such as pianos, brass and stringed instruments, male quartet music books, radios, turntables, and records as well as furnishings for day rooms (deck games, indoor games, writing materials, projection machines, films, various sporting goods, religious books and magazines, hymnals, Bibles and other reading materials).[7] The URC collected these items for the CSC at a workroom at the Los Angeles Farmers' Market.[8]

"We all recognize that . . . the chaplain needs, and must have, assistance from the outside . . . from the church . . . the home, from the community and from every single individual concerned with the mental, moral and physical welfare of our men," stated a CSC pamphlet. This meant providing "the concrete, wholesome, worthwhile things that formed the background of . . . civilian life," among them, "entertainment and discussion groups arranged and transported by the church."[9] To maintain high troop morale, donors were urged to write frequent "cheerful letters" that demonstrated "unflagging interest" in the work the troops were doing.[10]

As "an agency between the military chaplain and the churches of all faiths," the CSC took advantage of the interfaith membership and contacts of the URC. As in World War I, each military chaplain had responsibility for "ministering to . . . men of all faiths" when needed. To the twelve hundred men in his unit during the Second World War, the chaplain "is the spiritual leader during the most crucial period in many of their lives."[11] Glenn Moore thus suggested that the URC act as a clearing house to which military chaplains could "turn to easily make contacts with any religious group . . . [so they might better get to] know their men; that is, religious groups with which they are not particularly familiar, or to which the chaplain does not personally belong." He asked that the URC work with the CSC to "act as a clearing house for directing chaplains to headquarters of [unfamiliar] religious groups.[12] "People from every religious denomination" turned to the URC, and "they taught the Jewish rabbi what would be most comforting to a dying Methodist . . . or a Catholic. . . . And they talked to Catholics, what would you say to a Jewish . . . [soldier]," recalled former URC student Jean Burke.[13]

Drawing on previous experience in human relations, the URC also provided services to the Nisei (American citizens of Japanese background) and Issei (Japanese immigrants) who were removed to the internment camps and tried to ameliorate the hardships of removal. A flyer mentioned that the URC "has been handling the problem of Japanese discrimination on the U.C.L.A. campus and the Sawtelle area," offering "its experience in problems of minority discrimination."[14] Christian and Jewish URC students on the UCLA and LACC campuses "worked hard to relieve the pressure of their Japanese friends," by organizing student travel escorts to accompany the Japanese students to assembly centers and to set up a letter writing system "to keep them in touch with their college life while they were gone," wrote Guenther in a letter of 1942.[15]

Classes were held at Los Angeles City College where the URC had a branch. LACC offered classes for the Japanese students several weeks before they left, to help prepare them for life in the camps.[16] Classes offered included community leadership training, religious education for children, Bible study, community singing, journalism, and handicrafts. Once the Japanese LACC students began the evacuation process, other LACC students continued keeping in touch with the evacuees after accompanying them to the assembly centers. "The fellowship between the Caucasian and Japanese Americans [was] gratifying. Not the least of the benefits derived from this experience was the fine spirit of co-operation shown between the groups of the Religious Conference when they put their minds and efforts into a common task," reported Herman Beimfohr, then URC Methodist religious adviser at LACC.[17] The URC students at LACC wrote the student evacuees letters and sent them equipment for teaching and recreation, Beimfohr reported. He also mentioned how the students took advantage of the opportunities for broadening fellowship that the evacuation of the Issei and Nisei presented.[18]

As an organization that included not only students but prominent religious, civic, and business leaders of Los Angeles, the URC was in a position to work with other organizations to pressure those who administered the camps. One such organization was the Church Federation of Los Angeles, which had helped O. D. Foster in the founding of the URC in the 1920s. Alphonso Bell, a long-time URC Presbyterian supporter, was the president of the federation in 1942. In a letter to Guenther, the Church Federation's E. C. Farnham wrote, "We are all distressed over the sharp contrast in conditions which our Japanese friends are experiencing upon entrance into the evacuation camps" and "our concern over the fact that they must suffer incarceration and privation." The federation has "been in touch with the authorities . . . so far as diplomacy would permit," the letter continues, "urging that once the evacuations were completed, camp managers could be directed to relax regulations and allow for the release of inmates to the east coast and mid-west."[19]

It is clear that the URC was critical of internment, though never publicly condemning it. The evidence at hand indicates that the Conference supported amelioration of conditions of internment and early release of those interned, but it falls short of indicating outright advocacy to end the internment program. The use of such phrases as "so far as diplomacy would permit" and "relax regulations" to "release . . . inmates to the east . . . .and mid-west" reveals that the URC was cautious in its approach.[20] The URC was a moderate rather than a radical organization and seems to have welcomed the "opportunities for broadening fellowship that the evacuation of the Issei and Nisei presented."[21]

The URC expanded various existing service projects to help the war effort. Service projects in the community previously developed for Uni-Camp alumni and neighborhood children were broadened to include children of defense workers, many of them Mexican, as part of an overall program to prevent juvenile delinquency.[22] Participating in these activities were UCLA and LACC students who had gained training and experience working at Uni-Camp. Some of them had worked in the URC after-camp programs in Sawtelle. URC students also staffed a day nursery (under adult supervision), ran six afterschool clubs dedicated to children of defense workers, conducted Big Brother and Big Sister programs for about one hundred children in the area, and staffed and extended the hours of previous afterschool playground programs.[23]

URC programming of student and graduate speakers to address audiences

on campus and in the community was also adapted to helping the war effort. Since the early days, URC students had spoken at houses of worship, in
the community at large, and more recently, on the radio. They had spoken
about religious programs at the URC and the importance of religious brotherhood. During the war URC speakers gave talks on religious subjects related
to the war. "More than one hundred trained speakers, students, graduates
and faculty members from UCLA and LACC are available to discuss the role
of religion in world affairs under present conditions," stated a URC wartime
pamphlet.[24]

As the war progressed, the URC worked informally with the Student War
Board (SWB), set up by the UCLA Student Council and chaired by URC
member Robert Hine. Although the URC had no formal organizational ties
to the SWB, the two overlapped in personnel and shared similar values.[25] The
SWB worked on home-front activities such as supplying harvesters, steve-
dores, and salvage workers needed at home during the war.[26] "Maintenance of
democratic institutions," another category of SWB home-front activities, presented opportunities for URC students to write articles for the college daily,
the UCLA Bruin, and to speak about the close ties between interfaith tolerance, religious pluralism, and American democracy.[27] The war underscored
the need to publicize these values.

URC Veterans Abroad

During the war Guenther began a new URC project, collecting the letters of
former URC members serving in the military and redirecting them to others
in military service. She received letters from some two hundred former URC
students in the military and their fellow servicemen.[28] They corresponded
about their experiences in the war and their ideas about shaping the world
after the war. Guenther saved the letters, gathered them together, and retyped
them into a bulletin called *10845 Le Conte Avenue*, the URC's address. She then
mailed copies to URC servicemen abroad. At times she read letter excerpts
aloud at the URC annual meetings, without identifying the authors.[29] Some
of the letters reflect the influence that the Conference exerted upon these servicemen and upon their values and ideals. Other letters reveal how the war
influenced their hopes for the future.

138 CHAPTER FIVE

One serviceman wrote, "We almost had a fight here last night in the barracks arguing the racial and religious prejudice problems. You have been doing this for years, but I'm making some new observations. . . . I'm so glad to put across a little of what the Conference has given me. More and more I realize the value of it, and I burn with an eager desire to impart a little of the Conference idea of understanding."[30] Another letter, this one written from Belfast, describes a "Christmas Kids project" that, for the "first time in memory," got "Catholics and Protestants to sit down together . . . on a single job of Christmas cheer. . . . The affair went off in good shape with toys and sweets for the 4000 children who would otherwise have had nothing."[31] The third letter reveals the writer's thoughts about "the meaning of America to other peoples than our own." "Despite our motion pictures and our gangsters . . . the apparent turbulence of our political system, despite our treatment of the negro . . . we possess in the minds of other peoples a moral weight and importance which is quite astonishing. . . . the important thing is that these people . . . admire the states and our great free democratic institutions. . . . They know our great potential for good in world affairs, and they pray for our continued acceptance of responsibility in the world community."[32] All of these letters were read by Guenther at the 1943 URC annual meeting.

"There are two wars being fought today. . . . One is a physical war. . . . the other . . . is the one you talk about all the time at the Conference. The war of democracy vs. fascism, of truth and falsehood—the battle for the lasting peace. . . . and the one you folks at home must fight," wrote a URC graduate, then in the Navy. His letter continues, "It's the personal one . . . against prejudice, intolerance, religious hatred, castes, and racism. And I'm horrified to think how unsuccessful our fighting out here can be . . . unless there is a vigorous action to make the individual . . . understand these hatreds and allay them. There are many who see no connection between the individual, his prejudice and attitudes and peace among nations. No connection between the place of Africa in a post war world and the best nigger is a dead nigger; No connection between freedom of religion, and those damn Jews; no connection between Goodwill among the Americas and all Mexicans are lazy, dirty, good for nothings."[33] Guenther read this letter at the 1944 URC annual meeting.

By distributing *10845 Le Conte Avenue* to the servicemen abroad, Guenther hoped to keep together "those men in the service who had experienced the driving force of the Conference" while they were away serving in the military.[34] URC graduate Gilbert Harrison corresponded with Guenther while serving in the wartime military, but apart from that, he also corresponded widely with many fellow GIs about plans for the post war reconstruction. His correspondence formed the framework of a fledgling veteran's organization that eventually became the American Veterans' Committee (AVC). Guenther explained that she had "no strings on it" and that she played no substantive role in the actual formation or administration of the AVC. Gilbert Harrison confirmed her interpretation of events.[35]

While Harrison was one of the key URC men involved in founding the AVC, other URC men became involved too, among them Clifford Dancer, Merle Miller, and Donald Marsh. The veterans' organization "mushroomed" and "it will go far afield from here," predicted Guenther, describing how the idea of a veterans' organization was "an illustration again of Mr. Evans' idea that religion is a creative force, and you can't always tell where it's going to break through."[36] She also saw it as an illustration of the strong Conference bonds among the former URC students in the wartime military.

There were others in the AVC besides URC men, but the Conference's spirit of practical social activism seems to have set the tone at the founding of the organization and inspired some of those who joined it, noted Charles G. Bolte, a Dartmouth graduate, the first head of the AVC, and author of *The New Veteran*.[37] Bolte first met Adaline Guenther in 1944. She was in Washington, DC, and invited him to lunch, having heard of him through mutual friends. She was looking for someone to take over producing *10845 Le Conte Ave*.[38] "UCLA boys had one advantage denied the rest of us: they had been strongly influenced by the University Religious Conference . . . practicing democracy, practical work . . . This seemed to give them a social conscience with its sleeves rolled up, instead of the generalized diffuse air of good will . . . that emanated from so many of the college liberals I had known," Bolte wrote. He, continued, "They [URC former members] seemed not to suffer from 'the incompetence of mere unaided virtue or right-mindedness. . . . ' Their virtue and right-mindedness sounded essentially practical, armed with a knowledge of how the world runs."[39]

Harrison and other URC servicemen who played a significant role in founding the AVC seem to have been unaware of CIS and O. D. Foster's idealistic, even utopian, goals for society after the First World War. The American Legion, so different in outlook from the liberal inclusive outlook of Foster's

CIS, was the only new veterans' organization to have emerged from the First World War, as discussed earlier. Not unlike CIS, the AVC had a relatively short life, although it did continue after the war. There were disputes about whether the AVC should become a mass organization like the American Legion or a small, elite organization of influential, highly educated leaders (as Harrison and Bolte preferred). Ultimately, they and others left the organization when Communists infiltrated it.[40]

From Trialogue to Panel

The war brought changes to the trialogue program. In response to gas rationing, less time for community activities, and fewer speakers on hand, the number of trialogue events decreased. They were given mainly to new audiences at places such as military training camps in California. Since the outbreak of the war, many of the young men were away, and the URC began experimenting with new trialogue speakers.

One experiment involved replacing male students and recent graduates with ministers, priests, and rabbis. Another option was using mature women in the community as speakers.[41] But the most successful experiment was using a team of UCLA women students and recent graduates. "The college girls were the favorites," declared Adaline Guenther. These panels of young women eventually came to be called the Panel of Americans. They increasingly stood in for the male trialogue speakers and gradually replaced them, although both the original trialogue format and the newer wartime version with university women continued to coexist for a while.[42] The URC broke new ground during the war by having these young university women and recent graduates occupy the public spotlight and demonstrate a sense of camaraderie previously associated with men. Like the trialogue male speakers before them, the university women also answered audience questions.[43]

As the involvement of university women students and recent graduates took hold in 1942, there were other changes as well. The number of university women speakers increased from three to five or six; a moderator was added to field questions from the audience; the speakers were not only of different religions but also of different racial and ethnic backgrounds. They introduced the topics of racial and ethnic diversity in addition to religious diversity. These new programs quickly became popular. During that first year the university women averaged about twenty-seven presentations per month and spoke before some seventy-eight thousand people at high school assemblies, women's clubs, civic and educational organizations, and church groups. No doubt these presentations contributed to the fact that by March and April of 1945 one quarter of all the interfaith programs in the United States were given by the URC, observed Guenther.[44]

Daring as this experiment with university women speakers was, it was also an extension and continuation of the URC male trialogue speakers who dealt with religious inclusion, and before that, of O. D. Foster's tri-faith traveling male panels in the military camps to publicize CIS during the First World War. All of them attempted to broaden American identity, as did the Panel of Americans during the Second World War.

From 1944 to 1946 the university women addressed live civilian audiences numbering some 320,000 and live military audiences numbering about 250,000, in addition to radio programs broadcasted in northern and southern California.[45] These woman speakers drove all over southern California, often in groups. We "were all over the place . . . we went to every conceivable kind of organization, and we would speak . . . several times a day," panelist Marian Hargrave recalled. She told how they drove to the Los Angeles suburbs, to places like Fullerton and Placentia, to "speak to the . . . Rotary Club or the Lions Club." In fact, before 1947, they spoke at social and fraternal clubs more than at schools.[46]

The first group of young UCLA women speakers was composed of five members and included a Catholic woman of Irish background, a Jewish woman of English background, a Protestant woman of Russian background, an African American woman, and a Mexican American woman (the last two, of indeterminate religion).[47] At the earliest presentations, this team was called the United Nations Panel, but soon thereafter, in 1942, the name was changed to the Panel of Americans (POA). According to Marian Hargrave, "It would have a lot more punch and a lot more meaning if it would be a Panel of Americans. That's what we were talking about."[48] The POA program not only expanded and reinvigorated the trialogue format—by the addition of racial and ethnic issues—but the prominence of young women speakers attracted public attention as well.

Teams varied, but members of a typical six member POA team would include Catholic, Protestant, and Jewish panelists of European background, and African American, Mexican American, and Chinese American panelists. Guenther or G. Byron Done, religious adviser at the URC and later director of student work for the Church of Latter-Day Saints in southern California, often served as moderators. Done served when the POA made overnight presentations in California, and later too, when it went on a national tour.[49] These university women speakers demonstrated religious, racial, and ethnic diversity, more so than the previous trialogue presentations.

The diversity of the POA resonated well with the need for national unity during the war. Portrayed as examples of American inclusion, the panelists demonstrated how a group of diverse young women could get along. In fact, the experience of *being* a panelist—traveling together with others of different backgrounds, adjusting to trying conditions, remaining flexible, being of good cheer, and coming together afterwards to discuss the experience—was an experiment that enlarged the social circle of panelists and strengthened their ties.[50] The panels exemplified a URC principle important to Guenther: that diverse groups of people could work together to do a job. "The outstanding fact that must strike their audience is that these six girls of widely varying backgrounds . . . [form a] harmonious group. They have solved one of the greatest problems of society, of America, for themselves . . . they personify an American ideal," noted a contemporary press release, describing how each member of the POA "presents the case for her own segment of America, outlining the traits that differentiate her from the other[s] . . . and also the fundamental similarities which have made good friends and good Americans of all."[51]

The attractive, harmonious image that the POA projected was similar to the one projected by the earlier trialogue speakers. Like them, the POA speakers were to disarm the audience with a light and entertaining touch. They were to be nonthreatening amateurs, speaking from the heart, not professionals or experts.[52] They were to be likeable and presentable in their appearance. They "went in as civilized, pleasant, congenial people to whom anybody . . . could relate to."[53] The idea was for them, when possible, not to appear as outsiders but to look like neighbors or sisters or cousins, so they would be more easily accepted.[54] The panel team was to demonstrate how a group of wholesome, middle-class, well-educated amateurs could be good humored, unpretentious, and real Americans, regardless of religious, racial and ethnic differences. Like the trialogue speakers, the panel speakers also demonstrated to their audiences that they knew each other well, got along well with each other, and had an esprit de corps.[55]

Although the POA was thought to have educational benefits for the audience, its main purpose was to do so for the student panelists. As panelists, they needed to find out about their own religious, racial, and ethnic backgrounds and how they fit into the larger society. They needed to prepare personal stories and answer audience questions. To do this, they needed to learn about themselves and their families. This required research, reflection, and consulting with friends and family members. Sometimes it required consulting with the URC religious advisers, who seemed pleased by the attention. Watching the panelists earnestly grapple with questions about their own identity also appealed to the audience, Guenther observed.[56]

While each the panelists concentrated on the specifics of her own identity, they all focused on the strength of their bonds, as well as on the hopes and values they held in common as Americans. Among those were acceptance of difference, equal opportunities, and respect for themselves and others. Like the trialogue speakers, the POA speakers projected an image of highly assimilated Americans, by their dress, their speech patterns, their good manners, and sense of humor. Likewise, the panelists avoided some of the major disparities in American life that might occur to the contemporary reader, such as gender discrimination or class privilege. In the context of the war and its aftermath, such issues were inchoate or had receded, and the issues that the POA tackled, of religion, race, and ethnicity, seemed most central to the war effort.

Gender discrimination and class privilege seem to have remained invisible to the POA panelists themselves. Perhaps they were unaware of these disparities, disregarded them, or just took them for granted. The same was largely true of differences between those like themselves who had a formal college education and those who did not, although UCLA was a public university, for those of reasonable means, not for those who were rich. In any case, the POA speakers accepted such norms of the day without comment and concentrated instead on bridging racial, ethnic, and religious differences, rather than class.

Even when they touched on racial segregation, the panelists did so gently rather than confront it with hostility. One the one hand the Panel program arguably reflected the racial, ethnic, and religious multiplicity of the United States—a 1944 URC pamphlet called it "a cross section of America, a collection of the people you might find in any community anywhere in America," "concrete evidence that America is a land of many peoples." Yet, thanks to racial, religious, and ethnic barriers in Los Angeles and in American society generally, it is not unlikely that a POA presentation was the first time that a Caucasian, Protestant audience member had even seen an African American, a Mexican American, a Chinese American or a Jewish American up close, well-dressed, and in the spotlight, much less asked them a personal question.

Panel presentations gave racial, religious, and ethnic differences a human face. "Each member of the panel has a story to tell—a story about her own family and why they came to America. Each story is different, because none of the girls are alike, but each story carries one thought. 'America is a good place in which to live because here people have the right to be different,'" the 1944 pamphlet points out.[57] All of us are "members of a unique society," Hargrave agreed. "It is "a wonderful, positive getting together of all people under common values."[58]

Most of the panelists had undoubtedly experienced discrimination, and each of them was "articulate and constructive about talking about that so . . . others would understand what it's like to . . . stand in somebody else's shoes," Hargrave declared.[59] They went beyond victimization, however, to talk about the promise of American diversity. Guenther emphasized how the POA avoided talking about victimization but instead talked about the opportunities offered by American society.[60] "Yes, there are problems and there is victimization . . . and those are things that definitely must be addressed." But "we have to address them together . . . the solution . . . would have to flow from a larger overarching point of view . . . that we are a nation of diverse people and diverse belief . . . that was what the Religious Conference was talking about," explained Hargrave.[61] The Protestant panelists avoided taking on blame for being in the majority but generally spoke optimistically about the necessity and responsibility of the latter to live up to stated national values and to respect the rights of others. "Over and above all," Hargrave observed, "we were fighting a war . . . to try to support those values, and that's what it was all about."[62]

The message of the panel was an optimistic one. It was to raise the morale of the audience, as well as to demonstrate the values that Americans were defending in the war, aspirational as those may have been. Despite racism and racial segregation in the military and in civilian life, and discrimination against Jews in housing, jobs, and at certain clubs and universities, the panel was to take a positive attitude rather than protest or complain. The idea was that if all Americans worked together the situation would improve. Once the values were demonstrated and defined by the panel, they could be achieved. If victimhood were the subject of the panel discourse, then presumably the audience would lose heart and victimhood would grow.

In the Second World War, white Catholic, Protestant, and Jewish troops again served together in the same military units, as they had in the First World War. Again, as in the First World War, the military separated African American troops into racially segregated units, despite the fact that the military recognized religious, racial, and ethnic diversity as an American value that needed to be propagated. Notwithstanding this cognitive dissonance, the Army Department of Education and Information invited the Panel of Americans to give presentations on diversity at racially segregated Army and Army-Airforce training camps in California, as part of the American Orientation Program.

Guenther and the POA happily accepted these invitations. Those in the Army command who arranged the visits made sure the panelists were well cared for. Army planes ferried them from one California base to another. "You name a base in California at that time, and we went." The POA gave several panels a day at these bases. The Army organized the POA base visits and treated the panelists "so warmly and so courteously and with such interest." The panel was put up comfortably in Army quarters and was fed "royally" by the Army. There was rationing in civilian life, but not "on the Army bases" and "we ate gloriously," recalled Hargrave.[63]

The POA presentations fit in with the war effort in helping the military "take all of these disparate kids who were in the service and try to not only bring them together . . . so they could . . . communicate . . . but so that they had some kind of an idea of what in the world they were fighting for. It wasn't just fighting Hitler which was bad enough but we had so many positive values that we should be talking about." Nevertheless, speaking as they did to racially segregated audiences at the military bases, the POA message was "terribly ironic" as Hargrave put it, adding that "we were imbued, all of us, with the idea that we were one nation, indivisible. And, we had all of these differences with a lot of problems, but the problems could be solved because we were . . . optimistic . . . and it was the new generation."[64]

"We supposedly were attractive and could come into . . . these huge audiences of all these guys . . . whistling. . . . Imagine what a thrill it was for this bunch of girls. . . . I have to tell you that the whole thing . . . appealed to everybody's ego . . . there was a lot of massaging going on," recalled Hargrave.[65] Under the protection of Army personnel, on stage with male moderator G. Byron Done, and with chaperone Edith "Picky" Pickney nearby, it is likely that the panelists were not fearful but rather enjoyed the attention they were receiving from the young military trainees, as Hargrave's recollections indicate. Guenther mentions that the panelists were attractive, some of them beautiful. At times the audience gasped when, for instance, an Anglo-looking woman, someone who might well have resembled their cousin, identified herself as Jewish.[66] Gilbert Harrison described a somewhat analogous experience he had had with a trialogue audience. Once, before the program started, the trialogue members asked the audience to identify the religion of each speaker by his appearance, and the audience got the identities all wrong. No doubt both the panel and trialogue programs were dealing with assimilation. The thought was that if someone on stage looked like you or your cousin, they must be like you and thus not a stranger.

This use of university coeds as panelists reveals how gender was used to gain attention at the military bases. Not unlike the participants in the Miss Brotherhood contest described earlier, the women panelists were young, attractive and eye-catching, especially in the male context of training camps. Although the message of American racial, ethnic, and religious inclusion was serious and central to the war message (or maybe because of its importance) using young women to deliver the message added sex appeal that made the message more memorable. The women panelists were meant to give the trainees pause: if a Jewish woman could be so beautiful and persuasive, if she could look like my cousin, perhaps she (and her people) should be accepted as Americans. Of course, using women as sex objects to convey a message was nothing new, as the Gibson Girl drawings of Charles Dana Gibson from the 1890s indicate. Some fifty years later, the women panelists also made heads turn, in this case, to advertise American diversity.

The National Conference of Christians and Jews also launched speaker programs for the military in 1942. The NCCJ program promoted a concept of American democracy that was tied to religion, specifically to practicing tri-faith values and accepting tri-faith diversity. By the end of the war, the NCCJ had presented this program to over nine million American troops. But unlike the presentation of the URC Panel of Americans, the NCCJ presentations omitted women, as well as racial and ethnic speakers, and concentrated on religion alone.[67]

Wartime Losses and Postwar Resolve

The Second World War took a toll on the URC. Illness had caused Thomas Evans to be absent for prolonged periods of time and to retire as executive secretary in April of 1945. He passed away a few months later. His absence left Guenther unsure about whether to continue at the URC. Bereft of the mentor she had known for more than twenty-five years, first in New York City at the International Society for Religious Education and at the URC since 1928, she felt isolated and insecure without him. Evans was the one who had smoothed things over with the URC denominations and their student pastors, the National Conference of Christians and Jews, and other outside organizations that had cooperated with the URC. In fact, the NCCJ and the URC split up their partnership not long after Evans took ill. He had been a persuasive fundraiser and a source of wisdom and stability for Guenther. Speaking of his absence, she wrote "all who had in any way been part of the Conference felt themselves in deep and unchartered waters."[68]

Adding to Guenther's troubles was a critical editorial that appeared in the UCLA student newspaper, the *Daily Bruin*, on February 5, 1945. The editorial complained that URC religious activities had become less active and that the panel presentations "tried too hard to promote goodwill." Another complaint was that "religion had been commercialized." In addition, the student programs such as the summer camp and afterschool activities were "handled by mere amateurs which cannot even half offer the necessary solutions to the existing problems."[69]

Another worry was the loss of the Catholic advisers and Newman Club. During the war, they moved from the URC building to the new Newman House in Westwood, located a few blocks away. Although no longer at the URC building, the Catholic group continued to participate in URC activities and contribute to the URC budget.[70] The loss of the Catholic advisers and the Newman club students was nevertheless a blow to the URC. Recognizing the need for more space, the URC built a new, larger building several years later, in 1951, on a site located near the UCLA campus. The larger accommodations at the new building were an improvement over its cramped, twenty-year old predecessor, although the Catholic participants stayed in their new location.

Despite Guenther's misgivings, she remained at the URC. At first the board of trustees offered her the position of acting executive secretary. She turned it down, holding out for executive secretary. Notwithstanding the fact that Guenther had been assistant executive secretary since the URC's founding, the board, almost entirely male, may have had trouble picturing a woman in a position with primary responsibility for dealing not only with male students but with the male-dominated denominations, religious advisers, academic faculty volunteers, administrators, leaders of the community, and prominent religious figures in the Clerical Division. But when the board relented, and offered her the job of executive secretary, at the same salary they had paid Evans, she accepted the offer.

In her new position, Guenther worked under difficult circumstances. She was then without an assistant executive secretary to share the work load. Meanwhile, student enrollment at UCLA was growing apace with increasing numbers of veterans returning from the war. Most of the new students at UCLA had never heard of the URC, and shorthanded, Guenther devised ways of attempting to reach them and reestablish the popularity and reputation that the Conference had enjoyed before the war.

Once at the helm, Guenther found her footing and continued as the URC executive secretary for almost fifteen more years. She applied her leadership and charisma to expand and develop projects to help students understand the new, larger role of the United States in international affairs and to demonstrate inclusive diverse values in postwar society. Both of those goals were associated in her mind with national responsibilities that had emerged during the Second World War. The URC became her vehicle for helping to achieve them. As before the war, Guenther was always on the lookout for new student projects, often seemingly secular ones but imbued with underlying religious purpose. Her intention was to keep the students engaged in religious cooperation and service in the community and beyond. She kept her ear to the ground to find out about current trends and incorporated them into her innovative student projects.

Among other things, Guenther started a URC project that reached out to foreign students. In 1948 some 260 students from forty-four countries were attending UCLA. In response, the URC organized the World Student Associates

to welcome those students from abroad, to teach them about American society and to give them practical help such as small loans, scholarships, guidance in finding jobs and housing, providing transportation, hospitality, and
"friendly encouragement." In addition, the URC took advantage of the opportunities the foreign students and visitors on campus presented for teaching
UCLA students not only about distant cultures and religions but also about
American culture.[71] She wanted the American UCLA students to learn about
other perspectives from the foreign students and be prepared for the new and
enlarged international role the United States would be playing in world affairs
after the war.

Another of Guenther's projects was the URC Intercultural Committee,
which provided housing for UCLA African American women students by
opening up a four-apartment residence. The residence accommodated twenty
students and a house mother. The URC Intercultural Committee consisted
of a group of adult URC women volunteers who raised the money to buy the
apartment house and refurbish it. They named the residence Stevens House
after the late Episcopal bishop Bertram Stevens, one of URC's founders, officers, and supporters. Located at 1411 S. Westgate Avenue, in Los Angeles,
Stevens House was a ten-minute bus ride from campus and situated beyond
Westwood's racially restrictive housing covenant.[72] Before Stevens House
opened, there had been no place near the UCLA campus to live for women
(or men) who were not white. One exception was a small dormitory in the
URC Building. This small dormitory provided accommodation, under the
radar, where Tom Bradley lived in the 1930s, as mentioned earlier. Bradley
and a handful of other male student members of the URC lived in the small
dormitory in exchange for doing chores. Bradley lived there because housing
was racially restricted in Westwood. John Krumm lived there as well because
he could not afford to live in a fraternity house on campus or a rented room
in Westwood.

Much work remained to be done in helping to realize the stated wartime
national values of religious, racial, and ethnic inclusion that Adaline Guenther
and the URC hoped to achieve in the postwar era. The Panel of Americans
with its diverse membership, good will, fellowship, sharing of personal stories,
and winning manner must have struck Guenther as well suited to help spread
the aspirational, wartime American values of diverse inclusion. As for the
student and graduate panelists themselves, Guenther likely thought that the

experience of living and sharing their everyday life on the road with others of different backgrounds would itself be an education, one akin to an education in religious fellowship. Having toured California military camps and appeared at hundreds of venues in and around Los Angeles during the war, the panelists had built their confidence and effectiveness in giving presentations. It seemed that the postwar era was the right time for the POA to present its message to a national audience and that their experiences during the war had prepared them well.

"... Behold how good and how pleasant it is for brethren to dwell together in unity!"

An America United!

By strengthened religious convictions.

By inter-faith cooperation on common principles of justice and charity toward all.

By common defense of freedom through common opposition to all divisive movements preaching bigotry and hate.

THE UNIVERSITY RELIGIOUS CONFERENCE

COMMUNITY PROGRAM

CAMPUS PROGRAM

URC pamphlet cover of five student members of various religious, racial, and ethnic backgrounds demonstrating brotherly ties. Below them are listed three URC goals. Adjacent are the titles of sections on URC activities. URC Files.

A TEACHER, GENTLY WISE

A Tribute to
Thomas St. Clair Evans
at the time of his
retirement from
The University Religious Conference
April 30, 1945

Thomas St. Clair Evans, the first executive secretary of the URC, served from 1928 to 1945. His projects of service on campus and in community brought diverse URC students together in common purpose. Herman Beimfohr served as a Methodist minister at the URC. In 1978 he compiled a printed, spiral-bound, multipage commemorative history of the URC to mark its fiftieth anniversary. This photograph is from Beimfohr's commemorative history. URC Files.

A Uni-Camp counsellor teaching a camper how to use a bow and arrow. Uni-Camp was a popular URC project. It was staffed by URC counsellors, who served a diverse mix of disadvantaged Los Angeles children. The purpose of Uni-Camp was not only to serve the campers but also to promote bonding among the counsellors. This photograph is from Beimfohr's commemorative history. URC Files.

Three URC members standing in front of a military aircraft in 1940. They were members of the URC trialogue, a program in which three URC speakers, an Episcopalian, a Jew, and a Catholic, would make public presentations on their respective religions and demonstrate fellowship and unity. The aircraft was to take these speakers to military training camps in California and demonstrate American unity in diversity to the military trainees. The three speakers, from left to right, are Stuart Ratliff (Catholic), Gilbert Harrison (Jewish), and John Krumm (Episcopalian). Panel Files of Marian Hargrave.

ON THE AIR...

In its program of education for inter-faith goodwill, The Conference is making increasing use of radio. The forms of effective radio presentation are being thoroughly explored and cooperation of major radio stations is obtained for the presentation of many different type of radio broadcasts that are arranged by Gilbert Harrison and the radio committee of The University Religious Conference, headed by Mr. Thomas A. McAvity.

Approximately one thousand radio programs have been given over the air during the past year by the Conference, many of these programs covering the entire Pacific Coast. In Los Angeles, series of inter-faith programs have been given over stations KFI, KECA, KNX, KHJ, KFWB, KMPC.

Pioneer development in the field of "listenable" inter-faith programs has resulted in the following series of broadcasts, given during the past two years over local or network release: "Youth Demands An Answer," a round-table of four young men, from four different religious faiths, who discuss each week a problem of common concern to all religionists; "The Pastor's Study" (MBS coast network), an informal interview with an outstanding priest, minister, or rabbi in his own study; "Well, You're Wrong," the facts about current religious prejudices, given by a prejudice-expert, Mr. John Wright; original dramatic sketches, written, produced, and musically backgrounded by persons in the Conference interested in dramatizing the story of goodwill; "The Book of Books," readings from the old and new testament, integrated with classical musical recordings; "The West Coast Church of the Air" (CBS from Los Angeles), an inter-faith round-table discussion on a common theme; "The Religious News Reporter," news in the world of religion prepared by the National Conference of Christians and Jews office; "To Keep Our Freedom," talks by an educator and clergyman on what we must do to preserve and extend freedom.

Special radio event programs are also staged, as for example, during Brotherhood week when thirteen special broadcasts were taken in 1940 by stations in Los Angeles, Long Beach, and San Diego. The Radio Division of The University Religious Conference also assumes responsibility for the creation of a nation-wide radio program from Hollywood commemorating Brotherhood Week.

The aim of the Radio Division is two-fold: to utilize radio to counteract subversive movements based on racial or religious bigotry; and to encourage positive expressions of the finest in all religious traditions.

Radio Committee

Thomas A. McAvity, Chairman.
Gilbert Harrison, Secretary.
Rev. Ralph Mayberry, Baptist.
Rev. S. Mark Hague, Congregational.
Rev. Arthur Braden, Disciples of Christ.
Rev. John Krumm, Episcopal.
Rabbi Morton Bauman, Jewish.
Rev. Clifford Holand, Lutheran.
Rev. Glenn Phillips, Methodist.
Rev. Glenn Moore, Presbyterian.
Rev. Benjamin Bowling, Roman Catholic.
Rev. Ernest Caldecott, Unitarian.

WEEKLY PROGRAMS

"The Book of Books"—KFI, Sunday morning, 8:15.

"To Keep Our Freedom"—KFWB, Saturday night, 7:45.

The URC formed a radio committee of students, clergy, and radio professionals to produce programs for broadcast. The programs were broadcast locally, and some of them were broadcast over national radio networks. They were educational, sometimes with university faculty members invited to give talks on the air. All the programs were intended to build interfaith goodwill and combat bigotry. Some of them were dramatizations, roundtables, and musical programs. The National Conference of Christians and Jews had helped smooth the way for URC participation in radio programming by providing formats and religious news. URC Files.

URC women of different religious, racial, and ethnic backgrounds participated in the URC Panel of Americans during the Second World War. Here are six of them standing in front of a military aircraft that will take them to military training camps throughout California where they will give presentations to the military trainees on American diversity and unity. Members of this group, from left to right, are Ernie May Maxie (African American), Francis Toy (Chinese American), Marian Hargrave (Protestant), Marian Taylor (Jewish), Jeanne Farrell (Catholic), and Maria Elena Ramirez (Mexican American). Panel Files of Marian Hargrave.

Formerly the assistant secretary of the URC, Adaline Guenther became the executive secretary in 1945. Dynamic and indefatigable, she energized the URC and gave it cachet. Here she is with five members of the American Veterans Committee (AVC) after World War II, some of them former members of the URC. During the war Guenther received letters from former URC participants then serving in the military. Those letters discussed ideas about the role of the United States in the postwar world, which led to the founding of the AVC. Most of the former URC veterans left the AVC soon after its founding when Communist influence increased. URC Files.

Six members of the URC Panel of Americans seated outside the University Religious Conference Building with the names of the member religious groups inscribed on the wall behind them. The photograph was taken in 1947, when the panel made a successful national tour to promote acceptance of American religious, racial, and ethnic diversity. From left to right are Marian Hargrave (Protestant), Frances Toy (Chinese American), Ernie May Maxie (African American), Jeanne Farrell (Catholic), Maria Elena Ramirez (Mexican American), and Marian Taylor (Jewish). Panel Files of Marian Hargrave.

Six pretty girls tackle world's biggest problem!

These young Americans have the right idea...

A few months ago, these girls were strangers—just six young students at the University of California at Los Angeles. Now they're touring the country—telling young people how American unity is the key to solving the world's biggest problem: lasting peace; how Americans of every race, creed and ancestry, living and working together in harmony, can set an example to the entire world. ...

They're all different—but they're all Americans...

Protestant—Jew—Catholic . . . Mexican—Chinese—Negro . . . they represent you . . . your appreciation of your neighbors of every creed and color . . . your devotion to good citizenship . . . your faith in your country's future, today and every day. ...

You belong in this picture too!

You—in your church, school, club, labor union, community center—you have a chance to do your bit for unity at home, peace abroad. Stand up for your neighbors! Spike false rumors based on racial or religious prejudice. Combat discrimination in education . . . employment . . . housing. Clear the road for postwar progress in your town. ...

PANEL OF AMERICANS

From left to right:
Top row—Maria Elena Ramirez, Frances Toy, Jeanne Farrell;
Bottom row—Marian Hargrave, Marian Taylor, Ernie May Maxey.

This is National Citizenship Week—Time for Unity!

Flyer of the Panel of Americans publicizing National Citizenship Week. The flyer urges Americans to build unity at home and peace abroad by standing up for your neighbor, standing against religious prejudice, and combatting false rumors and discrimination. Panel Files of Marian Hargrave.

CHAPTER SIX

The Panel of Americans in the Postwar Era

The war against prejudice, intolerance, religious hatred, caste and racism. . . . This is one of the post-war problems we can't wait to solve.
—*URC participant then in the US Navy, May 1944*

Issues of religious, racial, and ethnic exclusion were in the limelight after the Second World War. As word spread of the millions of Jews and others murdered in the Holocaust, the need for American religious tolerance and acceptance gained public notice. Cold War rivalry with the Soviet Union further intensified concern. Religious identification and church attendance became symbols of American patriotism, contrasted to the atheism associated with Soviet communism. Yet social clubs, restaurants, and college fraternities and sororities continued to exclude Jews, while restrictive covenants excluded them from certain residential areas, some of them built during and after the war.[1]

Racial exclusion was the rule not only in the South but in much of the rest of the nation. Over one million African Americans had served in the military during the war, in racially segregated units. While serving in the military and when returning home, both during and after the war, African Americans faced racial conflicts and race riots.[2] Moreover, after the war, it was hard for them to find good jobs.[3] Racial exclusion in housing nationwide became more visible as increasing numbers of African Americans migrated from the South to the North and West and encountered restrictive covenants limiting where they could live. Some of those restrictive residential covenants were put in place after the war as new suburbs were built. Others, like the covenant governing Westwood, dated back decades. Meanwhile communists here and abroad were highlighting American racial hypocrisy.

The wartime internment of the Nisei and Issei illustrated the second-class status of Nisei citizens and Japanese immigrants. In 1943, about a year after removal and internment began, Nisei volunteers were organized into the 442nd Regimental Combat Team, which became one of the most highly decorated units in the US Army for its performance in the Italian campaign and elsewhere in Europe. At the same time, most American military units in both the First and Second World Wars consisted of ethnically diverse troops that served together in combat. Many of them served with distinction. Yet not only for African Americans and Japanese Americans but for those of Mexican, Native American, and Chinese backgrounds, among others, segregation and exclusion continued after the war. Their wartime service was largely unknown, ignored, or feared.[4]

President Harry S. Truman voiced support for measures to increase the civil rights of African Americans and other excluded groups. Addressing Congress on February 2, 1948, he called for enacting legislation to strengthen civil rights and "fulfill its obligation of insuring the Constitutional guarantees of individual liberties and of equal protection under the law."[5] Both the address and a report by the President's Committee on Civil Rights, *To Secure These Rights*, recommended several measures, among them establishing a commission on civil rights, a joint congressional committee on civil rights, a permanent Civil Rights Division in the Department of Justice, federal protections against lynching, strengthening the Fair Employment Practices Commission, providing home rule and suffrage for the District of Columbia, equalizing opportunities for US residents to become naturalized citizens, and settling the evacuation claims of Japanese Americans. In the face of congressional inaction, five months later Truman issued Executive Orders 9980 and 9981. Order 9980 set forth regulations to end discrimination in the federal work force based on race, color, religion, or national origin. Order 9981 aimed to end discrimination based on race, color, religion, or national origin in the armed forces.[6]

The court system moved slowly in protecting the rights of marginalized groups; this applied not only to the US Supreme Court but also to courts on the state and local level. Nevertheless, some court cases did break new ground in recognizing the rights of racial and ethnic minorities as citizens, limited as they might seem to the contemporary reader.[7] The Supreme Court ruled unanimously in the test case of *Ex parte Endo* that Mutsuyo Endo, a woman of Japanese ancestry and an American citizen, be granted release from the Tule Lake Internment Camp in Northern California on a writ of habeas corpus.[8]

She, along with approximately 120,000 other American Nisei citizens and Issei, were still being forcibly held in internment camps. The camps were under
the control of the War Relocation Authority, a result of President Franklin
D. Roosevelt's issuing Executive Order 9066 in February 1942. Speaking for
the court in 1944, Justice William O. Douglas stated that the War Relocation
Authority had no right "to detain a citizen . . . at least when his loyalty is
conceded."[9] It was a narrow decision based on citizen loyalty, not on constitutional grounds, and it was hardly an affirmation of full rights of all Nisei.[10]
The decision nevertheless stated that a Nisei could be a loyal American citizen
at a time when the United States was still at war with Japan.[11]

Another narrow decision was handed down in 1948, in *Shelley v. Kraemer*,
in which the Supreme Court ruled unanimously that racial and other restrictive
covenants governing residential ownership could be ruled unconstitutional by
the courts because they violated the equal protection clause of the Fourteenth
Amendment. But the ruling applied only to restrictive covenants created by the
government, not to those created and carried out by private groups.[12] Six years
later in *Brown v. Board of Education of Topeka*, the court ruled unanimously
that the concept of separate but equal in public education violated the equal
protection clause of the Fourteenth Amendment. This decision overturned the
1896 *Plessy v. Ferguson* decision. The *Brown* decision was broader than the other
cases, but it was aggressively resisted, especially in the South.[13]

These issues of exclusion and inclusion were controversial, and many cities and towns in different parts of the country, including Los Angeles, set up
human relations councils or unity committees to defuse tensions and promote harmony. As discussed earlier, the Panel of Americans also embraced
these goals. But the POA differed from the human relations councils and unity
committees in several ways. The panel presentations *demonstrated* harmony
by appearing as a unified but diverse group, rather than telling the audience
what it *should do*. Also, the POA comprised ordinary students—not prominent experts, attorneys, professionals, or political leaders—and they told personal stories and answered audience questions in good humor, without lec-
turing. Moreover, the POA had had practical prior experience in dealing with
issues of religious, racial, and ethnic diversity. During the war, in addition to
radio broadcasts, the POA had traveled to twenty-seven California military
camps and to multiple civilian sites in and around Los Angeles, as well as to
thirty-five California cities in various parts of the state.[14]

Positive results seem to have followed from the Panel program approach. In 1946 the Tulare Chamber of Commerce, the Ventura Board of Education, and the Lancaster Civic League called upon the Panel of Americans for help in easing racial tensions. These organizations liked the POA's "method of handling potential difficulties better than they did other more widely publicized . . . political methods, all think the Panel . . . did a job for them in terms of a harmonious community," Adaline Guenther declared.[15] Personal and nonthreatening, the panelists seemed equipped to calm the tensions of the day and demonstrate how those of various religions, races, and ethnicities could get along as good Americans.

Adaline Guenther and other leaders at the University Religious Conference thought that the next step for the POA was to go on a national tour. In preparing for the tour, Guenther sought an endorsement from Joseph T. McGucken, auxiliary Catholic bishop of Los Angeles. McGucken was a UCLA alumnus and a longtime URC supporter. He had served as the URC Board President for 1946–1947. "It brought out with great force the message of Americanism and Democracy and . . . had a strong inspirational effect on the audience," McGucken wrote in a letter about the Panel to Dan Dodson, a member of the Unity Committee of New York City, assembled by New York City mayor William O' Dwyer.[16] "The fact that our democracy must draw its life and its unity from spiritual roots is clearly depicted by the Panel of Americans," the bishop wrote to panelist Marian Hargrave.[17] The spiritual roots of the POA message were in line with the religious and educational goals of the URC. The goal of panel presentations was to reenforce these spiritual roots for the panelists themselves and strengthen the bonds among them, as well as communicate them to the audience. The tour would also give the panelists direct, practical experience in living and traveling with a diverse group of URC participants.

The Panel of Americans on Tour: From Los Angeles to the East

On February 10, 1947, six young women, funded mostly by special individual gifts to the URC, boarded a train and set out for Philadelphia.[18] They visited more than sixteen cities and towns, from Philadelphia, New York City, and Chicago, to Antioch, Yellow Springs, and Xenia, Ohio, from Kansas City to Denver and Salt Lake City. They gave more than one hundred and fifty panel presentations to audiences numbering more than 140,000, mostly at high schools. "The reason for the High School audiences was the insistence of the panel members that their message was more easily assimilated by the younger groups."[19]

Considered a "first string" panel, the six panelists on the tour included Jeanne Farrell (Catholic), Marian Hargrave (Presbyterian), Marian Taylor (Jewish), Ernie May Maxie (African American, unidentified religion), Maria Elena Ramirez (Mexican American, unidentified religion), and Frances Toy (Chinese American, unidentified religion).[20] Hargrave and Maxie were recent graduates of UCLA; Farrell, Ramirez, Taylor, and Toy were current UCLA students who took a semester's leave of absence to go on the tour. They were accompanied by a chaperone, Miss Edith Peckham, described by Guenther as being of "uncertain age," and by panel moderator and manager G. Byron Done, a URC Board member and Mormon religious adviser, UCLA alumnus, and professor of sociology at USC. Both Peckham and Done had accompanied the panelists when they toured the Army camps in California during the war. Hargrave was fond of "Pecky," whom she described as a New Englander "with a ram rod straight back to prove it."[21]

The trip was undertaken not "because we had any ambitions to become a national organization," stated the 1947 URC annual report. It was done with the idea that "the Religious Conference might be considered a laboratory for the development of techniques . . . made freely available to anyone." The report goes on to say that such an idea was in line with the "philosophy of our Education Division," a URC division consisting primarily of university faculty and other educators who volunteered in support of URC educational projects.[22]

"These girls are neither theologians nor scientists nor experts. All they have to tell you is their personal story. . . . The crux of the whole thing lies in the simple statement that the split atom demands a united world—and we cannot hope for a world united on principals [sic] of peace and democracy if we cannot have a united nation." Although the panel "does not pretend . . . to solve all . . . problems . . . it can share . . . personal experience," said Done at the beginning of the Panel program. He then introduced the panelists. After the six panelists had each given a five-minute talk, Done fielded audience questions for panelists to answer. He then concluded the program. "You won't remember all we said, but we hope you won't forget the picture, nor the spirit of seven people of different races and religions, together working toward a solution of the American problems," Done told the audience.[23]

The first stop on the panel tour was Philadelphia, where the *Philadelphia Record* and the United Nations Council made the arrangements. The panel's first appearance was before the United Nations Council of Philadelphia, at a luncheon in the Burgundy Room of the Bellevue-Stratford Hotel, with retired Supreme Court justice Oren J. Roberts presiding. "People were turned away from a complete sell-out," Guenther reported, adding that the next day the panel broadcasted a program on the local station of the National Broadcasting System "by local demand." The panel was also scheduled to appear at a local town hall meeting.[24]

Philadelphia mayor Bernard "Barney" Samuel greeted the panelists at city hall with an official reception, at which the panelists presented Samuel with a letter from LA mayor Fletcher Bowron.[25] The following day the panel resumed school presentations, at William Penn High School, Springside School, and the Drexel Institute of Technology. Writer Emily Kimbrough helped to publicize the panel in Philadelphia. She was an enthusiastic panel supporter who had spent some time in Hollywood and was a graduate of Bryn Mawr College. The panelists spoke at Bryn Mawr, where they met with renowned historian Arnold Toynbee.[26]

Although panelists spoke primarily to high school audiences, they also addressed adult groups, small college groups, and large public audiences. Averaging seven appearances per day in Philadelphia, to a total of about sixty-one hundred audience members, the panelists could not reach all the Philadelphia high schools during their seventeen-day stay, so the local board of education made recordings of their presentations, to be played at the schools they missed.[27] "Our girls took Philadelphia by storm—everybody who heard them loved them. . . . they won friends for the cause they represent and the ideals they embody," Kimbrough wrote, summing up the panel's Philadelphia visit.[28]

The next panel stop was New York City, where Guenther met the panel members for a brief visit in support of the tour and to raise funds before returning to California.[29] When she left the panelists, "they were dashing from place to place, from dawn until late at night, unable to fill half the requests for their program."[30] While in the city the panel met with Eleanor Roosevelt, as had the Trialogue some six years earlier. She spoke favorably about the panel's efforts to bring about racial and religious understanding. Pearl Buck also extended an invitation to the panelists, asking them to join her for lunch.[31]

The Office of Superintendent of Schools of the New York City Board of Education arranged the schedule of the panelists.[32] During their two-week stay at the Barbizon Plaza Hotel in Manhattan, they addressed some 34,700 students in thirty appearances in most parts of the city. This included presentations at public high schools, and the occasional junior high school, from the Bronx and Queens to Brooklyn and Manhattan, as well as at Columbia and New York Universities. They also broadcasted a one-hour program to seventy-eight high schools that reached a total of 240,000 students.[33] Despite the cold weather, the sniffles, laryngitis, and other winter illnesses the panel stuck to their schedule.[34]

Letters from New York City teachers and principals in praise of the panel speakers reached Byron Done at the Barbizon Plaza Hotel. Commenting on the panel's "absence of histrionics," John Loughran, principal of Christopher Columbus High School in the Bronx, wrote, "Though I have been alive a long time, this is the first presentation of the essential problem of democracy and tolerance of just this kind that I have seen." "The sincerity and naturalness of the girls, the unstudied honesty and thoughtfulness of their answers, the lack of formula or stereotype, gave us a tremendous impact. I doubt any of our students will ever forget it and I am sure it will show results in their attitudes in the future. Critical as I have been of many projects with the same purpose as yours, here I could find nothing to criticize," wrote Edith Ward of Flushing High School in Queens.[35]

The diversity of the panel seems to have resonated with the diverse student body at Long Island City High School in Queens. "You cannot have any idea the lift it seemed to give our pupils and the electric charge in the atmosphere of the school. . . . I think in one morning you have done as much in the direction of combatting prejudice as we could have done in a year," wrote principal David H. Frank, who described "a constant stream of teachers telling me how fine the program was and how favorably the students reacted. A cross section of our student body would give us a grouping similar to this panel—all faiths, all races. I think every pupil in the school is a member of some minority group, and at some time, has been exposed to some form of intolerance. The fresh and sympathetic handling given this group will be invaluable to them."[36] Done's notes reveal that when the panel spoke to audiences numbering some fifty-five hundred at New Utrecht and Prospect High Schools in Brooklyn, the principal of Prospect High, Dr. Thomas Shiff, and his secretary, "cried!"[37]

From Manhattan came a letter for Done written by Dan Dodson, "a big lanky Texan" on mayor O'Dwyer's Unity Committee. "From every source in our city where conflicts are perhaps as acute as anywhere in the country, I have heard nothing but the finest reports of their work. You are setting a pattern whereby a college . . . can serve its constituency and contribute profoundly to the cause of better inter-group relations in America," wrote Dodson, commenting that the Panel program proves "even to the most skeptical that it is possible for us to discuss our differences and stress our likenesses in such a fashion that we know what the common mortise is which holds our culture together, and at the same time what are the unresolvable differences which we must come to respect and appreciate."[38]

After their stop in New York City, the panelists boarded a train bound for Cleveland, where they were met by reporters from the local newspapers. On the train they often attracted attention. "Everywhere the gang went curious people crowded around to ask who they were. Everyone was excited and enthusiastic, from the dining car waiter to the mayors."[39] Sometimes the panelists held "bull-sessions with passengers in crowded trains."[40] "We're not crusaders in the sense that we have a light in our eyes, but we feel we do some good, just traveling. People on trains are so curious that they ask questions about us, and we just sit down and talk with them. It does more good than a lecture," Marian Hargrave declared.[41]

"Girls all well/schedule here calls for fifteen engagements in schools in next five days," Done telegrammed Guenther upon arriving in Cleveland, later adding that the city was a "tough assignment," probably because of illnesses and the blizzard they encountered.[42] The panel nevertheless stuck to the scheduled fifteen meetings and was heard by some 17,050 people "who were not in bed with the flu or blown off the street by the blizzard." While in Cleveland, panelists Jeanne Farrell and Maria Elena Ramirez did spend some days in bed with colds. The other four panelists incorporated their speeches into the program, so "little was lost," thought Done, acknowledging Edith Peckham's care. "The chaperone . . . is very careful of their health and as the weather improves, they should all continue well," he wrote.[43]

One of the first programs the panel gave in Cleveland was at an "all Negro high school." Another was at a boys' school. The "Negro audience was perfect" and those at the boy's school "were a close second." Done reported that the principals told him that the Panel program was "the best yet in the field of understanding." Mr. Moles, the "principal of the Negro school, felt we had done more good in a single program than has been accomplished by all the intercultural activities-organizations in the city to date."[44] Another presentation took place at John Hay High School, where Dilworth Lupton, pastor of the First Unitarian Church of Cleveland, heard them. He wrote up a column about the POA for the *Cleveland Plain Dealer*. Lupton was so impressed with the panel's sincerity and the enthusiasm of the audience that he followed them to Glenville High School later that morning to hear them speak again.[45]

Commenting on how the panel mixed humor with serious discussion, Lupton described Jewish panelist Marian Taylor and her talk about how her grandfather had changed his name from a "'Russian jawbreaker'" as his ship passed the Statue of Liberty. Here Taylor uses humor, as Lupton observed, to identify with the audience, but she further identified with the audience by demonstrating how assimilated she was, not even attempting to pronounce her ancestor's difficult name. Next was Catholic panelist Jeanne Farrell, who credited her Catholic faith with helping her understand that whatever the differences, each of us is "a brother human soul" and "child of God." Next spoke Chinese American panelist Frances Toy whom Lupton quoted as saying of herself and her Japanese American friend, "We both have the same glossy hair and the same slant to our eyes and both are patriotic Americans." Yet her friend wound up in a "concentration camp" while Frances was seen as a "noble and courageous ally." Maria Elena Ramirez spoke about how hard it was to mediate between the Mexican culture of her parents and American culture. Ernie May Maxie spoke about how difficult it was for African Americans to secure good jobs. Finally, Marian Hargrave urged the audience to show tolerance and understanding to minorities in American society, recalling how her Puritan ancestors in England were "sneered at" for following a minority religion and got away "in a leaky old boat called the Mayflower."[46]

After the presentation Lupton asked the panelists which questions audiences asked most often. They replied that the popular questions were those about intermarriage (the panel privately agreed that it was a bad idea but maintained a neutral stance in their public presentation), how to get rid of prejudice among parents, and what young people can do overall to get rid of it (education for both). Some in the audience wanted more panels like this in high schools and colleges so students could be trained and there could be "interchanges between institutions and even between cities. We need more chances for discussion."[47]

Done's report contains a quote from E. E. Smeltz, the principal of Cleveland's John Adams High School: "The comments from teachers and students have been universally favorable, and everyone has mentioned the good they felt would come to the cause of racial and religious understanding because of it. Your program is the only one I have ever heard on the subject that is constructive and dignified. All others defeat their own purposes." Smeltz presented Done with a check for $25 on behalf of the high school.[48] Other schools and organizations in eastern cities also "contributed money to extend the panel's tour after hearing the girls," although the panel never asked for donations from the audience and the URC had enough money to pay for the tour on its own.[49]

From Cleveland the panel traveled to Pittsburgh, where "they really rolled out the red carpet for us, providing the school physician for the four of us who were ill at one time or another, riding us around in school cars and being excellent hosts."[50] The panel stayed at the William Penn Hotel, made sixteen appearances, and spoke to audiences numbering 14,200. The panelists' speeches were growing "better with practice and experience and their morale is high," reported Done.[51]

"Young people enjoy hearing others near their own age discuss problems," Roy Mattern, principal of Allegheny High School, wrote to Done. Mattern thought the panel was a good example for them and "presents living proof that differences in race and religion can be intelligently explained and this in turn promotes better understanding."[52] Ernest Dimmick, Pittsburgh superintendent of schools, asked whether the panel would be returning to eastern high schools next year. If so, "please consider this a request for their return to Pittsburgh where pupils and teachers alike are praising them. . . . It was good for our high school youth to see in demonstrable manner six of their contemporaries actually and successfully practicing those principles. . . . they professed." In closing, he noted "the simple personal vivid examples each girl gave" and exclaimed, "TAKE YOUR PANEL TO AS MANY PLACES AS YOU CAN, AND DO RETURN TO PITTSBURGH."[53]

The next stop was Detroit, the site of wartime race riots.[54] There "we were handled with gloves," and the panel's schedule included speaking seventeen times to audiences numbering 15,075.[55] J. J. Powels, principal of Eastern High School, wrote about the panel's "gripping message," which he thought was needed to build a "sound foundation for future peace among nations." He thought that "presenting this philosophy of living which involves a better understanding between the intercultural and interracial groups of this country" needs to start "in our high schools" and that the panel was "performing a great service to the schools."[56] The panel was "the best program ever put on for these pupils—best in terms of the importance of the message and the quality of presentation," stated Paul Rankin, the Detroit superintendent of Schools.[57] "I can think of no one program which has been as provocative of serious thought as this one. . . . it gave our students many new ideas which they will talk about among themselves, discuss with their parents, and keep in their subconscious minds until the time comes to put them to use," wrote William R. Stocking, principal of Redford High School.[58] While in Detroit the panel made an appearance at Marygrove College, a small liberal Catholic women's college. "Our sincere thanks for the Panel. . . . You may not be able to actually count conversions, but certainly you are making them," wrote Sister Maria Honora in her letter to Done.[59]

The Panel National Tour Continues: Westward and Home

After leaving Detroit, the panel returned to Ohio, beginning its second visit to the state in Cincinnati. The Mayor's Friendly Relations Committee described the Panel program and how "eager" the committee was to "share them [the panel] with other Cincinnatians." For this reason, it arranged a Panel program at the YMCA. Admission was free of charge, "but we don't guarantee seats to latecomers. These girls have 'boxoffice!'" The committee described how the panelists expressed "the all-American credo. Simply and winsomely, each . . . [tells] about herself, her family and her ideas and ideals of 'one nation indivisible.'"[60]

In Cincinnati, the panel made sixteen appearances to audiences of more than sixteen thousand.[61] L. P. Stewart, principal of Walnut Hills High School, wrote to Done that the pupils at the school "always give excellent attention to speakers, but in this instance, there was something far deeper than merely courteous attention. All young men and women who do any thinking realize that race and religious differences constitute a real menace to American life. . . . The pupils at once perceived they [the panel] had a message and were delivering it in the language that they, the pupils understood and appreciated." "If a program such as this doesn't reach the active consciousness of our young people, we may well despair of making much progress on this subject," Stewart warned.[62] G. H. Reavis, from the office of the superintendent of schools in Cincinnati, told Done that "we had a meeting of the principals, and they were unanimous and emphatic in their commendation of the program." He went on to praise the community meetings the panel addressed, saying that they were "met with equal fervor. Perhaps the most unusual thing was the fact that the Rotary Club of 400–500 men which usually adjourns its luncheon meeting promptly in order that the men may return to their work, was prolonged for approximately half an hour in order that the question period could be extended."[63]

From Cincinnati the panel ventured for four days into Ohio's smaller cities, towns, and rural areas, as well as to Columbus. It included fourteen appearances to audiences numbering about sixty-five hundred. Some of the towns they visited included Springfield, Xenia, Yellow Springs, Plain City, Mechanicsburg, and Dayton.[64] In Yellow Springs they spoke at Bryan High School and held a public assembly at Antioch College. The college served as their headquarters for this portion of the tour, and some of the panelists stayed in the dormitories and others with faculty. In Springfield they spoke at the Masonic Temple and the Springfield Congregational Church. Near Xenia they spoke at Wilberforce University, a historic Black university in the town of Wilberforce.

In Dayton they spoke at Kiser, Stivers, and Wilbur Wright High Schools. "I think most of us would be tolerant if we were given a clear understanding of the problems of others as we were this morning." "Our parents and other older people should hear such a program." "If we want to get race and religious hatred out of other countries we must first get it out of ours." These words were written by three of the students at Stivers High School. Done had received them in a letter from F. F. Carpenter, principal of Stivers, who enclosed them.[65] The panelists spoke as well at Mechanicsburg, Plain City, and Marysville High Schools.[66] At one unnamed "small city . . . the high schools refused to admit them."[67] The outlook in some of these Midwestern rural areas and small towns resembled those where Guenther and O. D. Foster had grown up.

The panelists spoke not only in high schools, churches, and synagogues but in private houses and to women's groups in these towns and rural areas. The panel "was remarkably effective in every case, and we had many reactions which consistently indicated that what they said and were doing struck home in a most thought provoking way even in those places where the rural young people were too surprised to respond quickly with questions," stated the hostess who set up the trip, commenting that she was impressed with the panel's superior preparation and skillful handling of audience questions and their "ability to make vivid each person's part in better faith and race relations." Their "personal charm and their natural approach" helped them win over the audience "in this prejudice ridden section of the nation." She called the panel's technique "the best technique we have ever seen used. You also go direct to the heart of the matter when you recognize the pre-requisite place religion holds in the solution of all these problems."[68]

When the panel left Ohio they headed to Chicago, where they stayed at the Sherman Hotel. The local office of the National Conference of Christians and Jews apparently had offered to handle the scheduling. However, "there was some resultant misunderstanding, conflict of purpose and methods—for which the Religious Conference must take its share of the blame," the URC Annual Report stated, explaining that in the confusion, the panel made only eleven appearances and spoke to audiences totaling 12,250, a disappointing showing.[69] Nevertheless, there was some success. "I cannot begin to tell you how pleased I was with the splendid presentation the young women made and with the entranced rapture of our students. These young women . . . are . . . bringing before our American public the ideals of our democracy. Just being seen together does an enormous amount of good. Their presentation is simple, direct, and forceful. They challenged a number of traditions and invited spirited discussion," wrote Maudelle B. Bousfield, principal of Wendell Phillips High School.[70]

After Chicago the panel went to Kansas City, Missouri, a place, "we had so dreaded," perhaps because of its southern heritage and explicit racial segregation, but where they wound up having "a wonderful experience."[71] The panel spoke seventeen times, broadcasted a radio program, and appeared before audiences numbering 17,200. C. O. Williams, principal of East High School, wrote that he had "talked with a large number of our pupils and teachers and all were well pleased with your program. . . . Several felt your program was the very best that we have had this year." He commented that the panelists "were good speakers . . . knew their subjects, and they impressed our pupils and teachers." He ended with the hope that the panel will come back again.[72]

D. H. Holloway, the principal of Westport High School, wrote about the panel's "refreshing point of view to an age-long problem." He commented on how the "earnestness, enthusiasm and sincerity of the girls brought into clear focus the inter-racial and inter-religious difficulties that face us." He went on to describe how the teachers were taking the content of the Panel program into their classrooms, "the chairman of our English department . . . as a text in pointing out the joys of intellectual activity. Our social science teachers are using the ideas presented by the panel as examples of the best in present day thinking." The speech teachers are examining the "clarity and 'It made me understand how they feel toward better thinking and more wholesome living."[73]

Done and the URC received hundreds of student letters and compositions sent by the principals encountered on the tour. Of those, only two have survived, both of them from Kansas City. One was a letter by Jay Sears, who identified himself as "just one of the students." He wrote, "It was the best program we have had, not merely a chance to stay out of Geometry, but a chance to become better acquainted with the separate races. It made me understand how they feel. I think that when I own a business, I will not hesitate to hire somebody for any position if he qualifies, regardless of race or religion. There are others like me who heard you speak and feel the same, and this will make you know you are accomplishing something. With your help this country should be able to become the real America toward which we are striving."[74]

The other piece of writing was a composition by an unidentified pupil from Westport High School, who wrote, "I think the Assembly today was wonderful. The girls said many things that need to be said. They put their meanings in such a way that everyone should try to do better. . . . it was a very good idea to travel and express their feelings as individuals. I know that after this I am going to try to be kinder to everyone. I did not have everything clear until this morning. I wish that older people who are not in school could have been here to hear these girls. I hope the pupils at Westport help as individuals to straighten this problem out. I feel that until we have straightened this problem out that the world will not be a completely happy and neighborly world."[75] After Kansas City the panel finished its national tour with stops in Denver and Salt Lake City.

It is clear that the inclusion of racial and ethnic diversity in the Panel program brought up new issues. In comparing the Panel program with the predecessor Trialogue program, religion lost prominence and issues of fairness, jobs, cultural, and generational differences came to the fore. All of these new issues were central to being a good American. Of course, religion was still implicitly at the center of the presentations in communicating the humanness of each panelist, and in moving the audience to recognize themselves in others who at first appeared so different. The panelists sought to show the audience that underneath it all, they were not only fellow human beings but true Americans.

The two students whose writing was referenced earlier grasped that panel message. Writing about "the separate races," Jay Sears comments that "it [the Panel program] made me understand how they feel." As a result, when he grows up, he intends "to hire somebody for any position if he qualifies, regardless of race or religion." He sees doing so will help make "the real America." The composition written by the other student states that she will do her best to make the world a better place: "After this [the Panel program] I am going to try to be kinder to everyone. I did not have everything clear until this morning. I wish that older people who are not in school could have been here to hear these girls. I hope the pupils at Westport help as individuals to straighten this problem out. I feel that until we have straightened this problem out that the world will not be a completely happy and neighborly world."[76] Perhaps the authenticity of the panelists, perhaps their youth (the panelists were only about seven to ten years older than the pupils), perhaps having the pupils see the panelists in person and hear the panelists speaking extemporaneously made the issues of empathy and citizenship come alive for these Kansas City pupils.

When the panelists returned to Los Angeles, UCLA held a Provost's Tolerance Convocation in Royce Hall. Classes were cancelled so all could hear Provost Clarence Dykstra and the six returning panelists present their program to an audience of fellow-students.[77] That evening the panel gave another presentation, at the Ambassador Hotel, where they were honored at the URC annual meeting and dinner.[78] Guenther thought that the panel tour and presentation were so successful that they would need to continue and expand them.

As if to confirm Guenther's assessment, a few days after the panel returned, a letter arrived suggesting that she "might find it mutually advantageous" to have "the inspiring" Panel of Americans appear on the program "These Are

Your Neighbors" jointly sponsored by the County Committee on Human Relations and broadcasted over KRKD. The letter was from Frank E. Cane, Executive Secretary of the Los Angeles County Youth Committee.[79]

Soon after returning from the national tour, the *California Daily Bruin* published an article describing how the panel had set out in February "to demonstrate to the nation their successful solution to race differences, one of America's gravest social problems. For three months they have lived and worked together as closely as six people can. . . . [and] have addressed well over 100,000 students."[80]

New Demands on the URC

The success of the national panel tour raised the possibility of starting a URC national Panel program. But as this idea was developing, demands on the URC were increasing. Requests to help start URC programs at colleges and universities kept coming. As mentioned earlier, one request arrived from Santa Barbara, asking for help in setting up an organization like the URC at the University of California at Santa Barbara (UCSB). The newly established University of California at Riverside was also setting up an organization like the URC. Gordon Watkins, the first provost at Riverside, had been a strong supporter of the URC when he was an economics professor and dean at UCLA.[81] The URC Clergy Division authorized Guenther to offer the requested help, a process that at times continued for several years.[82] The newly established Universities of California at Santa Barbara and Riverside were indicative of the overall postwar expansion of public higher education throughout California. Universities, colleges, and junior colleges were growing at a robust pace. This growth of higher public education in the state, and especially in Los Angeles, placed new demands on the URC.

At UCLA the student population had increased from about five thousand in 1928, when the URC was founded, to about fourteen thousand in the late 1940s. The university was adding more faculty, a new counselling program, graduate and professional schools—all of which required more URC staff and administration to maintain its name recognition and religious engagement among the students. The religious advisers for the denominational groups, some of them part-timers, were already overstretched and poorly funded, ill-equipped to provide adequate pastoral care and religious guidance to the growing student population.[83]

Meanwhile the student body of Los Angeles City College had grown to more than twelve thousand students, almost rivaling that of UCLA, and soon to surpass it with a student population of seventeen thousand.[84] The new East Los Angeles City College, on Brooklyn Avenue, established a branch of the URC, and Harbor City College in the Wilmington district of Los Angeles, was to follow. It was estimated that some seven or eight junior colleges would open in Los Angeles during the 1950s and soon thereafter, with an anticipated new enrollment of fifty-eight thousand.[85] In 1940 California had a population of just under seven million, making it the fifth largest state. By 1950 the population was about ten and half million, making it the second largest state. With this increase in population, there was pressure to enlarge and found new public colleges and universities.

Moreover, this population surge required not just enlarging the URC staff and physical plant but also maintaining the personal religious message of the URC while reaching a larger body of students, many of whom were secular. These new circumstances required new programs to develop a religious sense in the students. "We are working at an institution which has gone in for mass education. Mass religious movements once in five hundred years are effective—most of the time . . . religious education is an extremely personal thing," wrote Guenther. "Mr. Evans used to say that religion was caught as well as taught—and that means that 14,000 students must have someone to catch it from." Guenther thought about how meagre the church and synagogue support for the URC religious advisers had become, and how few their number in comparison with the increasing student body. "Church apathy is matched by student apathy," she commented, estimating that of the fourteen thousand UCLA students, perhaps three to four thousand are active in some sort of Conference or denominational program. Most students think that religious education "is not keeping pace with the rest of their academic careers."[86]

Student materialism and apathy toward religion, lack of adequate church and synagogue support for the religious advisers, and the failure of organized religion to keep pace with the academic standards of secular higher education were problems of long standing. O. D. Foster had attempted to solve them more than twenty years earlier, and Evans and Guenther had continued on that path. All three of them had met with some success, but much still remained to be done. Adding to Guenther's difficulty was the need to manage this daunting situation essentially on her own, without a full time, paid permanent assistant and without a partnering organization.

One response was to experiment with cultivating a URC following among younger students by building student boards in local high schools. The URC recruited UCLA Student Board alumni volunteers to work with high school teachers and students to set up these boards. The first three were set up at Hollywood High, which had one co-ed student board, and Beverly High, which had two, one each for male and female students. All of the boards had between sixteen and twenty members. They mainly hosted programs and held discussions on timely issues. One of the programs was a trialogue presentation, another, a discussion on racial prejudice. The goal was to have high school students "gain a better understanding of other peoples by discussing . . . [their] different backgrounds, aspirations, and convictions."[87] The URC hoped to "indoctrinate" students who would later attend UCLA and other schools "with the idea of the Religious Conference . . . and ready [them] to respond to appeals from the Conference and the constituent groups."[88]

Another option was to establish several Bruin Boards at UCLA. The Bruin Boards were smaller versions of the main URC Student Board. Composed of promising lower division students, the boards undertook such programs as sponsoring speakers and discussions and volunteering for social service projects, less extensive activities than those of the main Student Board but with a similar spirit of cooperation. "By such a plan it is hoped that more and more students will become instilled with the Conference spirit, so that spirit may, in turn, be spread over the entire campus."[89] The Bruin and High School Boards helped to spread the influence of the URC and prepare students for service on college and university campuses. Both experiments placed importance not only on recruiting young participants but also on a personal rather than a mass approach to religion by instilling feelings of religious fellowship among students of diverse backgrounds.

Guenther's heavy workload continued, with ongoing activities such as Uni-Camp, afterschool programs for neighborhood children, and trying to fill requests for panels, trialogues, and for help in setting up URC branches. Guenther puzzled over the best future direction for the URC Panel program after the successful 1947 national tour. The URC lacked the necessary resources and staffing to satisfy the demand. Should the URC partner with another organization as it had previously done with the NCCJ in Southern California? That partnership had helped enlarge URC programs, resources, and national contacts, as well as giving the URC increased visibility. Without doubt, the 1947 national tour of the Panel of Americans had also raised the visibility of the URC. But now, lacking a sponsoring partner, could the URC take on a national Panel program as its next major project? If so, what was the best way to deploy URC resources? Should the Conference serve only students at UCLA, LACC, and other partners at local colleges, or should it also include a national POA program?

When the 1947 national POA tour was planned, it was not intended that the URC would become a national organization, but merely that, through the POA, the URC might become a laboratory for the development of techniques made available to others. Yet the success of the national tour caused Guenther and others at the Conference to ponder whether the influence of the POA should continue nationally. In the meantime, they took a break from the overwhelming pace of URC activities. From May of 1947 until October of 1948, POA appearances and expansion were put on hold while a small subcommittee of the URC Education Committee, chaired by M. J. Karpf, considered the future of the POA and whether to team up with a national organization.

For the next eighteen months new projects were extremely limited. Trialogues were substituted for POA appearances in local community and campus venues, while queries about the URC and the panel continued apace.[90] "We are receiving from other parts of the country questions about our organization and its value, not merely in terms of . . . the panel but in terms of bringing together in one community all the spiritual forces," yet owing to "lack of time and staff" there has been no URC "cooperative effort in the human relations field," Guenther's report complained.[91] Partnering with another organization now appeared to be a realistic solution.

The American Jewish Committee (AJC) was a promising prospect, and both Guenther and the URC Education subcommittee discussed the idea of sponsoring a national Panel program with the AJC. Founded in 1911, the AJC was organized in New York City to protect the civil rights of Russian Jews in the wake of pogroms in Russia. During the First World War the AJC had helped to found the Jewish Welfare Board, one of the organizations that joined the Commission on Training Camp Activities and Comrades in Service. In the 1920s, when Foster was helping to organize the interfaith American Association on

Religion, he consulted with some of the early AJC leaders, among them Louis Marshall, a prominent Jewish lawyer and the first AJC president, who served until 1929, and Cyrus Adler, a highly respected Jewish scholar and educator. Since the First World War the AJC had promoted not only the civil rights of Jews but also the rights of various diverse groups in American society.

Both the URC and the AJC had worked to counter prejudice. Both organizations believed that American democracy could give scope to different religions, races, and ethnicities without splintering off into narrow provincialism or chauvinistic nationalism. At that time, the AJC had supported the idea that Jewish Americans were American in their nationality and Jewish in their religion, analogous in that respect, to Protestant, and Catholic Americans, as well as to Americans of other religions, a point that Gilbert Harrison had made in his trialogue speeches during the 1930s.

In short, the AJC and URC were natural allies, and negotiations between them began in 1948. The final proposal agreed upon called for Guenther to travel to cities where there were universities that had the potential to become sites for local panels, and the AJC would supply the contacts. Although Guenther continued as the executive secretary of the URC, the AJC would pay her salary and expenses while she traveled to these potential sites. She would evaluate each based on the dynamism and commitment she observed in the prospective local sponsoring group and local student panelists. After one or two return visits for some follow up work, Guenther's participation at the sites would conclude, and the individual sponsoring group would take over directing the local panel program.

Under pressure from the AJC and the URC Education Committee, Guenther agreed to this plan, whose implementation began in October of 1948 and continued through the following spring. Her first trip lasted for three weeks. Soon thereafter she made return visits for follow-up work and to other sites as well, some of them the same ones visited by the URC panel on their 1947 national tour. When she boarded the eastbound train from Los Angeles, she had "the blessing of her board" and was "wearing the orchids of enthusiastic students."[92] Guenther made these trips by herself.[93]

Meanwhile, in October of 1948, the URC Panel program at home was reactivated. Some thirty panel speakers began their training and the following spring undertook an active schedule in the Los Angeles metropolitan area. From the following January to May, they made appearances at high schools, civic and service clubs, and PTA meetings. They averaged about two programs per week and met audiences totaling some 13,560. During the course of the year, demand for URC local panels continued to exceed the number available.[94]

As she was setting out, Guenther must have been ambivalent about the trip ahead, and she must have worried that her absence would cause problems for the URC at home. Others at the URC had misgivings as well. Edward Goodspeed, a member of the education committee, feared that Guenther's absence would "imperil" the Conference. He expressed this fear in a letter he wrote to Guenther the summer before she left on her travels.[95] The annual report of the URC Student Board confirmed Goodspeed's fear. The student program at the URC "has had a difficult time, chiefly due to Miss Guenther's frequent absences from the campus," noted Loyd Mc Cormick, chair of the URC Student Board, in May of 1949, as he looked over the past year.[96]

Nevertheless, the AJC, URC leaders, and most on the education committee approved of her travel, no doubt partly for the funding and prestige it promised to bring the Conference. Perhaps another factor that contributed to Guenther's acceptance of the plan was a fear that if she were to decline, it would be difficult to prevent "irresponsible individuals in other places [from] jeopardize[ing] our results by an ill-advised attempt to duplicate them."[97] All these factors likely played a part in her yielding to the pressure to travel.

Guenther's Evaluations

After her visits to several universities, Guenther wrote evaluations for David Danzig, program director of the AJC. At the time he was a professor of social work at Columbia University. During the First World War he had participated in O. D. Foster's Comrades in Service; since then, he had worked extensively in the area of intergroup relations.[98]

Among Guenther's several site visits, was one to the University of Cincinnati, where she found some reason for hope. She worked with interested students at the university and was confident that "there will be some good speeches there." She also found two women who would be helpful, including a Mrs. Wunder, an "intimate friend" of Mrs. Dykstra, wife of University of California provost Clarence Dykstra. Mrs. Wunder was head of the local chapter of the League of Women Voters and had promised to help get community backing. But there were problems. Guenther comments that "Cincinnati is a mess." Most of the problems had to do with finding the right sponsoring group at the university. There, Guenther found that the faculty, and one faculty member in particular, had a "large amount" of what she called "residual prejudice," by which she meant a "general feeling" of suspicion, some of it held "perhaps unconsciously," toward what they considered "ax-grinding groups" such as Jews; moreover, they harbored doubts about what these Jews are "trying to get us to do." Her report continues, "The University here resents . . . being pushed into something, no matter how good, by one segment of the community."[99]

Another stop in Ohio was at Cleveland College which she reports "is a little less messy." The faculty is in support of having a panel, but the "students are a little apathetic." Apart from that, there was also residual prejudice. Like the University of Cincinnati, "here too, the barest hint . . . that the AJC was in it produced a vivid show of resentment."[100]

Guenther also went to Washington University in St. Louis, where she found even more "unrecognized prejudices" than in Cincinnati. The "feeling that there must not be any group pressuring the University and the extent of unrecognized prejudice was almost calamitous." The head of the Speech Department "has unrecognized prejudices lying around all over the place." The student panel, however, had made six appearances in St. Louis, the last time at a high school where the respect of the audience "surprised and delighted the faculty." This made Guenther hopeful that perhaps the effort would "result in something good."[101]

Nevertheless, her evaluation for Danzig was pessimistic. Guenther's introduction expressed real doubts about "whether we have yet found the right answer." Putting together the right local sponsoring groups and supervising how distant embryonic panels would develop was problematic. "I don't think we will get what we want. And I'm willing to take my share of the blame for not foreseeing this or not arguing about it enough—you know I have such respect for your brains that I usually don't have the courage to argue about something very long if you say decisively that you think one way or the other."[102] Guenther explained that when she agreed to trust organizing the panels to "local people elsewhere, with only hit-and-miss help from the outside, I betrayed the whole thing. It CAN, but we have not to date found the people—with the motivation, the ability, the platform on which to stand."[103]

Guenther admitted that when she met with Danzig, she "should have insisted at the first meeting . . . that the job could only be done by those who had certain experience and training."[104] She continued, "I still have the feeling that just the hiring of the [URC] Panel and the sending them around the country for a few years would have done a lot to alter the prejudices we want to eliminate." "It would have been costly, but I'm not sure that dollar for dollar, it wouldn't have been the best expenditure that AJC could have made."[105] After all, the URC panels were well trained, experienced, and had a good track record, as their wartime appearances at military bases and the 1947 national tour had shown. In addition, Guenther could select and train the best URC panel candidates as well as control the panel's future direction. Expressing frustration and resignation, Guenther wrote to Danzig that "[I can] see you shaking your head and saying, 'for gossakes, I thought we had that out once,'" adding that "but to my mind *they* [the URC panelists] were effective."[106]

Guenther summarized several problems for Danzig with the current proposal. One of them was that it left "no channel for offering help, supervision or advice. We told the Universities to do it." She continued, as long as "it does them good, and no harm, and isn't too much work, they'll go along. When any one of those factors fails to play into the idea of the Panel, it will stop."[107]

Another problem Guenther found on her travels was the resentment of faculty toward outside Jewish groups like the AJC. Guenther thought some it was subtle "unrecognized prejudices;" but other resentment was brutal in the "depth of the feeling . . . against the Jewish segment of the community organizing to do something." Even those who displayed the more subtle resentment "have no appreciation whatever of the cancerous growth that prejudice is." In her view, "They would all deprecate race riots, or any of Hitler's more blatant activities, but things are pretty much all right here."[108]

She lamented the shallowness of the commitment to fighting prejudice and the narrowness of vision that she encountered. She thought that many of those she met would let the Panel program flounder and even eliminate it for the sake of convenience. What was missing at these sites was missionary zeal: "That missionary zeal is only available, I think, from people who know what prejudice is, or from people to whom it is a personal thing, or from those who are driven to it by religion."[109] Otherwise, acquiring such zeal or what she called a "religious sense" required experiencing the kind of religious diversity and inclusion that was present at the URC, where "respect for those of other religions, races and ethnicities . . . flows from the belief that all are fellow children of God."[110]

In view of the prejudice she encountered, and the comparatively small size of the Jewish communities in these local sites, Guenther thought the plan was impractical. She argued that "the only way we could help that would be to have a section of the community which cuts across many faiths and interests." She argued that the Panel program and other "interfaith movement[s] should always wherever possible be carried or fronted by Protestants. We just showed our hand too openly here,—or perhaps not openly enough—it amounts to the same thing."[111]

Her observations confirmed her conviction that missionary zeal in fighting prejudice flowed from directly experiencing diversity, cooperation, fellowship, and service. To her mind, such experiences were necessary for untrained faculty and students to direct and present an effective Panel program. Foster, Evans, and Guenther had committed themselves to building institutions in which university students of different religious groups could work together for common goals with a spirit of fellowship, cooperation, and service. Guenther's travels convinced her that only institutions like the URC captured that spirit and embodied those ideals.

None of the local sites Guenther visited had an effective interfaith organization or a sponsoring group with the spirit and drive of the URC. The URC was an organization of many faiths, begun primarily by Protestants, with Protestants in positions of visible public leadership. Also needed were a highly developed religious sense among its participants, and the missionary zeal needed to spread interfaith inclusion. In the absence of an organization like the URC, Guenther thought that the local sites she visited needed someone *from* the URC to play an active and ongoing role.

Although she ended the report to Danzig with discouragement, Guenther's travels seem to have impressed upon her all the more the need for keeping the panel idea alive, not just in California but in the nation at large. The experience of the panel national tour of 1947 was a source of hope. It had brought together, in common purpose, students of different religious, racial, and ethnic backgrounds. Each of them differed from one another in important ways, but each panelist was treated as worthwhile and with respect. None of them were slighted, demeaned, trivialized, or forced to surrender or compromise on their fundamental values. Guenther now had to think anew about how best to convey the spirit of the panel to young people on a national basis, throughout American society. Although she wanted an interfaith organization comprised of members of various faiths as a sponsoring organization and the AJC had a specifically Jewish identity, she needed the contacts and funding of the AJC to expand the Panel program into a national project.

Over the next two years Guenther and others at the URC developed a plan: the URC would organize a Panel Extension Division similar to the Extension Division that had coordinated the activities of the URC and the NCCJ in Southern California. It had been chaired by Judge Marshall McComb and staffed by URC participant and former UCLA student John Burnside in the 1930s, as seen earlier. Unlike the Extension Division of the 1930s, the Panel Extension Division would be located in New York City, but it would report to the Panel Advisory Board of the Intercultural Associates at the URC, which would in turn report to the URC Board of Trustees. Both the Intercultural Associates and the board of trustees would be located at the URC near UCLA.

This new URC Extension Program would send a field representative to New York. From there, inspired by the spirit of religious inclusion and cooperation, as well as the experience of service and fellowship gained at the URC, the field representative would travel to prospective university panel sites across the nation, to help found local university panels and provide the ongoing guidance needed for an effective Panel program. In New York the AJC would act like a silent partner, remaining in the background but providing the national contacts, the financial backing, and office space for the field representative. As a URC organization, the Panel Extension Division would have a diverse religious organizational identity rather than the strictly Jewish identity of the AJC. Meanwhile, Guenther could retain some influence over the Panel program from afar while remaining in Los Angeles to direct other URC programs at UCLA and within the community.

CHAPTER SEVEN

Building Panels Nationwide

As a white Protestant American I believe that differences—racial, religious,
cultural—should not be minimized. They should not just be tolerated, but rather be
understood. American society, our very freedom, is founded on a principle of unity
without uniformity. Living and studying at Temple University has taught me to look
beyond an individual's religion or race, to look at his personality, to listen to what he
has to say and try to learn from him.
—*Temple University student member of the Panel of Americans*

The goal of the Panel Extension Division was to build student panels at university campuses throughout the nation. The field representative, having had
the experience of service, cooperation, and fellowship gained at the URC,
would presumably be well prepared to travel to prospective university sites
across the nation to help found local university panels, and provide the ongoing guidance needed for an effective Panel program.

Adaline Guenther chose Marian "Onie" Hargrave, a Protestant, as the field
representative of the URC Panel Extension Division in New York City. Hargrave was a UCLA graduate and an experienced panelist. She had toured the
California military bases with the POA during the war and had participated
in the 1947 national panel tour. A hardy traveler, adventuresome, and open-
minded, Hargrave was a good choice. Guenther no doubt thought that Hargrave's years at the URC had given her the necessary experience to cooperate
with others across lines of religious, racial, and ethnic division. She assumed
her new duties during the 1950 to 1951 academic year.

During that first year Hargrave traveled from her New York City office to
university sites east and west, starting new panels. She worked with university
administrators, faculty, and students and helped them see the benefits of the
Panel program for the students, the community, and the public status of the
university. Hargrave discussed the necessary time commitment, the role of

the panel sponsor (a faculty member, administrator, or a graduate student). She also undertook panelist training; her job also included building community support and finding out about the demographic composition of the student body and surrounding area.

The URC annual report in May of 1951 paints a rosy picture of panel expansion: "Panels are functioning out of the University of Washington in Seattle which reports one appearance per day for the last two and a half months." In her report to the URC Intercultural Committee, Hargrave wrote that Syracuse "will go ahead I hope," and that St. Louis "is on the way"; she had received "quite a terrific letter about them." The report goes on to list other universities where panels had been launched: the University of Cincinnati, Washington University in St. Louis, Wayne University in Detroit, Western Reserve in Cleveland, and San Francisco State College. In addition, Boston University, Carnegie Tech in Pittsburgh, Brooklyn [College] in New York City, and Syracuse University, as well as eight others, were in the formative stage. There was also "great interest" at Wayne University and Carnegie Tech in starting their own respective Religious Conference organizations, probably as supporting institutions for future panels. "There will be without doubt some form of cooperative organization modelled on our Religious Conference before this year is over."[1]

Panels at Indiana and Syracuse Universities, organized the previous year, were now making presentations, and their "effectiveness has been just as observable as that of the parent group here [at the URC]," states the annual report of 1952.[2] Confirming this assessment was a memorandum to the dean of Syracuse University by B. L. Fox of the Sociology Department. "Seldom has it been my privilege to see a top-notch performance of the kind put on by the [Syracuse] student team of the Panel of Americans," wrote Fox, who went on to describe the speeches of the student panelists. Dave, the Jewish panelist, "won the audience with his forthright presentation" on "the common heritage of Jews and Christians." Lorna, the panelist of color, spoke about "the venom of discrimination in a land where she sees the possibility of a more nearly perfect achievement of the true meaning of our democratic heritage." Her speech was a "combination of logic and emotional appeal." Frank, the Catholic panelist, "refuted many common prejudices" and "his frequent light touches of humor made him very effective." Vernon, the Protestant panelist, described himself as "the World's Luckiest Man" and "probed into the prejudices of most of us and forced us to think of the terrible responsibility we carry."[3]

By then, the URC Panel Extension program had established functioning panels at sixteen universities, some of them with several panel teams in the field. Wayne University had "fifty to sixty Panelists who present eighty to one hundred programs a year." During the 1952 academic year, "approximately 375 programs were conducted by some 300 students, and panels made ten appearances on radio and television in Cincinnati, Pittsburgh, Cleveland and Detroit." In addition, new panels were in process at other universities: Purdue, Temple, UC Berkeley, Kansas City, and Omaha.[4]

Despite the success of the URC Panel Extension Division, the URC Board voted in 1952 to end it the following year. The explanation offered gave two reasons. One was that the grant of the American Jewish Committee would soon be expiring and that "unless answers to requests which have been made by the [URC] Board, to certain other foundations, are forthcoming, this rather unique extension of the Religious Conference idea will come to a halt."[5]

It seems strange that the URC would give up on the national panel program when it was gaining strength for lack of about six thousand dollars, especially with such steadfast panel donors as Sol Lesser and Dore Schary, among other Hollywood figures. More credible is the second reason hinted at in the 1952 URC report: that the national panel program "under the direction of Miss Marian Hargrave of the Conference staff has now reached such proportions that. . . . the Panel Advisory Board . . . recommends . . . that we confine our work with the Panel of Americans hereafter to California and Arizona." If other communities wish to use the Panel technique, the URC "would make available whatever help they could without . . . assuming responsibility." That recommendation was accepted by the URC at the 1952 annual meeting.[6] Meanwhile the local panel program remained popular and continued as before in Los Angeles, but the URC dropped the national program.[7] Thereafter the URC local panel made a tour to Arizona in 1953, and to Texas in 1955, but these panelists were from the URC and under Guenther's immediate direction, not as part of the New York-based national panel program.

It seems likely that Guenther found the national URC Panel Extension in New York, and the many new panels it had helped set up, too much of an undertaking to oversee. The panel idea had become so popular that it had outgrown the URC. Founded by a charter approved by the California Board of Regents in 1928, as previously discussed, the URC was an extracurricular, multifaith, educational institution. It was intended to encourage religious

cooperation and understanding among university and college students in the
state of California. But the URC was not founded as a national organization.[8]

Moreover, unlike the Extension Division that John Burnside had staffed
and coordinated with the NCCJ in Southern California, the Panel Extension
Division was now offering services to university students and communities
not only *unaffiliated* with the URC but also *distant* from California. Although
the ideas and approach of the URC were appropriate for a national program,
such a program exceeded what the URC itself could do. It became clear that a
new national organization was necessary if the program of expansion was to
continue.

The National Council of the Panel of Americans

The National Council of the Panel of Americans (NCPA) was formed soon
after the URC eliminated the national program. The NCPA was to provide
"the realistic national structure so urgently needed" and "the highest type of
leadership and support." Over the course of the next few years the NCPA organized a board, hired an executive director, assembled an executive committee, brought together a supporting sponsoring group to raise funds, and was
incorporated as a nonprofit organization in New York State.[9]

Marian Hargrave and John M. Krumm were central to the founding of
the NCPA. Like Hargrave, Krumm was a UCLA graduate who had been a
URC participant and, in the 1930s, had been a member of the URC Trialogue
program. After he left the URC, Krumm became an ordained minister in the
Episcopal Church and eventually became the Episcopal chaplain of Columbia
University. He would later become an Episcopal bishop.[10]

The board assembled by the NCPA was impressive and eventually came to
have more than forty members. The sponsoring group, responsible for raising funds, and organized several years later, counted twenty-five members.
Both groups included educators, religious leaders, philanthropists, and business leaders, as well as figures prominent in public life and cultural circles.
They were drawn from diverse religious, racial, and ethnic groups and hailed
from many parts of the country, from Missouri and Indiana, to the East and
West Coasts. Among them were Ethel J. Alpenfels, professor of anthropology
at New York University; Ruth Harris (Mrs. Ralph Bunche); Harry J. Carman,

dean at Columbia University; the public intellectual Norman Cousins; Dorothy Height, president of the National Council of Negro Women; Rabbi Edgar Magnin of Los Angeles; Jackie Robinson of the Brooklyn Dodgers; the Rev. James H. Robinson, Presbyterian pastor in Harlem; and the San Francisco ceramicist and author Jade Snow Wong. Former URC participant Gilbert Harrison, at the time owner and editor of the *New Republic,* also served on the NCPA Board.

The NCPA sought to continue the work pioneered by the URC in building new university panels nationally. Each university was to create and sponsor its own panel program, while the NCPA would provide various field services, such as consultations on how to organize, initiate, and develop new university panels; visits to existing panels for stimulation and enrichment; writing, printing, and circulating publications such as bulletins, training manuals, and bibliographies of research materials; facilitating informal communication among the panels nationally; and holding periodic regional and national conferences where panelists received training and shared information at workshops. The NCPA also occasionally made small grants to university panels, helped build community support for the panel programs, and attracted local and national publicity.[11]

Notwithstanding the national structure and professionalization provided by the NCPA, the spirit and sense of mission of the URC was retained. Marian Hargrave continued in New York City with the NCPA from the start, first as the field representative, and in 1956 as the associate director. Hargrave was assisted in 1954 and 1955 by Joan Meyersieck, another former URC participant. They worked together helping to establish new panels and guide them. John Krumm became the chair of the NCPA executive committee. With their leadership and Guenther's occasional participation from afar, the influence of the URC remained strong, and the panels reflected the same values of acceptance and inclusion. In fact, except for organization and funding, the URC panels and those of the NCPA were much the same and are treated here as one continuous movement.

The American Jewish Committee continued to offer office space for the panel until 1956, when the National Council of the Panel of Americans moved to its own office several blocks uptown. The AJC was no longer the major financial supporter of the NCPA, but it continued to make small grants and a loan to the panel program. New sources of revenue became available from donations of various universities and panel communities and community leaders in Cincinnati, Cleveland, Los Angeles, New York, and San Francisco. Grants were also given by the Goldwyn Foundation and the Lucy Stern Foundation. The year after its founding, the budget of the NCPA was nineteen thousand dollars, and its goal was to reach forty thousand dollars the following year, 1955–1956. The projected increase was to develop and launch panels at Hunter College in New York City, Northwestern University near Chicago, the University of Pittsburgh, Wisconsin State College, and Vanderbilt University in Nashville. There was particular interest in Vanderbilt, in the hope that it would become the first university to set up a panel south of the border cities of Kansas City and St. Louis.[12]

Like the URC panel program before it, the NCPA program was unusual in involving university students in what was then called intergroup education, not only on campus but in the community. "We all talk about the genius of America," stated John Krumm, "but it is young people who have the gift for dramatizing it and making it real to us. . . . demonstrating before public audiences their conviction that religious diversity, racial and cultural variety can be one of America's greatest strengths." "When a man understands and appreciates his own tradition . . . and has confidence in those around him—however profoundly they may differ in faith, experience or culture—he will not fear, he will not hate," Krumm explained. "Such confidence, springs from common belief in God and . . . without it democratic institutions cannot endure." He wrote, "For the student it is a constructive alternative to the arm-waving, irresponsible left or right wing action groups."[13]

The impact of the panel was primarily emotional, to motivate a sympathetic listener to find out about opportunities for community social action. In this sense, the Panel of Americans served as "catalysts of community action," rather than as community activists themselves. Only in unusual circumstances would the panel convert a bigot into someone who embraced an outsider, but it was a first step that could be followed up by education. In fact, the panel was intended to be educational, rather than a vehicle for advocating a specific social policy. It relied on modeling and persuasion. Panelists were not experts. They gave no advice. But their very appearance likely raised eyebrows. The poise and the neat, attractive look of all the panelists, be they of Protestant Catholic, Jewish, and African background, or of Mexican or Asian background—the last two, typical of panelists in Los Angeles, but different elsewhere depending on local demographic composition—may have surprised some in the audience. The deep personal faith discussed by Jewish and Catholic panelists (Protestant too) may have surprised other audience members. The confidence of the African American panelist and the personal experiences and personal stories that each of the panelists told, at times emotional or even humorous, spoken in proper English, and the articulate, conversational tone and spontaneity of the panelists were intended to create ease and rapport between them and the audience. So were the honest and tactful response of panelists to audience questions asked after the presentation or at the occasional social mixing later between panelists and audience members. Perhaps most memorable was the spirit of fellowship, acceptance, and cooperation that each panelist displayed toward the others, even when they disagreed, and the pride of each of them in their own background and simultaneously in being a good American.[14]

Both the URC panels and the panels assisted by the NCPA were based on the same premise: "that people are weary of the suspicious voices . . . which are producing misunderstanding among us," in the words of John Krumm. "We think that people are ready to hear voices which encourage confidence and unity among us. We think that the Panel of Americans is a powerful and dramatic way of doing this by creating an atmosphere in which every man has the freedom to be himself—even though he be different."[15]

Krumm wrote these words in March of 1954, during the height of the Cold War, about four years after the Senate had established the Internal Security Committee, and little more than a year after Senator Joseph McCarthy had become the chairman of the Senate Permanent Subcommittee on Investigations. While the Panel of Americans was far from a political action organization, its message of confidence, unity, and acceptance of difference was suspect in that environment of fear. Nevertheless, there were people at the URC who had spoken up in the past in times of division. O. D. Foster had spoken at the University of Oregon in 1923 of accepting Jews and Catholics during the rise of the second iteration of the Ku Klux Klan. The URC's John Burnside risked suspension from UCLA for standing against the vigilantes on campus when he protested the cancellation of Upton Sinclair as an invited university speaker. And now John Krumm and those associated with the Panel of Americans were presenting a message of acceptance and inclusion in the face of division.

Two months after Krumm wrote those words about the Panel of Americans as a force for unity in the face of division, the US Supreme Court decided the case of Oliver Brown and that of four other related suits, stating that racial segregation in the public schools was unconstitutional. The firestorm of protest and violence that *Brown* set off, especially in the South, created additional opportunities for the panel "to bridge the gap between legal enactment and popularly accepted practice," much needed in cities like Kansas City, where tensions surrounding race ran high even before the *Brown* decision of 1954.[16]

The Kansas City University Panel: A Case Study

In late October of 1952, Marian Hargrave arrived in Missouri, at the University of Kansas City, where she stayed for two days to follow up on the progress of the Panel of Americans, recently organized by Phyllis Printz, activities counsellor at the University, with help from Hargrave. During the visit Hargrave was scheduled to give a lecture at a university coffee hour and, the next day, to meet individually with the fifteen students then participating in the panel program at the university. The program had teams of four or five panelists, comprising a Protestant, Catholic, Jewish, and African American, and at times, a first- or second-generation American. Each panelist spoke for three minutes on "racial and religious prejudice and ignorance in the community" before answering audience questions. It seems likely that Hargrave wanted to find out more about the local religious, racial, and ethnic landscape and attitudes at the university and in the community. It is also likely that as an experienced panel member herself, she coached the panelists on their talks and demeanor.[17]

Perhaps it was the October visit that brought the desired results. "The organization is rapidly becoming a popular drawing card to community groups," stated an article in the student newspaper, the *University News*, three months later. Panel appearances were scheduled at the Village Presbyterian Church, in front of the board of directors of the local chapter of the National Conference of Christians and Jews, at the Lincoln High School student council and PTA, Southwest and Paseo High Schools, the Junior Chamber of Commerce, and the Hadassah, a Jewish Women's organization. There were also several other engagements, just in time for February's Brotherhood Week. The KC University panel was "the most sought after program from requests received so far," reported the *Kansas City Star* in February 1953. By then, the UKC panel had scheduled some twenty engagements.[18]

Hargrave returned to Kansas City in March of 1953, to observe "the activity in this area." An article in the *Kansas City Star* described the KC University panel as "pointing out the positive potential in religious, racial and cultural differences among people." Since last November, the Kansas City University panel "has appeared before several Kansas City organizations and will present more programs this spring with a view toward bettering human relations by lessening social tensions." The paper reported that "the students with a diversity of background tell of a common misconception and prejudice associated with each group. Each [panelist] in the many programs speaks both as an individual and as a member of a particular racial, cultural or religious background. . . . They seek to show people a positive value in appreciating differences. An awareness of people as individuals is a result. Social tensions may also be reduced."[19]

Tending to the ongoing progress of the Panel of Americans was a vital part of Hargrave's duties as a field representative. Helping to set up and maintain effective university panels had many moving parts: gauging student interest, finding panel sponsors or coordinators, adjusting to preferences of faculty and administrators, suggesting appropriate office space, coming up with available funds, and building community awareness. It is no surprise that panels sometimes came and went in a year; others, like the panels at Purdue and Wayne Universities, continued for about a decade. Keeping all these moving parts in working order, often at great distances, required constant attention. Much of the time, Hargrave did this work by herself with occasional secretarial help, but in 1954 and 1955 she received assistance from fellow UCLA graduate and URC participant Joan Meierseick.

In December 1954 Meierseick wrote a letter to Earl C. McGrath, president of the University of Kansas City. She began by noting the high quality of students in the UKC panel program and commenting that the panel program generally attracts students of the highest caliber. She then described the panel program as being more than a student activity; rather, it was something that required a special coordinator who could devote time and attention to provide the ongoing evaluation and resources necessary to maintain high quality panel programs. Not only time, but mature guidance, she argued, was also required to coordinate an effective program. In her letter, she listed three goals that a panel program must accomplish: widen audience awareness about human relations, educate the participating student panelists, and promote positive public relations and public service for the university.[20]

She wrote her letter in response to the recent appointment of William Weifenbach as a special assistant to President McGrath while still designated as the sponsor of the UKC panel program. In a forceful tone, Meierseick declared that with his new responsibilities, Weifenbach would lack the time to be an effective panel coordinator. Her letter assumed that McGrath agreed with her that the panel program was worthwhile and should be done properly. Urging McGrath to act, she suggested either appointing a faculty coordinator with release time, or continuing to run the program on an emergency basis, with plans to staff the position the following year, or employing a special assistant or staff member on a part-time basis with an office, qualifications, and a title. She went on to relate how four other universities—Wayne, Western Reserve, UC Berkeley, and Purdue Universities—were handling their panel programs and made the point that although there was no one pattern for all, whatever the pattern, there must be one key person responsible for the program. Finally, Meierseick mentioned that she was sending a copy of her letter to leading businessman Edward G. Gilbert and highly respected lawyer Anthony P. Nugent Jr., both prominent citizens from Kansas City and members of the Board of the National Council of the Panel of Americans.[21]

After conferring with Weifenbach and other UKC administrators, Mc-Grath wrote to Meierseick that he hoped to add personnel to the student activities staff the following year to assume responsibility for the UKC panel program, and in the meantime, he would likely have to continue the panel program on an emergency basis.[22] In March of 1955 Edward G. Gilbert proposed to donate eight hundred dollars that year for a fellowship to support the Panel of Americans at UKC. It was to be granted to a graduate student who would have no other duties aside from coordinating the panel and pursuing graduate studies. The administrators at UKC agreed to waive tuition for the panel coordinator position so that the recipient of the grant could devote twenty hours per week to the UKC panel, while the director of student activities would provide the supervision.[23]

Meierseick arranged to visit UKC the following month. Her purpose was to help the university plan and provide continuity to the panel program for the next academic year.[24] Gilbert renewed his eight hundred dollar grant, and the UKC administration also renewed the tuition waiver of the graduate student panel coordinator for 1956.[25] Thanks to the persistence, high standards, and patience of Meierseick and Hargrave, the generosity of Edward Gilbert of the NCPA Board, as well as the cooperation of the UKC administration and the interest of the university students, the panel program at UKC continued successfully through 1956 and for a time thereafter.

The UKC student panel program became a model for an adult women's panel in the Kansas City community, later called the Panel of American Women (PAW). At its peak in the 1960s and '70s PAW grew to some sixty chapters across America. PAW turned to Marian Hargrave and the NCPA for materials and guidance to investigate "possible new directions for our . . . group. Even though our circumstances are different, we certainly share common objectives and essential format," wrote PAW member Beta K. Smith.[26]

Panel Training Books

Achieving the NCPA's goal of building an effective national panel network required teaching university students and panel coordinators about the rationale, format, mechanics, and impact of the panel approach. Great was the need for instruction on constructing and delivering panel speeches, answering audience questions, and working together as a team—all without notes while maintaining spontaneity. Panelists also had to learn how to project themselves both as members of a particular religious, racial, or ethnic group, and most important, as individual Americans who amiably agreed to disagree. Different as each panelist was from the others, they all needed to demonstrate that they were unified as Americans, worthy of respect and acceptance, and that their diversity strengthened America. This was no easy task. But it was precisely the message that needed to be conveyed.

To help with this task the NCPA printed and distributed instruction manuals. Although the original URC panels had begun this practice, it became especially important in maintaining uniform standards as the panel network expanded across the nation. These manuals not only provided instructions on building a panel speech, working as a panel team, and answering audience questions but also listed specific questions likely to be asked of each of the panelists, special instructions for the moderator, and reminders for all the panelists to dress neatly and conservatively and model good posture and decorum both when presenting and when informally mixing with the audience afterward.

In an effort to help panelists gain information about their respective religious, racial, or ethnic group and contribution to American culture as a whole, most of the NCPA manuals included a bibliography of resources. It listed books, articles, pamphlets, films, and organizations that dealt with the achievements, advantages, goals, history, social context, and sociology of each group, as well as the prejudices and other problems that they faced. The sources included, for example, Gordon W. Allport, *The Nature of Prejudice*, Milton L. Barron, *American Minorities*, Rabbi Philip S. Bernstein, *What the Jews Believe*, Kenneth B. Clark, *Prejudice and Your Child*, Oscar Handlin, *Race and Nationality in America*, Will Herberg, *Protestant-Catholic-Jew*, Ernest F. Johnson, *American Education and Religion*, Jacques Maritain, *Reflections on America*, Gunnar Myrdal, *An American Dilemma*, Reinhold Niebuhr, *Pious and Secular America*, and David Reisman, *The Lonely Crowd*. The manuals also advised panelists to consult with family members and with religious, racial, and ethnic community leaders in preparing their personal stories and answering audience questions. Needless to say, being panelists involved more than just performance, developing social skills and confidence, or interacting with members of the audience. It also meant delving into their own identity, the diverse backgrounds of their fellow panelists, and their common ground as Americans.[27]

The NCPA manuals or handbooks gave instructions on how to build a speech. Panelists were to speak for themselves only, not for their group or for other panelists. "The most important element in your Panel speech is YOU." "Who are you? What is your identification. . . . Your personal introduction may describe your family briefly, or some dramatic experience you may have encountered as a member of your . . . group." The manual cautioned panelists to limit their speech to clarifying three or four basic points about their group, often misunderstood. "Information about your group will help your audience share your pride and interest in being what you are." "How have your religion, your family or your education helped you appreciate the differences among people, [and] to meet the problems arising from these differences? "What is the relationship between your group and the total pattern of American culture?" The handbook then asks, "What are some of the specific problems or opportunities growing out of the differences among us?" As a person, a member of your group, and as an American, how are you affected by these problems? "Are you concerned about prejudice against groups other than your own?" If so, what can a panelist do to help?[28]

The handbook goes on to discuss two other points about speeches. First, the panel is a team, and panelists should avoid repetition. They should plan their speeches knowing what other panelists plan to say. This approach "serves to stimulate a variety of questions from the audience and encourages panel integration . . . with five individuals applying five different insights and viewpoints to the same ultimate purpose."[29] Second, speeches should evolve. They may need to be revised over a period of time or may need more humor, or more dignity, or may need to be changed to fit a new audience. Find out about the prospective audience, the handbook suggests. "A speech appropriate for a high school assembly will need reshaping for a Rotary Club . . . a PTA group, a foreign student group or a classroom of elementary school children."[30]

The handbooks also discussed audience questions, reminding panelists that audiences consisted of individuals. "As individual challenges individual, the audience questions stimulate the panel's honest examination of issues, clarifies misconceptions, dispels rumors." They are a "high point of a Panel appearance and . . . the most rewarding aspect of the entire program." Occasionally, when more than one panelist responds to a question and there is a friendly disagreement, the handbook counselled that such "friendly differences of opinion are natural and will arise" and that the occurrence could demonstrate the "'unity in diversity' of the Panel philosophy" and "the friendship and mutual respect" among the panelists.[31]

It was the role of the moderator not only to introduce and conclude the panel program but to be a gatekeeper between the audience and the panel speakers, to field the audience questions, to repeat or rephrase them, and to direct them to the appropriate panelist. On occasion, the moderator would ask a question to the panel to get things started. In addition, the moderator needed to balance questions among the panelists, and, when necessary, step in and ease a tense or hostile situation caused by a bigot, heckler, or an otherwise antagonistic questioner. The moderator, often a university faculty member, had to remain calm and decisive to avoid disruption. The moderator also needed to speed up a long-winded questioner and clarify a question that was too technical. As for the panelists, they needed more than facts to answer questions effectively. "Tact is essential; forthrightness and the earnest assumption that a questioner is speaking in good faith; [also required of panelists] were friendliness and dignity; [and] brevity."[32]

The manual lists over two hundred sample audience questions, divided into such categories as white Protestant, white Catholic, and white Jew, as well as Negro and Ethnic. The Ethnic category included those of Puerto Rican, Mexican American, Indian (Native American), Japanese, and Chinese backgrounds. All the questions were drawn from actual questions asked of past panelists. "Some are petty, some superficial, some searching." "The Panel speaker needs to be forewarned about the variety of questions. . . . Audiences will not all be in sympathy with the Panel. Local situations differ and will lead to different audience responses and different questions asked." Panelist "will need to get the facts and background relevant to . . . [that specific, local] area and . . . [its] frame of reference." Perplexing as some of the questions might be, panelists nevertheless needed to find "constructive ways of meeting the difficult questions or questioner." Sometimes they needed to admit that they just didn't know the answer. At such times, another panelist or the moderator might take the question.[33]

Some of the sample questions listed in the manual were: "How do you feel about intermarriage?" "Don't groups ask for prejudice against themselves by putting up barriers between themselves and others?" "Can you legislate against prejudice?" "Will education eliminate prejudice?" "Can an atheist be a good American?"[34]

"Should Jews be assimilated or retain their group identity?" "Are the Jews a race, a religion, a movement or a nationality?" "Why don't Jews accept Christ as the Messiah?" "Should a Jew in this country owe allegiance to America or Israel?" "Why do Jews try to cheat other people?"[35]

"Do you as a Catholic believe that non-Catholics will go to Heaven?" "Must Catholics believe everything the Pope tells them?" "In confession why do you have to go through a priest?" "Why can't you go straight to God?" "Do you believe in the separation of church and state?"[36]

"What does it mean to be a Protestant?" "Why are there so many Protestant denominations?" "Do Protestants believe in the Resurrection?" "Why are Protestants so disunited?" "Why does the Masonic lodge refuse Catholics as members?"[37]

"What do Negroes want?" "What is your race doing to help its own members?" "What contributions have Negroes made throughout history of civilization to prove that they are equal to the whites?" "Have you ever been turned down in a restaurant or for a job?" "Why is it that Negro sections of town are always so run down?"[38]

"Why do Puerto Ricans come to New York to get on the relief rolls?" "Why are so many Puerto Ricans delinquents?" "Why are all Puerto Rican neighborhoods so run down?" "What contributions have Puerto Ricans made to our society?" "Why do Puerto Ricans stick by themselves and speak Spanish all the time?"[39]

Some of the other ethnic questions listed in the manual were: "Why should we let ourselves be overrun by foreigners pouring into the country from all over the world?" "If we let down the bars on immigration won't our jobs be threatened by the cheap labor of immigrants and new citizens?" "Why do Indians drink so much liquor?" "Has there been any feeling against the Chinese Americans as a result of the Communist government in China?" "Why were the Japanese Americans put in camps during World War II instead of the Italians or Germans?" "Why do Mexicans try to sneak into our country?" "Why do Mexicans hold education in such low esteem?"[40]

After the panelists answered the questions and left the stage, the program often continued with conversations among the panelists and the audience over coffee, lunch, or dinner. Tired as the panelists might have been, they had to maintain their composure, poise, tact, good posture, and good humor, as they earnestly discussed points that were on the mind of audience members. This personal contact sometimes would turn out to be the most effective interchange of the day.[41]

As soon as possible after the program the panelists and the moderator conducted evaluations. These detailed assessments were divided into sections on audience questions, panelists' answers and statements, the program as a whole, overall preparation, program length, relevance, humor, and the interrelationship and coordination among panelists, as well as the effectiveness of the moderator.[42]

In addition to the panel instruction manuals, the NCPA held periodic national and regional conferences to keep panelists abreast of current affairs, to promote communication among panelists near and far, to discuss common issues, and to provide panel training.

National and Regional Conferences for Panelists

The first national panel training conference was held at Purdue University in March 1957. One hundred student and faculty delegates from Boston University, the Universities of California at Berkeley and Los Angeles, Carnegie Institute of Technology, University of Cincinnati, Indiana University, University of Kansas City, University of Minnesota, New York University, Ohio State University, University of Pittsburgh, Purdue University, San Francisco State, Temple University, University of Texas, Washington University, Wayne State University, and Western Reserve University attended this two day event.[43]

The program began with a ninety-minute morning session on "Intergroup Tensions and the Public Schools: Religious Questions." The speakers included the Rev. James J. Maguire of Notre Dame University; the Rev. H. Richard Rasmusson of the University Presbyterian Church, West Lafayette, Indiana; Rabbi Gerald Engel of the Hillel Foundation, West Lafayette; and Dwight W. Culver, then executive director of the NCPA, on leave as professor of sociology at Purdue University. A "Buzz Session" followed the four presentations, with lunch afterward. The afternoon session included a session on panel speeches and panel questions with "Buzz Sessions" and analyses following.

That evening after the banquet, the Rev. James H. Robinson of the Harlem Church of the Master, director of the Morningside Community Center, and NCPA Board member, gave an address on "The World, the Opportunity and Our Responsibility." It was followed by a panel party at the University Presbyterian Church.

The session the next morning began with a talk by Ethel J. Alpenfels, professor of anthropology at New York University and NCPA Board member, who spoke on "Race, Ethnic Groups and Culture: How to Handle the Basic Facts." The talk was followed by "Buzz sessions" and then a talk by Edwin B. Bronner, professor of history at Temple University, titled "Background of the Present Crisis." Subsequently, Kenneth B. Clark, professor of psychology at City College of New York and session chair, gave a talk on "Where Do We Go from Here and How Fast?"[44]

Following lunch, a session was held on "The Panel and the Community," chaired by Dr. Dale E. Strick, dean of students at the Carnegie Institute of Technology. It included talks on "Housing" by George W. Culbertson of the

Pittsburgh Commission on Human Relations, on "Public Accommodation" by Marshall Bragdon of the Cincinnati Mayor's Friendly Relations Committee, and on "Employment" by John G. Feild, [sic], representing the State of Michigan Fair Employment Practices Commission, Detroit. The talks were followed by a discussion among Religious Activities Counselor Hubert Locke and Raymond Wright, both from Wayne State University, and Florence Inghram and Earl Onque of the Carnegie Institute of Technology. "Buzz sessions" followed until dinner, at which recorders of the sessions made reports, and plans for the 1958 national conference were announced by the Conference Committee. After dinner light entertainment was offered.[45]

Several regional conferences were held over the years, among them an event on a Saturday in February 1961. This was the day-long Eastern Regional Training Conference at Columbia University, chaired by the Rev. John Krumm, chaplain of Columbia University and chairman of the NCPA Steering Committee. On the roster were the Rev. Joseph P. Fitzpatrick, S.J., chairman of the Sociology Department at Fordham University; Dorothy I. Height, president of the National Council of Negro Women, specialist in leadership training, and a supporter of the NCPA; Harold T. Hunton, of the NYC Mayor's Intergroup Relations Commission; Cerona D. Johnson, intergroup relations consultant, National YWCA, and former Urban League director in Oklahoma City and Fort Worth; Joseph Monserrat, director, Commonwealth of Puerto Rico, Department of Labor, Migration Division; and Mannheim S. Shapiro of the American Jewish Committee. They formed a resource panel to train attendees and hold discussions with them centered on answering the following six major questions:

1. What are the major attitudes toward (my) group?
2. What kinds of personal experiences help to communicate ideas?
3. What are the major in-group attitudes, feelings, and convictions that I need to understand as I speak from my own experience as a member of my particular group?
4. What are some of the blocks to understanding that need to be faced?
5. What are some of the major ideas and convictions that I want to share about my group today? and
6. What makes it difficult to be oneself and at the same time an interpreter of a group?

Attendees worked with the resource panel member corresponding to their own religious, racial, or ethnic group., who demonstrated ways to handle these questions. For example, John Krumm addressed the problems Protestant panelists faced.

"We had lots of people in our group who thought they were Protestants because they weren't much of anything else," Krumm began. "There is a lack of self-identification among Protestants," "a catch all for everybody else," complacent, and defenders of the "status quo." "Protestants are . . . the lump and everyone else is the leaven." "We certainly have thought that this is *our* country and this is *our* tradition." But, Krumm goes onto say, "many of the activities in a community which seek to improve relationships have Protestants in them, but they don't identify as Protestants. They just are human beings who are interested in improving things."[46]

Krumm then asks about the panel format and whether "religious divisions . . . [are] more significant [than] those of class?" Do educational background, economic status, sociological history matter more than religion, he wonders. "Do Protestants of a certain social status . . . feel more identification with a Roman Catholic of a similar level than they do . . . with Negroes who may be Protestant? This is part of the problem of a group that isn't . . . clearly identified to itself or to the community at large."[47]

The disunity of Protestants was another issue for Krumm. He refers to James Hasting Nichols's *Primer for Protestants* and states that Nichols suggests that 'the commonest meaning of Protestants today in western countries is simply any Christian who denies the authority of the Roman Pope." From there Krumm argues that Protestants relate to both Judaism and Roman Catholicism. "Protestants do feel themselves as part of the people of Israel, the covenant community. They claim alliance and that of fellowship with Abraham, Moses, the prophets and also that they are a part of the Christian tradition of Western society. Therefore, they understand what St. Augustine was talking about and St. Thomas Aquinas."[48]

The Reformation and the general biblical tradition, Krumm explains, gave rise to various Protestant movements that see "all men as children of God, all men as having been created by God, as potentially part of the divine purpose for the fulfillment of human life, that every individual is seen in his distinctive individuality as a product of God's creation, and that God apparently wasn't terribly interested in making everyone in the same pattern." As a result, "the human community is to be discovered in the midst of diversity, that to deny diversity is to deny divine creation." Thus, "the question is not . . . whether you are a Negro first or an American first, but . . . are you first of all a human being?" From there, Krumm talks about Americanism, diversity, and their relationship to Protestantism. Protestantism is a religious tradition with "a distinctive perspective" that "can begin to tackle the problems of the total human community, the fellowship of the whole human race."[49]

Krumm describes Protestantism as a religion of diversity and individuality, a faith that touches both Judaism and Catholicism and is ultimately about being human. His description brings to mind his days in the URC trialogue program, when he often was joined by Gilbert Harrison. Harrison too spoke about diversity in Judaism and how there are Jews in the diaspora, all over the world, of every race and nationality. Those Jews and Protestants that Harrison and Krumm describe are ultimately united in their humanity. It is striking that Krumm is drawing on his URC experiences of some twenty-five years earlier to train new generations of Protestant university panelists.

After the two-hour session with Krumm and the others on the resource panel, lunch was served at the Columbia Faculty Club, where the Rev. Joseph P. Fitzpatrick gave a talk on "Facing the Facts of Difference." The afternoon sessions featured "Leadership Skills for Difficult Panel Audiences," given by Dorothy I. Height, and a demonstration presentation by the New York City Panel of Americans, followed by an evaluation of the panel and a discussion. The training conference adjourned at 4:30 that afternoon.

Publicity and Public Acknowledgements

The NCPA and the national network of panels led to increased publicity, not only in local and university newspapers but also in a NCPA newsletter, in a variety of university pamphlets, and even in national periodicals and publications. Among the universities that housed panels, several distributed pamphlets advertising their panel programs to the local community. Examples included the Bay Area Panels, namely at UC Berkeley, San Francisco State, and Stanford University. Others in the rest of the country included Carnegie Tech, the University of Cincinnati, the University of Omaha, Purdue University, Temple University, and Wayne State University.[50]

A national publication, *American Unity: An Educational Guide*, edited by Annette Lawrence and James Waterman Wise and issued by the Council against Intolerance in America, published an article on the Panel of Americans. It stated that "from one half to one million Americans of all ages are reached annually by the Panel of Americans in communities from coast to coast." At the end, the article included speeches by three panelists: Betty Yaki, a Japanese American, Vivian Robinson, an African American, and Esther Nathan, a Jewish American.[51]

At the beginning of her speech, Betty Yaki says that she thought her childhood was much like that of other American children, "except for one thing. I spent three unforgettable years in a relocation center surrounded by barbed wire and military police. . . . and I was all of seven years old." "America is one nation out of many cultures and that is what makes us strong. . . . I will always have slanted eyes—you can eat potatoes and I can eat rice—but these are only superficial differences compared to our common loyalties. . . . If our country ever begins to insist that all Americans must look alike, think alike, worship alike, we will have one grand assembly line—and much stagnation and boredom."[52]

"I have found intelligent people frequently asking," declared African American panelist Vivian Robinson, "what does the Negro really want?" "He doesn't want any special privileges, special drinking fountains, special schools, a special seat on a bus, a special military unit to die in. But he does want any job he can qualify for, any house he can afford to buy. He wants the responsibilities of being a full-class citizen. And he thinks he has the right to expect these things because he has helped to build what we so proudly call our American heritage. . . . He has worked at every job that has needed to be done. He has fought in every war in which the United States has been engaged." She continued, "He merely asks that the gap be closed between the American way and the way Americans live."[53]

"'The Jews have all the money in this country.' 'Watch out, the Jews try to cheat you!' The funny part is that most of these people don't mean any harm. They are just . . . saying what everyone . . . says at one time or other," stated Esther Nathan, the Jewish panelist. "I am puzzled by these generalizations. For America has developed the ideal that the individual is . . . most important and should be judged right or wrong as an individual. I could never understand the people who think they can identify a Jew by his . . . characteristics or

. . . occupation and yet think they [themselves] are Americans." She shared, "When I say I am a Jew, I do not mean that I am a member of a race or nation. I mean that I am a member of a people who believe in the Jewish religion." Furthermore, "With my heritage as a Jew comes pride and responsibility. I am proud that it was my people who first gave to the world the ideal of One God and the principles written in the Bible and the Ten Commandments. I am proud that many of these principles exist today as a basis for moral and ethical and legal codes. I am proud that . . . [Jewish] adherents have held together . . . for over five thousand years whether they have been black in Ethiopia, or brown in India, or white in Europe . . . As a Jew, as an American, it is my responsibility to be eternally vigilant . . . so that man will be free to contribute the best that is in him to make our nation a better nation and our world, a better world."[54]

The Panel of Americans gained notice on the national level as well as locally. In 1955, in its "Education" section, *Time Magazine* featured an article and photograph of one of the panels at UC Berkeley. This particular panel was addressing the American Federation of Labor Temple in Oakland. The article also mentioned panel programs at other universities: Western Reserve, Wayne, and Purdue. In 1957 *Coronet Magazine* published a photograph of a URC panel and an article by Andrew Hamilton, titled "Kids Who Speak for Brotherhood." The article mentions a panel appearance before a convention of the United Steel Workers of America. There the union men gave the panel a standing ovation. According to the reporting, someone at the presentation noted that the only other time this had happened was when famous union leader and president of the Congress of Industrial Organizations, Philip Murray, had spoken.[55]

An article in the October 1961 "Teenagers Talk" section of *Seventeen Magazine* concentrates on the question-and-answer portion of the panel presentation. This time the article focused on a New York City Panel of Americans, comprising a Puerto Rican panelist who was a junior at City College, a Protestant panelist who was a graduate student at Union Theological Seminary, an African American panelist who was a senior at Hunter College, a Catholic panelist who was a graduate student at Columbia University, and a Jewish panelist who was a pre-law student at City College. Marian Hargrave was the moderator. They all went to suburban Essex County, New Jersey, where they gave a presentation at Caldwell High School. The article reprinted about fifteen questions the students asked as well as additional high school student comments. The panelists answered the questions addressed to them, and other panelists often added their answers too. The dialogue was lively, the tone relaxed and conversational, and the questions the high school students asked were pointed and penetrating. The questions ranged from how to deflect the attentions of Spanish-speaking Puerto Rican young men on the street without causing problems (Just ignore them) to on which side would you fight on if the United States and Israel went to war? (The US.) Other questions concerned interreligious and interracial marriages (mixed responses) and was there racial discrimination in the North? (Yes, improving in North *and* South). This last question prompted the panelists to ask the student audience about racial discrimination at Caldwell High School (mixed responses).[56]

Soon after the article appeared, a letter from *Seventeen Magazine* arrived at the desk of Dorothy Bauman, then director of the NCPA. It quoted excerpts from several letters received from readers. "How I have waited for an article such as [this]. . . . Too many people today fight prejudice in their minds but haven't the courage to do anything about it. But only by words and actions can prejudice be destroyed." "Articles such as these are big steps toward increasing human understanding." "Your panel discussion was truly an inspiration designed not only for us teenagers but for the general public . . . If more adults had as much sense . . . as did the panel, this world would be a better place." One letter asked, how can one join such a panel? Another suggested forming a panel on the high school level.[57]

Over the years, the question about interreligious marriage continued to be posed, but the answers of the panelists evolved. Unlike the earlier trialogue and panel negative responses, the responses of the panelists at Caldwell High School were mixed, and a new question was introduced. It was about interracial marriage, and those responses were also mixed. The social context of the URC had changed, and the Panel Program it had created changed too. Unlike the URC Panel Program of the 1940s that saw only moderate changes in race relations, the program of the 1950s and 1960s saw dynamic changes in civil rights, affected by such events as the *Brown v. Board of Education* decision of 1954 to the Montgomery bus boycott of 1955 to the sit-ins and freedom rides of the early 1960s.

Vance Packard commented on the Panel of Americans in his book *The Status Seekers*. The panel that caught his eye was composed of students from

New York University, who had made a presentation to junior high school pupils one afternoon in Peekskill, New York, in response to rising hostilities among different groups at the school. That evening the panel made another presentation, this one to the Peekskill PTA. The junior high pupils prevailed upon their parents to attend the meeting, which drew a record crowd. Packard reports that the impact of that meeting lasted for weeks, and a friendlier attitude among housewives of various races and ethnicities was noticeable even in the local supermarkets.[58]

The Honorable Justine Wise Polier, a highly respected New York judge and vice chairman of the National Organization of Women, acknowledged the Panel of Americans in her February 1960 closing address at the NOW Conference in Washington, DC. She mentioned that "we rejoiced in the panel of Young Americans. We heard from a Negro youth, 'I do not want to be accepted as an exception. I want to be accepted and looked upon as a Negro. All that is part of my race, its history, its tradition, its culture, and its hurts are also part of me.' These words coming from a young Negro reflect not the drive to be accepted, to be assimilated but to live in dignity and to contribute in and to this land."[59]

New Panels, New Emphasis, New Direction

The first intercollegiate panel in the South was formed in the early 1960s. In Lynchburg, Virginia, Randolph-Macon Women's College, Sweet Briar College, Lynchburg College, and Virginia Seminary cooperated to form panel presentations. Similarly, the first panel in the Rocky Mountains was formed at Utah State University in Logan. At the time panels made presentations at Goucher College, near Baltimore, to a Wisconsin State Teachers Convention, at the Marble Collegiate Church in Manhattan where Norman Vincent Peale was the senior minister, and in San Francisco where the panel was in a television series.[60]

In New York City the national pattern of university-centered panels was expanded and supplemented by panels comprising individual students recruited from some twelve universities and colleges in and around the city. Unlike the national network of panels, which were organized and administered within the university and staffed by students, these NYC panels were supervised by the NCPA and included students from a variety of colleges and universities that included Barnard College, Columbia University, Fordham University, Hunter College, City College, College of New Rochelle, New York University, Union Theological Seminary, Jewish Theological Seminary, Lexington School for the Deaf, Rutgers Law School, and the New York School of Social Work. Usually, Hargrave organized these panels for a specific occasion and took on the role of moderator. Most often, these panels gave presentations in or near the city, but on occasion, they made trips out of town. One such trip was to Daytona Beach, Florida, where a panel of five students drawn from NYU and City College gathered in 1959, for a presentation at Cookman College. The event honored Mary McLeod Cookman Bethune, the educator, civil rights activist, and the founder of the National Council of Negro Women. The panel took place at the invitation of Dorothy I. Height, who, in addition to being the president of the National Council of Negro Women and member of the NCPA Board, was a good friend of Dorothy Bauman, then NCPA executive director.[61]

Another feature of the NYC panels was to expand a practice tried in 1957 at the National Training Conference at Purdue University, discussed earlier, at which members of ethnic, religious, and human relations agencies had been invited as speakers and resource leaders for training panelists. The NCPA expanded this practice and built up a pool of about twenty similar agencies and organizations, such as the Puerto Rican Association for Community Affairs and the New York State Committee against Discrimination, to help train panelists.[62]

This new pool of university and college student panelists made presentations not only to other college and university students and community groups but also to the public schools and the surrounding communities in which there were racial, ethnic, and religious problems. At the time, disagreement over issues such as open enrollment, bussing, and local control were leading to conflicts. Accordingly, "The Panel's emphasis has changed with the needs of the time. At the request of the New York City Commission on Intergroup Relations, the national office developed New York City panels capable of handling school and community programs in areas experiencing racial and religious tensions."[63]

From 1960 to 1962, NCPA panels made frequent presentations at NYC public schools and PTAs in various parts of the city. On March 7, 1961, William Lane, principal of Public School 175 in Queens, which was then receiving bused African American pupils, wrote to Hargrave about a panel presentation given the previous month to the pupils at their upper grade assembly and classrooms, and the next day to the local chapter of the PTA. "As you know, P.S. 175 . . . is a receiving school. In September, 1961, 29 children . . . will be entered into our 3rd, 4th, and 5th grade classes. Our neighborhood children have had very limited relationship . . . with Negro children. The presentation of the panelists and the subsequent discussions . . . were very effective in pointing up the principles of democratic relationships. I personally was thrilled with the response of our children." Lane's letter went on to talk about the response of the parents at the PTA meeting: "Whether or not the panelists were able to make a positive impression upon those parents who might be opposed to integration, it is difficult to say. I noted . . . a number of candid remarks revealing the feelings of members of the audience. . . . Such a meeting might be of even greater value next year when the new children are part of our student body."[64]

Dozens of similar letters, remarking upon panel presentations, were received by Marian Hargrave. Occasionally the letters offered suggestions for improvement, such as planning for follow up visits, and focusing on a particular conflict of values, but overall, they were enthusiastic and positive. On October 17, 1960, William Nosofsky, assistant principal of Junior High School 178 in Brooklyn, wrote to Hargrave that their recent appearance "was unquestionably the high point for all of us at 178. Your group brought understanding . . . to our youngsters. . . . when we came in contact with insight, enthusiasm, and a concern for important values. That our students found the program of great interest is evidenced by . . . the expressed desire of some students to form a junior high school Panel of Americans." Julius Raskin, principal of Junior High 178, also wrote to Hargrave that "I could not say enough in appreciation of the spirit of cooperation and sincerity of your Panelists. . . . they personified . . . those qualities which a democracy prizes." Describing the pupil response to the panel presentation, as "rich and deep." Bernard Friedman of Public School 157 in Manhattan wrote to Dorothy Bauman, "This is an impressionable age . . . and the best time to plant seeds of understanding, respect and fair play." "One measure of your effectiveness can be gauged," wrote Harold G. Walters, acting principal of Public School 77 in Queens, "by the imitation of your technique by the pupils themselves. Our fourth grade is now in the process of forming its own Panel of Americans to carry on where you necessarily had to leave off."[65]

In 1962 the panel participated in a pilot project: a Human Relations Course for Teachers on the Lower East Side of Manhattan. Hargrave was the moderator. The audience included twenty-six elementary school teachers, one junior high school teacher, and three school secretaries. According to the NCPA, "All are white, no Puerto Ricans . . . only one man. Quite a cohesive, homogeneous group. Most come from schools that are predominantly Negro and Puerto Rican. . . . several are Catholic. . . . some have 'Irish sounding names,' some are Jewish. One of the schools has many people of Italian background." It was felt that "the Panel can help . . . assess the feelings and attitudes of the members, the practical problems of intergroup relations . . . The Panel can also provide a model for frank discussion and for revealing one's own feelings."[66]

In 1962 Gladys Harburger replaced Dorothy Bauman as the executive director of the NCPA. With the arrival of Harburger, the focus of the NCPA shifted from sponsoring panels at universities around the country. The name was changed back to the Panel of Americans, and the organization turned to addressing the issues in the New York City Public School System. Described by Hargrave as a "fireball," Harburger had been president of the New York City United Parents Association, an association of all the PTAs in the New York City Public School System, the largest one in the country. With many contacts in the New York City Public School System, and in the face of the many problems of human relations facing the schools, Harburger used the panelists to help teach human relations and to train teachers, administrators, counsellors, and pupils to respond positively to the diversity in their midst and to calm the tensions arising from conflicts among the different groups. But this was a different mission than the one Marian Hargrave and John Krumm had had in building panels at universities across the country. Hargrave and Krumm had both been participants in the University Religious Conference, and had both been instrumental in bringing the influence of the URC to the panels at universities nationally. When they left, the national Panel program ended, as did the connection between the URC and the New York City panel.

CHAPTER EIGHT

The University Religious Conference
Goes to India

By their inquiring and open minds and their frank expression of views, the UCLA'ers are able to create a feeling of camaraderie with their Indian counterparts.
—Foreign Service Dispatch of 1960

After the Second World War, Americans envisioned a new and larger role for the United States in international affairs. Unlike the world inhabited by O. D. Foster after the First World War, the new environment had little isolationist sentiment. Americans saw their nation as a leader in world affairs, as a protector of democracy, and a builder of democratic institutions throughout the world. As the Cold War took hold and the United States, the Soviet Union, and China vied with one another for dominance, exporting American institutions, culture, and values became crucial to foreign policy. While projecting military power remained a priority, projecting American soft power also gained in importance.

The years following the war saw an end to the British and French empires, as their colonies in Africa, Asia, and the Middle East gained political independence. The Communist and Western blocs competed for influence in those areas. When India gained independence from Britain in 1947, it became one of several nations that remained neutral in this competition. In this context, the United States considered India an important nation in what came to be called the "nonaligned block."

Throughout the history of the University Religious Conference, the organization sought to create religious fellowship among diverse students by having them work side-by-side on social service projects. In India, Guenther saw the possibility that URC students could again create religious fellowship, but in an international context that would appeal to their interest in the new, larger role of the United States in world affairs.

The presence of URC students in India could also help create a positive view of Americans among Indian university students. Moreover, Guenther saw India as a nation where URC students could learn about a new democracy, demonstrate American democratic pluralism, project American soft power abroad, and increase religious understanding among the URC students themselves. The Indian population, which numbered more than 361 million in 1950, included a multitude of diverse ethnic, religious, linguistic, and racial groups, many of them little-known to URC students and to Americans generally. Traveling in India would expose the URC students to those diverse groups. Spending time in that country would expand the Judeo-Christian framework of the URC and open up the world of Hinduism and Islam for URC students. All these goals shaped Project India (PI), begun in 1952.

The idea of Project India developed from a talk given by James Robinson, pastor at the Church of the Master in Harlem. He briefly stopped in Los Angeles in January of 1952, on his way home to New York after six months on an international speaking tour sponsored by the Presbyterian Board of Foreign Missions. The tour had taken him to India, where he spent more than six weeks. While in Los Angeles Robinson contacted Cecil Hoffman, the Presbyterian adviser at the URC. Impressed by Robinson's charisma and message, Hoffman prevailed upon Guenther to set up a meeting between Robinson and the URC students.

Robinson addressed the students about the need for American young people to visit India as goodwill ambassadors who would show their Indian counterparts what American youth was really like. He noted that unlike other Americans in India—the formal diplomats, the rich elderly tourists, and businessmen—college students could put a youthful, sympathetic face on what was often seen at the time as the ugly American, later portrayed in a novel of the same name.[1]

As an African American man, Robinson had access to Indian attitudes and perceptions about American society that were less available to white Americans.[2] He thought that the vigor and idealism of American students might convince Indian university students that their impressions of American society as entirely imperialistic, racist, and materialistic were mistaken. Like the Panel of Americans, Project India could demonstrate how American students of various religions, races, and ethnicities traveling together harmoniously embraced their differences. Like the Panel program, one of the goals of this project would be to heal religious and cultural divisions through personal outreach. The timing was auspicious. Always on the lookout for new student projects, Guenther must have found Robinson's speech fortuitous, coming as it did when she needed a new project in line with current student interests and idealism.

When URC student Lee Nichols heard Robinson speak about American students going to India, he felt alive. Robison's speech was "my most vital memory of the Conference . . . the content, the meeting afterwards . . . the feeling that in our hands lay all possible futures," recalled Nichols.[3]

Guenther herself was surprised at the immediate success of Project India, which, along with Uni-Camp and the Panel of Americans, soon became one of the most popular URC programs. Looking back at its inception, she wrote that in 1952, PI "appeared to be a onetime outburst of adolescent enthusiasm for an impractical ideal, [but] has continued to win enconiums (sic) from hard boiled bureaucrats and hard headed foundations."[4] In addition to UCLA students, PI attracted several students and administrators from UC Riverside and UC Santa Barbara, when URC affiliates were formed at those universities.[5] In later years, the State Department suggested that the URC start a similar program, Project Ceylon, to defuse the increasing attraction of communism in Ceylon.[6]

Starting and Preparing for Project India

Project India was Adaline Guenther's last new major project at the URC, before she retired in 1959. It was a summer program in which she led URC students on trips to India where they would get to know and befriend Indian university students and further American goodwill. Project India lasted for eighteen summers, ending in 1969. For nine weeks during each of those summers, between seven and fourteen Americans, almost all of them students, traveled together in India accompanied by two adult URC leaders or recent university graduates. There they made presentations to thousands of Indian university students and met with them in small groups. They also met with Indian and American diplomats and public officials, among them Prime Minister Nehru, future prime minister Indira Gandhi, and political leader and diplomat Krishna Menin.

Anticipating the educational benefits of Project India, both in preparing for the trip and traveling in India itself, Guenther set rigorous standards for applicants. To prepare for the trip, applicants researched various aspects of life in India, the world's largest democracy, a distant, highly populated country of importance to the United States in the Cold War. As a key person in charge of selecting and training the applicants, Guenther required that they prepare for the trip by researching, writing, and presenting papers on various facets of Indian life. In addition, applicants were required to find out about American institutions and problems so they could speak convincingly to audiences in India and answer their questions. As a practical matter, Guenther could lead the PI groups during the summer while remaining in charge of URC activities during term time. For the first seven summers, she traveled in India with the students; for several years after she retired, she continued to work voluntarily as the key person in charge of selecting and training the PI students.[7]

As part of the selection process, applicants were asked several questions that tested their judgment, maturity, creativity, and moral compass. One question was what would you do if you were being entertained at a small Indian college and "it is apparent that they have spent their entire student budget on a feast they offer you." You know from past experience, however, "that eating it will make you ill . . . [and] lay a burden on the rest of the team." Yet refusing it "will hurt the feelings of the Indian students." Another question was what would you do if "an action has been determined . . . by a majority of the team. [However, it] runs counter to your idea of what is right and involves a matter of principle."[8]

Although the selection process varied from year to year, there was overall continuity. The process began in early October. The first phase consisted of written tests, "first for general intelligence, then for cultural background, emotional maturity and the ability to do rational thinking."[9] The number of applicants in the pool varied between a low of about one hundred to a high of about three hundred. From this pool, twenty-eight students of "varied racial, religious and academic backgrounds" were chosen for the initial cut. . Each finalist "was then given a topic on some phase of Indian life, history, or political affairs, and asked to prepare a thirty-minute report on it." A committee from the previous year's PI group "heard and rated the reports." After that the applicants were "divided into sections, put through a role-playing exercise, a series of leaderless discussions, and subjected to a certain amount of heckling. A weekend in the mountains followed, with the group divided into all possible combinations . . . for various jobs." The final test was "a peer-rating device." After all this, the "tests were correlated, together with the rating given to each applicant by the previous year's team, and [the] fourteen chosen for the new PI team were quickly revealed."[10]

Each successful applicant was expected to be articulate, quick-witted, well informed, a good team player, tough skinned, and well prepared for every situation. After the selection process was completed, those chosen had to learn about American history and culture, anticipate criticism and prepare a response, and practice sports and entertainments such as singing and dancing. Training for the trip "took the entire second semester—most Friday and Sunday evenings." In this phase, immersion in American culture began. "Each member of the team was given or took, a field in which he or she was to become as expert as possible—education, the social scene, history, economics, foreign affairs . . . [or] cultural background." Each was to write "a paper, and with it an outline which was given to each of the other members of the team." Sometimes two papers were assigned, "one to give the American point of view, the other of someone unfriendly to America. Periodic tests of material already covered pointed up . . . where his or her own weakness lay."[11]

Another important part of the training was "the extra-curricular training—at the close of each formal session there was an informal session over pizza or hamburgers where the acquaintance of each member of the group with the others was intensified." Jobs were given to each member. For instance, "two members of the team were dubbed 'cultural affairs officers,' and given responsibility for handling such singing, etc. as the group might be asked to do." In addition, each member "prepared and learned thoroughly a formal speech which could be expanded or cut and adapted, but which had a basic core covering what the individual wanted to say to Indian audiences." These speeches "were then correlated so that any four to seven of them could provide a whole well-knit program." In addition, "the group learned to sing together—patriotic, folk and popular songs." Singing, dancing, and proficiency in sports such as volleyball and baseball were important to Guenther. She wrote how the latter "can make more friends on occasion than even the best of speeches."[12] Sporting events between Indian and PI student groups became popular events.[13]

Funding PI was difficult. As it was a new program with no track record, individual donors and donating agencies proved scarce. The first team of PI students was funded by URC donors Paul Helms and P.G. Winnett, as well as the Episcopal Church and an anonymous gift of fifteen thousand dollars, later revealed to have been a personal gift from Winthrop Rockefeller, a friend of URC supporters Dore Schary and Robert Minckler. Some PI student travelers took extra jobs so they could earn enough money to contribute to the trip, something like two hundred dollars, in addition to the one hundred dollars for personal expenses. Despite the obstacles, most arrangements for the 1952 trip were in order before the PI group departed. Guenther reported that "the Indian government was setting up the schedule, the State Department had given approval, the University was cooperating." It remained only for the URC Board to "give its final sanction" and grant Guenther a two-month leave of absence, clearing the way for her and URC Presbyterian adviser Cecil Hoffman to lead the first PI group to India.[14]

Leaving for India

Taking advantage of the favorable publicity, Trans World Airlines (TWA) gave PI two free air tickets and served as the airline PI used for most of the trips.[15] As Project India gained increasing success and publicity, funding became somewhat more available but obtaining the approximately $25,000 to $30,000 needed each summer often remained a last-minute scramble, as major funding agencies such as the Ford Foundation and the US State Department varied their support from year to year. Returning PI students raised money as best they could for the following year's program. The URC also relied on grants from various local businesses, such as the Standard Vacuum Company and Standard Socony to help pay for the 1957 PI trip.[16]

Over the years the State Department became a major source of support as it recognized the benefits for American diplomacy. Invited to Washington, DC, in 1957, before leaving for India, the PI group met with Vice President Richard Nixon. After the meeting, the group went to the Indian Chancery and to the embassy, where they were introduced to the Indian ambassador, G. L. Mehta. Thereafter the State Department continued to provide briefings, sometimes by the office of the Secretary of State. The URC had to balance the need for independence with the need for funding and went to some lengths to avoid looking like a propaganda arm of the American government. When in

India, for instance, the PI group resisted hosting daily open houses for Indian students at the US Information Service (USIS) library.[17]

The State Department kept in steady contact with the PI program, not only through briefings prior to departure but through ongoing meetings in India. The department also scheduled PI appearances while the group traveled in India. Guenther herself sometimes took the initiative with the State Department. For instance, in 1957 she and some in the PI group asked USIS officials in New Delhi "very pointedly whether they considered the group valuable. We asked the question rather bluntly—'What difference does a bunch of college students make?'" She reported that the response was "very positive—they are not going to tip the scales one way or another decisively, but in . . . keeping relations between India and America friendly and cooperative, they have, and do, play an important role."[18]

Sometimes differences arose between the expectations and preferences of State Department officials and those of the PI students and Guenther. Officials tended to prefer what Guenther called "the road show" or the "pyramid" approach, whereby the PI students made presentations in front of as many Indian university students as possible. The presentations would include short speeches, answers to audience questions, and possibly a song or two. Guenther questioned "how valuable this sort of effort is—some of the Americans in official positions think that if only Indian students who almost never get to see Americans, can see a group of college students who are friendly, who make a good impression with their songs and honest answers to questions, all the good will result that can be expected." Even with audiences having little English comprehension, officials saw this type of program as effective. "One thing is certain, it takes a great deal out of the team in terms of energy and health." Guenther and at least some of the students favored settling down and "really becom[ing] part of the local scene." But American officials wanted to "cram into every day, every possible opportunity for Indians and Americans to meet." And "there were far more teas than were wise," thought Guenther, but she admitted that by the midway point of the trip, PI students had "a real sense of accomplishment."[19]

The amount of contact between Indian students and the PI groups was impressive. In 1957 the group visited 140 colleges and had contact with some sixty-five thousand Indian students during the nine weeks spent in India.[20] They "travelled for two months over 10,000 miles," PI student Lynn Phillips wrote, listing places they had visited: "Bombay, Ahmedabad, Nagpur, Lucknow, Delhi, Calcutta, Puri, Madras, and the cities of Kerala." She described a typical daily schedule: "9:00 A.M., spoke to a friendly student body of 3,000; 11:00 A.M., held an open discussion with a group of 100 students; 3:00, had the privilege of meeting the governor and learned about state administration; 4:00, spoke to a group of 500 and visited dormitories and common rooms; 8:00 attended a cultural evening given in our behalf."[21]

Needless to say, Guenther was alert to the educational benefits that awaited the students as they traveled in India: observing, meeting and interacting with the people of India, seeing the sights, eating the foods, traveling on the trains, and spending time with Indian students. They would see disease and extreme poverty on a level unfamiliar to them and the remnants of a caste system that, though officially abolished, still held powerful sway. Although English was widely spoken among the educated and among students at colleges and universities, India was a land of more than twenty major languages, thousands of different ethnic groups, and six major religions. All this would expose the American students to a scale of diversity and to social conditions beyond anything they had known at home. It would also expose them to a land that, in the course of gaining independence from Britain, became partitioned into two separate countries on the basis of religion: India as predominantly Hindu, and Pakistan as predominantly Muslim. The partition had separated families and led to violence and fleeing refugees. Periodic religious riots plagued India, and enmity between India and Pakistan remained an ongoing struggle.[22]

The partition and enmity was a reminder to the PI teams of how important it was to accept religious pluralism and the ideas of Evans and Foster, embodied in the founding principles of the URC: "that religious principles provide the most important foundations of all human society—moral, social, economic and political," that "an understanding of religious beliefs . . . are highly conducive to more perfect brotherhood between all people" and necessary for "promot[ing] goodwill and understanding between people of various religions and cultural backgrounds."[23] Similar ideas had inspired Guenther. The URC programs she implemented all embodied her assumptions that true religion leads to acceptance of other religions—strange and exotic as they may seem—and to treating their adherents with respect as fellow children of God. Like Foster and Evans, she believed that true religion results from experiencing service and cooperation with others. Project India seemed to present new opportunities for such service and cooperation.[24]

The panel format provided the basic framework for Project India. Following a format similar to the panel at home, the PI traveling teams gave brief talks to the audience and responded to audience questions. Preparing for the panel presentations required that PI participants become well-versed in their own respective religious, racial or ethnic identity and values, much as members of the Panel of Americans were doing at home. Like the Panel of Americans, PI panelists were Jewish, Catholic, and Protestant. In addition, there were panelist of African and Asian backgrounds. Some of the PI panelists were women; most of them were men. All of them took pride in being good Americans, and like the POA, they displayed attitudes of mutual fellowship and cooperation.

The different racial and ethnic groups on the PI panels, especially those of African American and Asian American background, surprised Indian students and led to many questions on racism. PI panelists did not deny the presence of racism and discrimination in American society, but they expressed hope that the very composition of the panels would offer a concrete and nuanced contrary view. Panelists pointed to programs like the URC Panel that were working to expand acceptance of diverse inclusion in American society. As at home, panelists in India wore neat Western dress and cultivated a good-hearted, light touch, using self-effacing humor as they thought appropriate.

When it began, Project India was a pioneering venture for students, although American religious missionaries, occasional scholars, and medical doctors had chosen India as a destination.[25] Despite the fact that the Experiment in International Living, the American Field Service, and other study abroad and cultural exchange programs were gaining popularity during the Cold War, there was no playbook for Project India when it began. The Peace Corps was nine years into the future, and the Fulbright Scholar Exchange Program, begun in 1946, had set up shop in India only recently, in 1950. All of these programs differed from Project India, a program in which small groups of American university students traveled to various towns and spent about a month in two of them. There they met Indian university students, spoke with them extensively, and when possible, worked with them side-by-side.[26]

Experiencing India

In efforts to befriend Indian university students, to bring back to the United States what they had learned from their travels, to share it with others at home, and to build bridges of mutual understanding between India and the United States, the PI students met and got to know as many Indian university students as possible. According to an early report, they encouraged them to ask all their questions and express all their fears and doubts about the United States, its people, values, and institutions. The PI students tried to answer the questions and allay the Indian students' doubts, all while learning firsthand about their problems, ambitions, and views about their own nation, which had so recently gained independence and set up democratic governance.[27]

The PI students also wanted to broaden typical American images of India as a land of "turbaned maharajas, elephants, yogi-practitioners and snakes" and "set in motion a continuing exchange of ideas and personnel . . . that there may be a real sense of unity and helpfulness between the two nations."[28] To do this, the PI students devised novel approaches. They not only addressed the Indian students at university assemblies but also, when possible, stayed at student hostels and adjacent guest houses and occasionally with nearby Indian families. PI students gathered with Indian students at coffee shops and tea rooms, even under a nearby Banyan tree when feasible, as well as arranging teas, parties, and open houses for Indian student leaders. By experimenting with off-campus venues and doing simple things like using a black cotton umbrella during the monsoon season, riding a bike, or traveling in trams and buses, the PI groups engaged in conversations with the local population. Many of them seemed comfortable talking to the PI students and asking them questions.[29]

On occasion, the PI travelers appeared as speakers at fraternal and service clubs like the Rotary in big cities such as Bombay and Calcutta. Guenther thought that the PI students "have no grandiose ideas about what they can do, but they honestly try to answer questions." She said, "They do not seek to make propaganda, but only friends—which gives them one superb advantage over . . . propagandists."[30] Like the Panel of Americans at home, the PI students projected a favorable image through honesty and humor.

Sometimes, PI teams met Indian students who were communists or otherwise hostile to the United States. With the Soviet Union, the Peoples' Republic of China and the United States all jockeying for advantage in India, it is not surprising that, as Americans, PI students sometimes found themselves in a sensitive position with no formal training in diplomacy. They relied upon their wits and good-natured, resilient, youthful student spirit. At times they had to stretch their imaginations to figure out what might appeal to their Indian peers and muster a friendly, informal attitude, reciting poems, conjuring up stories about life back on the UC campus, and displaying the UCLA banner they had brought along. They competed with Indian students at sports, performed square dances, and sang American camp and work songs. They seemed happy to interact with the audience members and to answer their questions, ranging from American dating patterns and educational systems to racial discrimination and sports.[31]

But, most impressive, they demonstrated their openness to Indian society, their respect for India as a fellow democracy, and their willingness to embrace India's culture when, for instance, they sang the Indian national anthem, "Jana Gana Mana," in Hindi. "All of them can sing quite well and some have picked up a few words to start a conversation in Bengali. PI student Joseph Colmenares knows how to say 'How are you?' or 'Thank you' in Bengali," according to an article in the Calcutta *Statesman*.[32]

In each town the process generally began with the PI team calling on the chancellor and vice chancellor of the university and the heads of the principal colleges, and then holding formal meetings with the Indian students. Usually, these meetings took place on campus, where each PI panelist spoke, "equipped for a very short talk on some aspect of student life in America . . . intended to stimulate and elicit questions." After these "'little speeches," the Indian students wrote down questions on subjects about American foreign policy, American history, family relations, religion, rock and roll, and the "Cowboy and Indian problem." "Why does the U.S. make arms available to Pakistan? Is divorce common? How can you call yourself a democracy of equal opportunities . . . yet practice discrimination?"[33]

After the formal part of the meeting, or what Guenther called "the road show," the PI panelists adjourned to one of the popular places, often off campus, where students gathered "to provide opportunity for small informal discussion . . . unsupervised by college administrators. These discussions continued as long as possible."[34] The sites of these informal discussions varied from one place to another. In Calcutta and Lucknow, it was the coffee house; in

Trivandrum, a Traveler's Bungalow near the main Training College; and in Hyderabad, the university faculty club. "Wherever possible, return visits were made to the college and those Indian students most interested were invited to further meetings at tea or dinner." Despite the many casual contacts, "every effort was made to find [Indian] student leaders . . . and offer them friendship on a more than casual, passing basis."[35]

The PI travelers were divided into two groups, which they called "batches." Each batch would have an adult leader, assisted by a student leader, and would stay together for much of the summer, remaining first at one site for about a month, and then for a month at a second one. This process was adopted so that the PI students could learn in depth about the local area and the local people, teach them about American society, and participate as fully as possible in the life of the community. In 1954, "one batch spent a month in Calcutta, and a month in the Hyderabad-Nagpur area; the second batch spent a month in Lucknow and a month in Travancore."[36] The batches would also unite for a short time at a major attraction such as the Taj Mahal in Agra or the Golden Temple in Amritsar.

Project India incorporated the basic armature of the Panel of Americans: small groups of American student presenters of different religious, racial, and ethnic backgrounds giving short speeches, answering audience questions, and overall demonstrating goodwill. PI also incorporated practical lessons from Uni-camp. Some of the PI travelers had been Uni-Camp counsellors. Like the counsellors, they were called upon to display stamina, patience, persistence, flexibility, and resourcefulness. As at Uni-Camp, they reached out to those who at first seemed unreachable, coped with unexpected health and weather crises, and overcame their own inhibitions so they could dig within themselves for the willingness to sing, dance, and tell stories as well as maintain patience and composure.[37] Other Uni-Camp practices adopted by PI included participating in cooperative construction projects, following up with service programs, and raising funds for future PI traveling groups.

Construction Projects

The idea of cooperative construction projects involving manual labor began during the first PI trip, in 1952, when one of the batches "hit on this quite accidentally . . . [having been] invited by the Rural Social Service League of Madras Christian College to help them build a school house at Tambaram village." The PI visitors thought that accepting the invitation would show their gratitude for the hospitality shown them.[38] Additionally, it would bring the PI program favorable publicity in the newspapers and on the radio.[39] It would demonstrate the high regard PI groups had for service and for the dignity of labor as well as their willingness to volunteer for physical exertion for the benefit of Indian society. Moreover, it would also counter communist and other views in India of Americans as entirely materialistic, unwilling to sully themselves on behalf of others and lacking spiritual values and idealism. This schoolhouse project was an idealistic one, and included the YMCA, the Student Rural Service League, the Young Communist League, as well as Project India students. "Many Indians . . . thought of America as a land of materialists, Cadillacs, low-cut dresses, cigarettes and champagne," as one of the PI students put it.[40] Having male and female PI students wielding hammers, picks, shovels, and other tools on construction projects would demonstrate that Americans of both genders, conscious of India's social needs, were willing to engage in physical labor to help them and present a contrast to the decadent images of Americans. They would present a contrast, as well, to gender customs regarding manual labor widely accepted by Indian university students.[41]

The schoolhouse at Tambaram village was to become the first of many construction projects. Perhaps owing to the remnants of the caste system, low pay, and the unpleasant nature of much manual labor, people of wealth and education in Indian society, including university students, had traditionally scorned such labor. But things were changing, and the PI spirit of cooperative work was in line with an increasing social consciousness then developing among Indian students. "We were particularly interested in noting signs of 'social consciousness' among the students, and signs of a positive and growing attitude toward helping others," wrote the PI students. At the time, programs for social service in India were being "set up" and "various social service leagues have been formed." This and other social service programs for Indian university students opened their eyes "to problems they never realized existed." Still, they were "hardly recognized by their college administrations or communities. It is often difficult for them [the Indian students] to obtain adequate information or funds for their projects." Despite the "growing" enthusiasm among this "enlightened minority, the greater part of the [Indian] students remain ignorant of and uninterested in [it]. The ... stimuli ... seem to be the Rotary clubs, missionary workers . . . and the Ford Foundation."[42] Nevertheless, the PI travelers hoped that their own willingness to work on social service projects would demonstrate their idealism and cooperative spirit, as well as increasing enthusiasm for serving social needs among Indian university students.

In 1953 one of the PI batches cooperated with students at a college in Calcutta to help build a school house under the direction of the West Bengal Commission on Refugee Rehabilitation. They also "spent some time working at a training center . . . in the Community Development Project at Annand, working with the students there on all the various projects, road building and village sanitation, etc. In 1954, all these activities were included," as possible cooperative work projects to be considered. A group of PI students cooperated with Indian students from about seven colleges to build a second refugee school in Calcutta. That year one of the batches spent two days in Travancore working on slum clearance with Indian students. All of these projects were organized under the sponsorship of charitable groups, educational institutions, or local government agencies, or all three. The projects that PI students participated in were a small part of larger projects to demonstrate American goodwill and a willingness of American young adults to work with their hands to help India. "Both in Travancore and in Hyderabad, from two to six days were spent in the community development projects and . . . [Indian] students were interested in what the government was doing and trying to lend a hand."[43]

Cooperative construction and service projects became a staple of the PI program.[44] Over the years the PI students undertook a variety of these projects, from helping to build schools, to constructing waterworks and dispensaries, to planting trees. PI travelers spent about four to six hours per day on these projects, typically in the morning, after which they continued their daily round of speaking engagements at Indian universities, followed by visits with the students at other more casual venues.[45] PI students found that cooperation with Indian students on work projects promoted goodwill as much as their speaking engagements.

The Bansdroni Project also promoted goodwill. "Built in the heart of a refugee village, [for refugees who had fled from Pakistan at the time of the partition in 1947], we worked, along with some of our new Indian student friends from 6:00 to 9:00 . . . every morning, carrying bricks, shoveling clay, mortaring walls, and pounding stones," described PI student Lynn Phillips, explaining how the whole village would watch them and some of the older village boys would "pitch in" and "even the children would be organized into brick passing lines . . . [singing] newly learned choruses of Ring Around the Rosy." Many in the village knew no English, yet by that "unspoken and universal language . . . everyone could understand what we were doing," she wrote.[46] The Bansdroni project gained favorable publicity in the press. A UCLA "team of three girls and four boys are extending help to local people to build a small dispensary," reported an article in the *Hindustan Standard* on August 14, 1957.[47] The article quoted PI student Joseph Colmenares: "We are helping to build this dispensary . . . because we desire to do something tangible, something meaningful to express our friendship to India and our need to help in any way we can."[48] Other construction projects included "school houses in Tambaram, Madras, [and] at Nandan-Nagar . . . a refugee colony outside Calcutta." As the article reported, "In 1955 the group [had] erected a tiny dispensary at Santoshpur under the guidance of the Commission on Refugee Rehabilitation."[49]

At the formal dedication of Bansdroni, newspapers reported that the California students were involved in its construction. They also mentioned how the dispensary would be used. "Welfare works—milk distribution, temporary medical dispensation, children's training and committee meetings—will be conducted in this building." The PI program donated money to the dispensary in addition to manual labor. Sri P. C. Sen, state minister of food, relief, and rehabilitation, cut the ribbon and dedicated Bansdroni in the presence of various Indian state officials, as well as American officials from the USIS. "I'm particularly impressed by the [PI] students' work, the criterion of which is not merely the money, but their fraternal love and interest in aiding the refugees. This is the basis for building the 'one world' we all seek," Sen commented.[50]

In Trivandrum, in the state of Kerala in southern India, the Communist Party had gained control in a recent election, and one of the 1957 PI batches had traveled there to work on a cooperative project. Working with students under a Communist government was a new experience for the PI travelers. One of them, James Beardsley, a political science major, commented that when he was in Kerala he saw "red flags for the first time in his life." A staff reporter at the *Statesman* remarked that although Beardsley had been in Kerala "a short while," he could talk about the politics there and his "mixed feelings."[51] Guenther confirmed this in her report that year, explaining that the PI students were "convinced that the success of the communist government in

Kerala had been a shocking blow to the Congress party, and that the religious people of the state were not ready to accept the status quo."[52]

In 1958 one batch of PI students built the first classroom for a Sree Colony school, near Calcutta. The site was then "little more than a 'bustee'" or slum area. "Almost all of its residents were refugees with little or no resources, and were . . . in the process of settling down and acclimatizing themselves to their new surroundings. They wanted a school for their children, and tried in every way they could to acquire one." "Four slim and sturdy young men and three women from Project India, on the lookout for a suitable work project" during their three week stay in Calcutta, took up work constructing a class room on the suggestion of the local education authority, recalled Anil Banerji, President of the Sree Colony Committee, as reported in a USIS news feature. "The local residents pooled what . . . they could spare," and the West Bengal Government donated one acre of land for the school." The PI students worked cooperatively with local Indian City College student volunteers and others. "They kept swinging their shovels until it was really dark," and a "bonfire was lit that night in their honor and the local youngsters had gathered round to converse with their new-found American friends." Before they left, "a 320 sq. ft. class-room took shape." Although they could not stay until the project was completed, the PI students did present "a black-board and foot-ball as their parting gifts to the new school."[53]

Three years later, in 1961, the school was "recognized as a High School," and in 1966, Bani Bhaban, as it was then called, "was further upgraded," with more classrooms. Plans were made for it "to be expanded further to include a vocational training school . . . to meet the increasing needs of the now prosperous Sree colony's enlarging community." S. Bhattacharyya, then headmaster of Bani Bhaban, recalled how it had all begun as a "tiny classroom that has been integrated into the main building and which still reminds the older residents such as Anil Banerji about those young American friends who spent three weeks working for us, with us and among us."[54]

Back Home in California

Teaching PI students to understand the different perspectives of the Indian students and how to explain them sympathetically to their fellow Americans was a major goal of the program.[55] During the 1950s, at the height of the Cold War, it was obvious that Indian students generally viewed communism more favorably than did the PI students. Indian students "admire greatly the material progress made in Russia or China; and while they recognize the loss of civil liberties in these lands, they do not place too much weight on it," observed a PI report from 1955. Another area of disagreement between Indian and American students related to whether Goa should become part of India, become independent, or remain under Portuguese control. Indian students tended to think that Goa should become part of India, and they saw Portuguese authority as a clear case of Western colonialism. The PI students tended to think that it was up to the people of Goa to decide for themselves. Thanks to their experiences in India, they could explain these different positions sympathetically, when they came back home.[56] Whatever the differences of opinion between Indian and PI students, their connection continued, as the latter raised funds for India when the PI students returned to California.

Each PI student "was committed to a year's work in speaking and interpreting what they had learned to the home community." They spoke to student groups and service clubs and charged a small fee for each talk. These funds were contributed to the following year's PI trip. Some groups started their own projects. Others participated in service projects begun by PI groups and in raising funds that were sent to India as gifts of money, or for books, magazines, or other needed items or equipment. The gifts sent in 1955 were for a motion picture projector and tape recorder given to the Social Service League in Trivandrum "for their work with slum children." Other gifts included funds for teachers to staff the schoolhouses built by the Refugee Commission in West Bengal and for a group of students in Calcutta to build a schoolhouse.[57]

In the fall of 1952, when the first group of PI students returned to the URC, two members of the group wrote a "To Whom It May Concern" letter explaining how the funds collected would be used. "The largest portion of the funds will be sent to Indian Colleges and Universities in the form of magazine subscriptions." Another portion would go toward care packages for food and milk to be sent to a child welfare center in Madras and other similar institutions. A third portion would go toward the purchase of equipment for a college psychology laboratory. The rest of the funds would go for "all services conducted by the Rural Service League, including the Child Welfare Center,

Cloth Weaving Center, Medical Service Center and Leper Work Center." In addition, funds would also be used to buy "kerosene lamps for the Adult Education Center in Mysore" and medical supplies for the Nagpada Neighborhood House in Bombay.[58]

Every gift and project from PI funds collected after the trip was documented, listing not only its name and description, but the background, why it was needed, and its overall justification.[59] One of the twenty projects of the 1952 returning PI students was to donate money to Mysore University Communal Hostel for purchasing dormitory furnishings such as chairs, tables, lights, as well as books, a medical unit, cooking facilities, blackboards and other visual aids, magazines, and periodicals. The justification for this project was to support the hostel as a way to bring the Mysore University students together and promote "democracy in action: the students of this hostel believe only through understanding of others can we learn to live together . . . In the same spirit of our University Religious Conference they are actively pursuing their . . . ideal."[60]

Another project was to help expand the Madras State Child Welfare Center in Tambaram Village to include family planning and birth control services as well as childcare and parent education. "At present they have two trained midwives who go out into the village, one examination room, [and] a wooden operating table. They want to add an additional room for instruction." They needed a projector, to show films on child and postnatal care, general health, sanitation, and first aid. They also needed graphs of bodily functions and magazines on parenting and health. The project justification stated that "this center is serving almost the entire village and is in demand yet restricted because of financial need."[61]

The 1952 PI students also kept detailed records of the funds collected for purchasing magazine and journal subscriptions. Much of it came from donations by UCLA campus sororities. Thirteen sororities contributed more than $480.00. A general fund on campus donated another $575.00. The Campus Community Chest Drive contributed another $166.00.[62] These funds went for subscriptions to about twenty different publications, which were sent to more than twenty colleges and universities in India, from medical colleges to agricultural colleges to teacher training colleges. The publications included, among others, *U.S. News and World Report, Scientific American, United Nations Bulletin, Annals of the American Academy of Political and Social Sciences,*

American Economic Review, American Medical Association Journal, American Journal of Pathology, Soil Science and Journal of Dairy Science.[63]

The various drives to raise funds and the projects they supported reinforced the bonds between the PI and Indian students. At times these bonds led to ideas for possible new projects. The 1957 PI group "came home much enthused about the idea of a reverse project," what was called Project Los Angeles, whereby "a team of Indian students . . . might come to the USA and specifically California, during . . . *their* summer holiday." They and the UCLA students would join together in a "workshop on student life," then visit other colleges in California, "ending with a visit to Washington, to match our visit to New Delhi," commented Adaline Guenther, explaining that at the time the idea was only "in the realm of enthusiastic conjecture."[64] It indicates, nevertheless, how excited the UCLA students were about Project India and their desire to reciprocate.

The Impact and Evaluation of Project India

The PI groups received positive notice from the State Department about how they gave hope and confidence to Indian youth about the United States. In a 1956 letter to California regent Edwin Pauley, Chester Bowles wrote, "Most students in Asia, and indeed through much of Europe, Africa and South America, are in a state of ferment. Under the impact of Western ideas of freedom and individual rights they have broken loose from their old family and religious patterns, only to find themselves at loose ends and unable to secure a sense of participation and belonging within a democratic framework. It is this restless frustration which has contributed to . . . many able young Communist leaders [who support] Moscow and Peking. I do not think it is too much to say that if a country like India ever ends up in the Communist orbit, it will not be because her people were hungry but because her young intellectuals were footloose, unattached, frustrated, and unable to develop a sense of security within free institutions."[65] Bowles was a Democratic politician, diplomat, and intellectual who served as ambassador to India from 1951 to 1953 and again from 1967 to 1969.

"On every campus in India . . . there is a nucleus of boys and girls who feel very friendly towards our country. Some of them have studied in our universities. . . . they are anxious to think well of the United States," Bowles continued. Yet the United States is "in conflict with their government. Our . . . foreign policy approaches . . . are no longer adequate to the world situation." They tend "further to create barriers and sow suspicion. Yet many young Asians cling to the belief that America must be what they always hoped and prayed it might be," Bowles continued, viewing Project India as a ray of hope for America's idealism abroad. "When a group of American students visits their campuses their hopes for the United States are vindicated. After the group is gone they proceed with a new confidence to continue the sense of friendship and understanding." He wrote, "My own experience has led me to feel strongly about the urgent need to continue this sort of thing indefinitely and perhaps to spread it to other universities."[66]

Guenther quoted the writing of a veteran Indian journalist: "Individually and collectively, these UCLA students have helped bring the younger generation in this country much closer to the U.S.A. And, as an Indian, I do believe that our students have a lot to learn from such student groups . . . Don't give us your money, but give us your spirit."[67] "The UCLA students, I have noted during the past six years have brought home to us the American spirit much more effectively than whole lots of political leaders. . . . It is my firm conviction that the UCLA students can match any other project sponsored or supported by USIS." So stated an Indian employee of the USIS, who described the impact of the [1957] PI group as "profound."[68]

"[Its] effectiveness was in part due to the boundless energy of the Californians who enlarged upon their full schedule wherever possible . . . [More essential] were the poise with which they addressed large audiences, their perspicacity in answering questions directed at vulnerable spots in American life and foreign policy, and the natural friendliness which . . . carried them easily across the cultural gap. . . . There is in fact no real substitute for the person-to-person contact so brilliantly executed by the UCLA group." So wrote Moses Hirschtritt, chief of the Educational Travel and Training Branch, International Educational Exchange Service of the State Department, to Adaline Guenther about the 1958 PI group, the last PI group that Guenther led.[69]

After Guenther retired, Project India carried on for another ten years under her successor Luke Fishburn, who became the URC associate secretary. Unlike Guenther, Fishburn traveled to India with the group only once, while others, some of them former PI students and URC leaders from UCLA, UC

Riverside, and Santa Barbara, filled in. Most of the PI trips remained success-ful under their leadership too, and the service projects of the returning PI students also continued.

In 1959 the PI groups participated in and cosponsored a model UN Secu-rity Council session with the United Nations Student Centre at Ruparel Col-lege in Bombay. PI student batch leader Tom Green presided over the session before an audience numbering some one thousand. The main subject was dis-armament, something of great interest to students in India. So exciting was the session that the speaker commented in his concluding thank you speech, "This model session surpasses anything done at the Security Council itself!" The event encouraged the local university to plan more such sessions in the future.[70]

That same year Winthrop Brown, the chargé d'affaires at the American em-bassy in New Delhi, took it upon himself to write to the chancellor of UCLA and the provosts at UC Riverside and UC Santa Barbara expressing his satis-faction with that year's PI group. Their dignity and modesty "made an abso-lutely first-class impression . . . upon everyone they have met and we can think of no better representatives of our country," he wrote, observing that "they have shown a deep interest in India and have made the Indian students . . . feel that the United States has a genuine interest in their problems and welfare." He continued, "There is an impression . . . in this country that Americans are materialistic, lax and easy going. The personal qualities of the . . . PI group and their attitudes toward family, work, church and community have done a great deal . . . to correct these misconceptions . . . to give Indians . . . a more balanced picture of the real America."[71]

John Lund, the first student leader of the 1952 PI group, wrote to Adaline Guenther in 1959. At the time he was deputy chief public affairs officer of the USIS in New Delhi, and one of several former PI students who later served in the American diplomatic service. The vice chancellor of Delhi University thought that the 1959 PI group, which had just visited the university, "was the best thing he had seen of American activities intended to promote better understanding." Lund related this observation in a letter to Guenther, adding that the vice chancellor had said that "for the first time he had seen a group of Indians and Americans mix freely and spontaneously in a spirit of good fellowship and understanding."[72]

The 1960 PI group was also highly praised. One Foreign Service dispatch of

1960 described how the PI groups had "maintained their reputation as student ambassadors of friendship and good will and once again proved to be one of the best means of contacting the college students in India. The effectiveness . . . has continued to grow with each passing year until today, Project India is practically a byword among many Indian college students." "By their inquiring and open minds and their frank expression of views, the UCLA'ers are able to create a feeling of camaraderie with their Indian counterparts." Commenting as well on the follow-up service project in California by the 1959 PI student group when they returned to UCLA, the dispatch states, "The highlight of this year's project was the presentation to Indian universities . . . of some 30,000 books."[73]

A 1960 dispatch from Madras noted how the PI students handled questions "very well, giving witty, brief and pointed answers."[74] "Not every visitor to India is received by Indians with Arti, vermilion, coconuts and other paraphernalia of worship which are associated with gods and goddesses. One such visitor . . . was President Eisenhower. . . . Project India 1960 too were accorded a similar reception," reported the dispatch from Bombay.[75]

In 1961, nine years after Project India had begun, the administration of President John F. Kennedy started the Peace Corps. Like Project India, the Peace Corps sought to teach Americans about the wider world while projecting American soft power. What PI had pioneered on a shoestring in a spirit of improvisation and experimentation, the Peace Corps launched as a government program, better funded and on a scale more extensive and elaborate than anything attempted by PI. No doubt similar program ideas were generally in the air at the time, a time of American confidence, world leadership, and prosperity. PI and the Peace Corps had certain things in common, of which the most notable was the animating goal: that American civilians, often young adults, could act as successful emissaries of the United States by traveling to what were then called "third world countries" not only to work on projects to help modernize their economies and improve their standard of living but also to demonstrate American idealism and good will.

The last trip of Project India was in 1969. One contributing factor to ending the program was the lack of funding from the State Department, which by then had looked to the Peace Corps rather than Project India to spread international goodwill. Moreover, by the late 1960s, American foreign policy had come to favor Pakistan over India as conflicts between President Nixon and Indian prime minister Indira Gandhi arose. Yet another factor was the changing outlook of American students.

Changing Times

During the 1960s, the Cold War became less compelling to many American university students as they became increasingly focused on other issues. Travel to India as American goodwill ambassadors no longer held the attraction it once had. The attention of students at the URC became focused on issues such as civil rights, protests against the war in Vietnam, university complicity in the war, resistance to the military draft, distrust of authority, and support for women's rights. There was passionate engagement on those issues, which sparked a range of student responses, from peaceful demonstrations and civil disobedience to the occupation of buildings on campuses. Some American campuses during the 1960s and thereafter experienced violence, at times carried out by authority figures in American society.

As university students became increasingly critical of the United States and less confident about the direction of American society, it is small wonder that service in India exerted less attraction upon those who came to believe that much urgent work needed to be done at home. Perhaps too, those American students came to wonder whether Indian culture had more to teach American culture than the converse. Opposition in India to the Vietnam War more closely reflected the outlook of many American university students than did that of the American government. Perhaps the loss of student confidence in American democratic institutions made it difficult for them to export American values. Paternalistic attitudes toward India gave way to admiration for Gandhi, Indian religions, philosophy, yoga, drugs, incense, and music. Indian influences surged in US society, as was illustrated for instance, by the popularity of the Beatles, who were strongly influenced by Ravi Shankar and gave concerts with him. Luke Fishburn undoubtedly grasped these changes. Little surprise that 1969 was the last year for Project India. That year he offered his resignation as associate director of the URC. It was to take effect in May of 1970, the same month that the Ohio National Guard shot thirteen unarmed, peaceful student antiwar demonstrators and bystanders, four of whom died.

Before the conflicts and mistrust between university students and those in authority had grown so intense, Luke Fishburn had achieved some successes as URC associate secretary. In addition to continuing Project India, he had worked on maintaining close relationships with the URC religious advisers, then called campus chaplains, opened up the UCLA campus to more URC religious activities, developed another Uni-Camp site called College Camp and a camp session that integrated sighted and unsighted campers. He had sent a team of students to travel in Ceylon, and another student team to Pakistan, both at the request of the State Department. He had instituted Project Discovery, a program of small discussion groups that looked at, exchanged, and evaluated ideas on racial issues. Other achievements were cosponsoring the first California conference on religion in the state university system and another conference with the URC and the Los Angeles Junior Colleges. Among his most significant achievements was bringing world renowned spiritual leaders to speak on campus. Among them were Rabbi Abraham Heschel, Bishop James Pike, Rev. Martin Luther King Jr., and Indian Prime Minister Jawaharlal Nehru, all of whom, among other things, were controversial, activist supporters of racial and social equality.[76]

Short of resources and responding to campus unrest and community criticism, the URC Board of Directors hired no new secretary to replace Fishburn. As a result, for the first time, the URC lacked a leader specifically dedicated to inspiring students and providing overall direction for student-centered programs. Instead, the board of directors reorganized the URC, giving leadership responsibilities to an administrative cabinet that consisted of several board members headed up first by Charles W. Doak (Presbyterian) followed by Luther Olman (Lutheran), both of them URC religious staff of long standing.[77]

Written in 1970, the plan for reorganization of the URC emphasized more formalized community outreach, academic study of different religions rather than direct social action, and forming a more academic and administrative relationship with UCLA.[78] "The current 'unrest' on campus . . . has opened us . . . to the realization that we have not formed the kinds of support systems into the community that we need to effectively interpret our work and that of the university," stated the 1970 plan.[79] The URC goal of building religion by inspiring and directing grassroots student activism now took a back seat to building community and alumni support. Community members and alumni were seen as a more reliable and practical constituency than current university students.

To strengthen its formal ties in the community the URC joined forces with established organizations by developing outreach relationships: recruiting for Operation Crossroads Africa, providing office space for the United Farm Workers of America, and helping the elderly in need by providing home de-livered meals through Meals on Wheels.[80] The URC also developed extension programs to offer educational opportunities for congregation members in the community "if possible on church property."[81] The 1970 plan organized activ-ities such as Social Issues Conferences, and Campus Tomorrow, which spon-sored campus tours conducted by URC students for disadvantaged youngsters to encourage them to start early in preparing for university. Worthy as those activities were, they lacked the hands-on, intense, steady, ongoing contact of projects from earlier days. Evans, Guenther, and Fishburn thought that proj-ects like the student board, the trialogue, the Panel of Americans, and Project India were necessary to build student bonds of fellowship, akin to religion. All of them were gone. Even Uni-Camp, the most popular of the URC projects, was taken over by UCLA in the late 1970s.[82]

Although the URC continued, it never returned to its former glory. It never regained the popularity and stature that it had enjoyed in years past. Once the URC set aside generating dynamic, new student social projects, secular as well as religious, and relied primarily upon academic study of religious teachings, without translating those teachings into direct student experience, student en-gagement at the URC declined. Perhaps it was no longer realistic for the URC to channel youthful student activism into institutions that were considered acceptable to the adult community. Perhaps the generational conflicts of the day were too great. Perhaps university students thought that they personally—not an institution—must initiate and direct their own activist projects.

In succeeding decades, the religious, racial, ethnic, and gender diversity of American society has continued to grow, and an increasing number of Amer-icans have found the secular sphere more hospitable and more effective for accomplishing positive social change than institutional religion.[83] Church-centered religion continues to lose ground, especially among liberal support-ers of inclusion. Yet even as the URC has faded away as a dynamic institution, its values of inclusion and diversity have remained.

URC Legacies

It must leave the whole lump and must make itself the servant of the whole.
—*E. C. Moore,* I Helped Make a University, *1952*

It was a Sunday in July several years ago. My husband and I were having brunch at a Denny's in Westwood near the UCLA campus when a group of about ten young men and women walked in together. They seemed excited about something. They appeared to be university students. Was it a class, a study group? Were they rehearsing for a play? The camaraderie among them was palpable. We could sense it even from our table. On our way out we went over to ask them who they were. They told us they were UCLA students just returning from a session of Uni-Camp where they had been counsellors. One of them was wearing a Uni-Camp tee shirt. Their enthusiasm was infectious.

What a surprise that a program begun by the University Religious Conference in 1935 could still engage university students when American life has dramatically changed since then. Today Americans are of many faiths, not just three dominant ones. Secular and spiritual activities have increasingly replaced institutional religion. A multitude of ethnic cultures abound. Racial and gender categories are more fluid, and the concept of race itself is widely recognized as a constructed artifact.

The URC programs from decades ago sought to stir young adults at universities to embrace those who differed from them, and to experience a mutual sense of fellowship. The hope was that these few students would become a light to the many, and that their legacies would continue in American life.

Historians look at the past for many reasons. Years ago, as a young teacher at a new college in a suburb of Kansas City, far different from New York City where I grew up, and facing large numbers of students having little interest in historical issues that seemed distant and abstract, I asked myself the same question that I imagine many new history teachers ask: How can I get my students excited about studying the past? I wondered if investigating the history of their nearby surroundings would spark their interest. Could they research historical sources like local newspapers, census tracts, cemetery records, and land titles, or conduct personal interviews? Possibly researching such sources would interest my students more than sources further afield.

In the course of finding out about the history of the Kansas City area myself, I encountered several suburban women active in the Kansas City community. They mentioned an organization called the Panel of American Women (PAW), explaining that it gave presentation panels by women of diverse religious, racial, and ethnic backgrounds who told personal stories about inclusion and exclusion in American life. It began in Kansas City in the 1950s, they told me, and had since formed numerous chapters nationally. I decided to attend one of its presentations. The program moved and inspired me. The women panelists gave American diversity a human dimension. As a historian, I wanted to learn more about the origins of the Panel of American Women. This book is the result of my research.

I found out that the Panel of American Women was based on the Panel of Americans, begun by the URC some fifteen years earlier, in 1942. Similar in tone to the original URC student panelists, the PAW adult panelists were not experts. In this case they were just everyday housewives without careers who told their own stories about the need for healing racial, religious, and ethnic divisions in American society. They were just ordinary people who could reach the public because they *were* ordinary, unlike the prominent leaders who typically addressed these issues. These women panelists accepted what they took to be American values of fairness, decency, and respect, and their stories told of their concern that those values were not being upheld. At times their stories were humorous, like one told by a Jewish panelist who said, "If you think all Jews are rich and clever, you should meet my husband's relatives." Other stories were sad. An African American panelist told a story about her small son "gazing at a carnival merry-go-round and asking 'where's the back? I want to ride.'"[1]

Like the URC student panelists, the PAW panelists also demonstrated diversity and fellowship in action. One difference between the two panels was that most of the members of PAW were mothers, and they would express their common fear that their children would continue to face prejudice. Their role as mothers further created bonds among them that transcended their religious, racial, and ethnic differences.[2]

Omaha, Nebraska, was one of the cities that PAW visited, even before it become an official organization. There PAW presented a panel at a luncheon held at a synagogue in 1961. Attending that luncheon was Lois Mark Stalvey, a middle-class, white, Lutheran, suburban housewife and mother of three children. Invited by her one Jewish friend at the time, Stalvey attended the luncheon only reluctantly, expecting to hear platitudes. Instead, it changed her life.[3] When Stalvey heard the panelists talk about how they felt alone and rejected, she began to think about her own childhood in Milwaukee, how as a child of divorced parents, the only child in her school whose parents were divorced, she had also felt that she was different and didn't belong.

Stalvey identified with the panelists and their stories of isolation and rejection. Her identification with them began a process of self-awareness and disappointment with the hypocrisy that she came to see in the society around her. She became aware too of how her own search for security and conformity had marked her adult years and how it had led her unknowingly to contribute to the racial, religious, and ethnic divisions in American society. These realizations ultimately forced her to give up the homogeneity and comfort of her Omaha suburban life and move with her family to Philadelphia, where she served as a panelist, lived in a racially mixed neighborhood, and sent her children to a school with mostly African American children. She wrote a book about her experiences, *The Education of a WASP*.

Shirley Chisholm was the first African American woman elected to the US Congress, serving from 1968 to 1983. Chisholm wrote the introduction to Stalvey's book. In it Chisholm argues that "the equality, the justice and the freedom of . . . the American dream . . . cannot be realized" because "those values often intentionally exclude other than white Americans." Stalvey's book demonstrates this "lie of democracy" "not with statistics . . . but with personal insight and pain," Chisholm wrote. To recognize this lie, "within each of us," is the beginning of progress, she argues.[4] This recognition was part of Stalvey's education, an education that began with hearing the PAW presentation and continued through her own hard-won experience.

The panel format was flexible and could be applied to a variety of situations. Panelists of many different types could participate. Consider the panel that Joan Meyersieck Rosen helped assemble in Marin County, California, in the 1980s. Rosen had worked with Marian Hargrave in New York City building panels nationally in the 1950s. She and her husband, Marty Rosen, both of them UCLA graduates and former participants in the URC, were volunteers with an adult community panel program in Marin County in the 1980s and 1990s. At times Marty Rosen would serve as a Jewish panelist or a moderator. The Marin County panels resembled URC student panels in having as members those of different religious, racial, and ethnic backgrounds. In the late 1980s and 1990s with the AIDS crisis taking hold, however, sexual orientation was added to panel presentations. Marin County put together panels that included a gay male panelist from central California. In his talk he said that he didn't grow up gay, "I didn't know you could." For years he didn't acknowledge his sexuality. "I fought it every step of the way." Engaged to marry a woman, he finally admitted, "I looked in the mirror and said to myself, 'it's over, goddamit, I'm gay,' realizing that what I thought of myself was more important than what you thought about me."[5]

Joan and Marty Rosen carried the URC values of inclusion into the wider world. The URC could look back on its many graduates who shaped American culture to become more inclusive. Some of them went into religious work. Most of them did not. Tom Bradley, the son of Texas sharecroppers, became the longest serving mayor of Los Angeles, and its first African American mayor. As mayor he formed durable coalitions with liberal Jewish and Latino Angelinos. Gilbert Harrison, a veteran of the Second World War, and the son of Russian Jewish immigrants, a scholar, and a public intellectual, became the publisher and editor of the *New Republic*, a weekly periodical he devoted to progressive causes during his tenure, from the 1950s until 1975. Harrison was an advocate for civil rights and an opponent of the Vietnam War. John Krumm became an academic and a bishop in the Episcopal Church. In the 1980s, he became an outspoken supporter of gay rights and of humanitarian assistance for victims of AIDS. Steven Muller, who arrived in America as a child refugee from Nazi Germany, served as a long-term president of Johns Hopkins University, where he advanced the natural sciences not only at the university but also at the Johns Hopkins Hospital.

Today new generations of Americans are working to realize a vision of diversity and acceptance that includes racial justice, same sex marriage, gender fluidity, and LGBTQ rights, as well as environmental justice and inclusion of many types. They are a leavening in the face of nativism, racism, misogyny, homophobia, intolerance, and division. Those who carry on this legacy of inclusion, on campus and in communities, secular or religious, probably never heard of the University Religious Conference or O. D. Foster, Thomas Evans, or Adaline Guenther. Would the latter themselves have recognized such causes as connected to the goals they pursued when they, as Protestants, worked to broaden acceptance of Catholics and Jews? But expanding inclusion is the work of many hands, and who knows where it will lead? The work of expanding inclusion is like the mustard seed, the least of all seeds that, when grown, becomes the greatest of the herbs, a tree large enough to become a sheltering place, perhaps for all.

Notes

A Word on the Sources

Owing to the time since I began the research for this book, the sources may have been reorganizd, digitalized, or transferred to other libraries or locations. Duplicates of some of them may also be found in other collections. I have cited the sources according to their form and whereabouts when I researched them.

Introduction: Education and Pluralism

1. The term "interfaith" as used here refers to cooperation among those belonging to two or more different faiths. Each component faith maintains its own separate identity, as well as liturgy, ritual, and belief system. It does not imply one faith combined with other faiths. In the 1920s, the term often used for this cooperation was "good will." It changed to "interfaith" thereafter. Muriel Clark Ezell, speech at annual URC student banquet, May 13, 1953, URC Files.

2. At its core, the ISR sought to have Protestant, Jewish, and Catholic clergy faculty on campus to teach credit courses on religion. The URC taught no credit courses on religion but housed off-campus offices for representatives (often student pastors) of many faiths who ministered to the university students. In addition to representatives of the Catholic, Jewish, and numerous Protestant denominations, the URC at times hosted representatives of the Greek Orthodox Church and the Church of Latter-Day Saints, as well as the YMCA. The book therefore refers to the URC as a multifaith institution.

3. Nancy Gentile Ford, *Americans All! Foreign-Born Soldiers in World War I* (College Station: Texas A&M University Press, 2001). This book discusses foreign language and other programs to train foreign-born recruits for service in the war; Jennifer D. Keene, *World War I: The American Soldier Experience* (Lincoln: University of Nebraska Press, 2006), 110–113. Keene describes some of the problems experienced by the foreign-born recruits and how the military attempted to deal with them; Christopher M. Sterba, *Good Americans: Italian and Jewish Immigrants during the First World War* (Oxford: Oxford University Press, 2003). This book discusses the impact of the war and progressive wartime programs on these two groups of recruits.

4. Ronit Stahl, *Enlisting Faith: How the Military Chaplaincy Shaped Religion and State in Modern America* (Cambridge, MA: Harvard University Press, 2017), 15–43.

5. K. Healan Gaston, *Imagining Judeo-Christian America: Religion, Secularism, and the Redefinition of Democracy* (Chicago: University of Chicago Press, 2019), 32–43, 46, 47, 59, 71.

6. Lila Corwin Berman, *Speaking of Jews: Rabbis, Intellectuals and the Creation of an American Public Identity* (Berkeley: University of California Press, 2009); Jessica Cooperman, *Making Judaism Safe for America: World War I and the Origins of Religious Pluralism* (New York: New York University, 2018); Daniel Greene, *The Jewish Origins of Cultural Pluralism: The Menorah Association and American Diversity* (Bloomington: Indiana University Press, 2011); Michael C. Steiner, *Horace M. Kallen in the Heartland: The Midwestern Roots of American Pluralism* (Lawrence: University Press of Kansas, 2020).

7. David Mislin, *Saving Faith: Making Religious Pluralism an American Value at the Dawn of the Secular Age* (Ithaca: Cornell University Press, 2015), 149–154.

8. Kevin M. Schultz, *Tri-Faith America: How Catholics and Jews Held Postwar America to Its Progressive Promise* (Oxford: Oxford University Press, 2011), 15–49.

9. "Rites Set for Miss Guenther," *Los Angeles Times*, October 11, 1975.

10. Diana Selig, *Americans All: The Cultural Gifts Movement* (Cambridge, MA: Harvard University Press, 2008).

11. Jeffrey E. Mirel, *Patriotic Pluralism: Americanization Education and European Immigrants* (Cambridge, MA: Harvard University Press, 2010), 156.

12. Christopher Capozzola, *Uncle Sam Wants You: World War I and the Making of the Modern Citizen* (Oxford: Oxford University Press, 2008), 173–214.

13. Clarence P. Shedd, *The Church Follows Its Students* (New Haven: Yale University Press, 1938), 84. Shedd agreed with Foster on this issue.

14. M. Willard Lampe, "Statement about O. D. Foster," given to the annual meeting of the board, ISR, May 9, 1966, Ora Delmer Foster Papers, MsCo211 SCUI (hereafter Foster Papers).

15. Julie A. Reuben, *The Making of the Modern University* (Chicago: University of Chicago Press, 1996), 58–60.

16. Reuben, *Making of the Modern University*, 55.

17. Reuben, *Making of the Modern University*, 136–137.

18. Foster, *Quest of Religious Reality*, 66, undated, box 7, Foster Papers.

Reuben, *Making of the Modern University*, 95–101; Douglas Sloan, *Faith and Knowledge: Mainline Protestantism and American Higher Education* (Louisville: Westminster John Knox Press, 1994), 2–8.

19. Foster, *Quest of Religious Reality*, 66–67.

20. Foster, *Memoir*, "The Depth of Jewish Scholarship," undated, chap. 9, 11–13, Foster Papers, box 23.

21. Foster, "Depth of Jewish Scholarship," chap. 9, 11–13. It is noteworthy that Foster uses the word "race" to describe Hirsch's Jewish religion. This was typical in the

nineteenth century and the prewar era, and it wasn't unusual for Jewish organizations themselves to use the word "Hebrew," for instance "Hebrew Union College."

22. Foster, "Depth of Jewish Scholarship," chap. 9, 11–13; Tobias Brinkman, *Sundays at Sinai: A Jewish Congregation in Chicago* (Chicago: University of Chicago Press, 2012), 132, 133. Brinkman states that Emil Hirsch saw a Jewish overlap with liberal Protestants, that they had common roots, and that the ethical teachings of Jesus "betrayed his Jewish origins."

23. Robert T. Handy, *A Christian America: Protestant Hopes and Historical Realities*, 2nd ed. (Oxford: Oxford University Press, 1984), 142.

24. Bennie Kraut, "A Wary Collaboration: Jews, Catholics and the Protestant Goodwill Movement," in *Between the Times: The Travail of the Protestant Establishment in America, 1900–1960*, ed. William R. Hutchinson (Cambridge, UK: Cambridge University Press, 1990), 193–230.

25. Ray H. Abrams, *Preachers Present Arms: The Role of American Churches and Clergy in World War One and Two with Some Observations on the War in Vietnam* (Eugene, OR: Wipf and Stock, 2009), 53–63.

26. William Adams Brown, a Presbyterian and secretary of the General War-Time Commission, who taught at Union Theological Seminary; William Herbert Perry Faunce, president of Brown University; and Harry Emerson Fosdick, author and faculty member at Union Theological Seminary, were three of the prominent Protestant leaders and thinkers who supported Protestant ecumenism during the war. John F. Piper Jr., *The American Churches in World War I* (Athens: Ohio University Press, 1985), 62–65.

27. Some examples of scholarly interest in Clinchy, Kallen, and Herberg include Gaston, *Imagining Judeo-Christian America*, 125–184 (Gaston discusses all three); Greene, *The Menorah Association and American Diversity* (Greene discusses Horace Kallen and Kallen's connection to the Menorah Society); Selig, *Americans All*, 84–88, 113–145, 260 (Selig looks at Kallen and Clinchy in the context of the Cultural Gifts Movement); and Steiner, *Horace M. Kallen in the Heartland* (Steiner devotes most of his book to Kallen and the influence of the Midwest on his legacy of affirmative cultural pluralism). Some attention has been paid to the ISR, but not to the URC. See for example Marcus Bach, *Of Faith and Learning* (Iowa City: University of Iowa Press, 1952); Bill R. Douglas, "Making Iowa Safe for Differences: Barnstorming Iowa on Behalf of Religious Tolerance," *Annals of Iowa*, 75, no. 3 (2016): 234–259; D. G. Hart, *The University Gets Religion: Religious Studies in American Higher Education* (Baltimore: Johns Hopkins University Press, 1999), 84; Stow Persons, *The University of Iowa in the Twentieth Century: An Institutional History* (Iowa City: University of Iowa Press, 1990), 41–44, 85–93, 188–89; Sloan, *Faith and Knowledge*, 25. In 1978 Methodist advisor to the URC Herman Beimfohr put together a spiral-bound chronology of the URC to mark its fiftieth anniversary, under the title *History of the University Religious Conference at*

U.C.L.A. Various books on Jewish attempts to expand pluralism have looked at Jewish efforts to gain acceptance in America. See Berman, *Speaking of Jews*, 132–136 (Berman discusses Morris Kertzer from a Jewish perspective. He was the director of the Hillel at the University of Iowa from 1939 to the early 1940s and taught a class there alongside Protestant and Catholic faculty members); Mislin, *Saving Faith*, 109–118, 150–155 (Mislin briefly discusses Foster and the AAR but says nothing on the URC). Books that mention CIS in the context of the First World War are few. See Jonathan Ebel, *Faith in the Fight: Religion and the American Soldier in the Great War* (Princeton: Princeton University Press, 2010), 171–172 (Ebel doesn't discuss Foster but does see the war as a Christian event); William Pencak, *For God and Country: The American Legion, 1919–1941* (Boston: Northeastern University Press, 1989), 149–50, 52–53, 55 (Pencak discusses CIS within the context of the American Legion and mentions O. D. Foster only in passing); William Hutchinson, *The Modernist Impulse in American Protestantism* (Durham, NC: Duke University Press, 1992), 226–256 (Hutchinson discusses the impact of the First World War primarily on the self-questioning and loss of esteem of those liberal Protestants who supported it and does not discuss American interfaith solidarity); William R. Hutchinson, *Religious Pluralism in America: The Contentious History of a Founding Ideal* (New Haven: Yale University Press, 2003), 137–138, 196–197 (Although Hutchinson views the First World War as a historical watershed of visible, collaborative efforts among Jews, Catholics, and Protestants, he sees it as a transient event); Schultz, *Tri-Faith America*, 15–49 (Schultz concentrates on Clinchy and the NCCJ and briefly mentions the First World War).

28. Robert Hine and Shirley Hine, "Adaline Guenther," in Beimfohr, *History of the University Religious Conference at U.C.L.A.*, 21.

29. David P. Setran, *The College "Y": Student Religion in the Era of Secularization* (New York: Palgrave McMillan, 2007), 214–215.

30. Virginia Lieson Brereton, "United and Slighted: Women as Subordinated Insiders," in *Between the Times: The Travail of the Protestant Establishment in America, 1900–1960*, ed. William R. Hutchison (Cambridge: Cambridge University Press, 1989), 140–164. Adaline Guenther was one of the few women at the time in a religious leadership position, although secular women social reformers like Jane Addams and Lillian Wald likely provided models for her. Like them, Guenther never married and devoted herself to institution building.

31. Selig, *Americans All*, 8, 21–22.

32. Allen F. Davis, Mary Lynn McCree, eds., *Eighty Years at Hull-House* (Chicago: Quadrangle Books, 1969).

33. David A. Hollinger, *Protestants Abroad: How Missionaries Tried to Change the World but Changed America* (Princeton: Princeton University Press, 2017), 10–11. Hollinger discusses how wide and long-lasting the divide between the evangelical family of Protestants and ecumenical Protestants was in the twentieth century. See also

Henry May, *The End of American Innocence* (Chicago: Quadrangle Paperbacks, 1964), 368–369. May discusses the fundamentalist opposition to the First World War and attributes it to various factors; ultimately he argues that one major factor was that the war demonstrated to fundamentalists the failure of modern liberal culture embraced by liberal, ecumenical Protestants.

34. Yaakov Ariel, "Jewish Liberalism through Comparative Lenses: Reform Judaism and Its Liberal Christian Counterparts," in *American Religious Liberalism*, ed. Leigh E. Schmidt and Sally M. Promey (Bloomington: University of Indiana Press, 2012), 270–290.

35. David Hollinger, *Science, Jews, and Secular Culture: Studies in Mid-Twentieth Century American Intellectual History* (Princeton: Princeton University Press, 1996), 18–22. Hollinger contrasts Catholics and Jews in American society of the 1930s, arguing that although Catholics were more numerous than Jews, Protestants perceived the former as less of a threat to Protestant hegemony than Jews who, lacking a single official hierarchy, were harder to lump together. Some Jews tended to be secular, skeptical, cosmopolitan free thinkers who traversed American culture and refused to become parochial in their outlook. Often, they were not religious at all and were stubbornly uninterested in converting to Christianity. They attended American public schools and universities when possible, and often excelled. No less than Protestants, some Jews thought of themselves as children of the Enlightenment, who dealt with big, seminal ideas and considered questions in universal terms, thus invading a terrain that elite Protestants had assumed was their own. See Jerome Karabel, *The Chosen: The Hidden History of Admission and Exclusion at Harvard, Yale and Princeton* (Boston: Houghton Mifflin, 2005), 98–99. Walter Lippmann, who attended Harvard, was one example of this type of secular, cosmopolitan Jew.

36. Kraut, "Wary Collaboration," 193–230.

37. Philip Gleason, *Speaking of Diversity: Language and Ethnicity in Twentieth Century America* (Baltimore: Johns Hopkins University Press, 1992), 282; idem, *Contending with Modernity: Catholic Higher Education in the Twentieth Century* (New York: Oxford University Press, 1995), 62, 124.

38. Tracy Fessenden, *Culture and Redemption: Religion, the Secular, and American Literature* (Princeton: Princeton University Press, 2007), 185–188.

39. May, *End of American Innocence*, 370–385.

40. Mislin, *Saving Faith*, 134–135, 147.

41. Cara Lea Burnidge, *A Peaceful Conquest: Woodrow Wilson, Religion, and the New World Order* (Chicago: University of Chicago Press, 2016), 106–125.

42. David Kennedy, *Over Here: The First World War and American Society* (Oxford: Oxford University Press, 2004), 383.

43. John H. Holmes, quoted by Wilson G. Cole, "The Church and the Returning Soldiers," *Methodist Review* 102 (1919): 257–258, cited by Ferenc Morton Szasz, *The*

Divided Mind of Protestant America: 1880–1930 (Tuscaloosa: University of Alabama Press, 1982), 88.

44. E. C. Moore, "Religious Education and the War," in *What the War Teaches about Education, and Other Papers and Addresses*, ed. E. C. Moore (New York: Macmillan, 1919), 209–211.

45. Christine A. Ogren, *The American State Normal School: "An Instrument of Great Good"* (New York: Palgrave Macmillan, 2005), 203–207. A national trend of converting Normal Schools to teachers' colleges and universities was underway during the period from the early twentieth century to the postwar years.

46. George M. Marsden, "The Soul of the American University: An Historical Overview," in *The Secularization of the Academy*, ed. Bradley J. Longfield and George M. Marsden (New York: Oxford University Press, 1992), 22; Gaston, *Imaging Judeo-Christian America*, 36–42.

47. Harry Levy, speech at annual URC student banquet, May 13, 1953, URC Files.

Chapter 1. Religious Cooperation in Wartime

1. Jennifer D. Keene, *World War I, the American Soldier Experience* (Lincoln: University of Nebraska Press, 2006), 106.

2. John F. Piper Jr., *The American Churches in World War I* (Athens: Ohio University Press,1987), 24–31.

3. Robert T. Handy, *Undermined Establishment: Church-State Relations in America 1880–1920* (Princeton: Princeton University Press, 1991), 179–180; Jessica Cooperman, *Making Judaism Safe for America: World War I and the Origins of Religious Pluralism* (New York: New York University Press, 2018), 36–44.

4. Nancy Gentile Ford, *Americans All! Foreign-Born Soldiers in World War I* (College Station: Texas A&M University Press, 2001), 11–14, 67–87; Jennifer D. Keene, *Doughboys, the Great War, and the Remaking of America* (Baltimore: Johns Hopkins University Press, 2001), 20–21. Keene discusses the middle ground the military occupied in Americanizing the immigrant trainees and letting them retain some of their cultural traditions.

5. Ronit Y. Stahl, *Enlisting Faith: How the Military Chaplaincy Shaped Religion and State in Modern America* (Cambridge, MA: Harvard University Press, 2017), 4–5, 7–8, 10, 15–17, 28–29. Although this framework was broad enough to include the three religions then prominent in the American military, it nonetheless combined divergent religious groups and entirely omitted others. Those omitted, or combined with unfamiliar others, included adherents of Native American faiths, Buddhists, Hindus, Mormons, and Muslims.

6. Cooperman, *Making Judaism Safe for America*, 18–34.

7. Matthew Frye Jacobson, *Whiteness of a Different Color: European Immigrants*

and the Alchemy of Race (Cambridge, MA: Harvard University Press, 1998), 62–67, 93. Jacobson looks at various markers of racial hierarchies outside the military.

8. Keene, *World War I*, 101–105; Chad L. Williams, *Torchbearers of Democracy: African American Soldiers in the World War I Era* (Chapel Hill: University of North Carolina Press, 2010), 108–112, 190–191, 202–205, 246–260.

9. George B. Dolliver, "Custer Frosts Y Revival Plan," *Detroit Free Press*, February 20, 1918.

10. Dolliver, "Custer Frosts Y Revival Plan."

11. Foster, *Memoir*, "Camp Custer," chap. 10, 8, part 2, World War I, undated, box 23, Ora Delmer Foster Papers, MsCo211 SCUI (hereafter Foster Papers).

12. Foster, "Camp Custer."

13. Foster, "Camp Custer," chap. 8, 9.

14. Foster, "Camp Custer." Foster distributed the cards to the recruits, as he was instructed.

15. Foster, "Camp Custer," chap. 10, 10–11.

16. Foster, "Camp Custer," 9.

17. *Camp Custer Bulletin* 1, no. 11, November 15, 1917, 1, part 2, World War I, undated, box 23, Foster Papers. Rabbi Edgar Drachman and James C. Sanford of the KofC were probably the men Foster encountered at Custer.

18. Foster, "Camp Custer," chap. 10, 7–8.

19. *Camp Custer Bulletin* 1, no. 11, November 15, 1917, 1, part 2.

20. Foster, "Camp Custer," chap. 10, 22–23. There was no official military record of the religious census of each unit.

21. "Reports of the Comrades in Service Clubs," part 2, World War I, undated, box 23, Foster Papers.

22. Verne Edwin Burnett, ed., "The White Comrade," *Trench & Camp, Camp Custer*, part 2, World War I, undated, box 23, Foster Papers.

23. Burnett, "White Comrade."

24. Burnett, "White Comrade."

25. Foster, "Camp Custer," chap. 10, 23.

26. George Dolliver, "'Forget Sects,' Is Custer Plea," *Detroit Free Press*, February 25, 1918, part 2, World War I, undated, box 23, Foster Papers.

27. Frank C. Parker, "Custer Y Aide 'Fired,' Is Charge," *Detroit Free Press*, March 5, 1918, 1, 3, part 2, World War I, undated, box 23, Foster Papers.

28. Parker, "Custer Y Aide 'Fired,' Is Charge."

29. Dolliver, "Custer Frosts Y Revival Plan."

30. Foster, "Camp Custer," chap. 10, 18; Clarence Barbour, letter to Foster, March 4, 1918. Both in part 2, World War I, undated, box 23, Foster Papers.

31. Parker "Custer Y Aide 'Fired,' Is Charge."

32. Foster, "Camp Custer," chap. 10, 30–31; "Dr Foster Is Given a Message for

Pershing," *Trench and Camp*, vol. 1, March 7, 1918, 1–2, part 2, World War I, undated, box 23, Foster Papers.

33. Foster, "Camp Custer," chap. 10, 22, 30.

34. Foster, "Camp Custer," chap. 10, 19, 30; *Trench and Camp*, March 7, 1918, part 2, World War I, undated, box 23, Foster Papers.

35. Foster, "Camp Custer," chap. 10, 23.

36. Foster, "Report of Executive Secretary, Survey of Comrades in Service," carbon typescript," 1, March 4, 1919, part II, World War I, box 23, Foster Papers.

37. Foster, "Camp Custer," chap. 10, 22.

38. Foster, "Report of Executive Secretary, Survey of Comrades in Service," 2.

39. Foster, *Memoir*, "American Expeditionary Forces," 41–42, part 2, World War I, box 23, Foster Papers.

40. Foster, "American Expeditionary Forces," 42–43; Stahl, *Enlisting Faith*, 17, 18. Stahl notes the merging of religion and the military during the First World War, as exemplified in a professional, tri-faith chaplaincy that carried rank becoming an integral part of the military.

41. Foster, "American Expeditionary Forces," 41. Unlike Carter and Brockman, King was a wartime appointment to the YMCA.

42. Foster, "American Expeditionary Forces," 55 (Foster's caps); Henry Churchill King, letter to O. D. Foster, October 28, 1918, Foster Papers.

43. The dues assessment of the YMCA was 40 percent of the CIS budget. See part 2, World War I, box 23, Foster Papers; and see R. H. Mc Kelver, Business Manager of the YMCA Religious Work Department, to O. D. Foster, March 4, 1919. Mc Kelver sent Foster an itemized list of YMCA payments to CIS. E. C. Carter letter to Foster, April 7, 1919. Carter objected to what he thought were needless expenditures and wanted to withdraw YMCA support.

44. Foster never worked for the Y again after the war and was fired from his position at the Y College in Chicago while on a leave of absence during the conflict. Foster to the Comrades in Service Continuation Committee, undated, part 2, World War I, box 23, Foster Papers, miscellaneous.

45. Foster, "American Expeditionary Forces," 46–47.

46. Foster, "American Expeditionary Forces," 45–46.

47. Foster, "American Expeditionary Forces," 47.

48. Donald Smythe, *Guerilla Warrior: The Early Life of John J. Pershing* (New York: Charles Scribner's Sons, 1973), 178. Brent first baptized Pershing's children, and soon thereafter, baptized Pershing himself, in 1910.

49. Foster, "American Expeditionary Forces," 42–43.

50. Once CIS was established as an autonomous organization, the Red Cross joined CIS for a short time before dropping out. It is unclear who paid the Red Cross 40 percent assessment once the organization left. While the assessment of the YMCA

remained at 40 percent of the budget of the Comrades, the assessments for the others were far lower: the KofC at 15 percent, the Salvation Army at 3 percent, and the JWB at 2 percent. Each assessment was to be based on the size of the group's membership. Part 2, World War I, box 23, Foster Papers.

51. "The Articles of Agreement," Comrades in Service, January 1919, 1, part 2, World War I, box 23, Foster Papers.

52. Foster, Memoir, "Comrades in Service at Work," chap. 15, 11, part 2, World War I, box 23, Foster Papers.

53. "Articles of Agreement."

54. Foster, "Report of Executive Secretary," 4–7.

55. Foster, "Report of Executive Secretary," 4–7.

56. One later example of interfaith touring teams was sponsored by the NCCJ in the 1930s.

57. Herbert Atkinson Jump, "Comrade," George Alexander Kohut, "Our Creed," mimeographed typescripts, part 2, World War I, box 23, Foster Papers.

58. O. D. Foster, "The Name," Comrades in Service, January 25, 1919, vol. 1, no. 2, 3, part 2, World War I, box 23, Foster Papers.

59. Comrades in Service, January 25, 1919, 1, no. 2, 3.

60. Comrades in Service, January 25, 1919.

61. Foster, "The Name."

62. CIS postcard, Comrades in Service, January 25, 1919.

63. Foster, "Report by Executive Secretary"; "Survey of Comrades in Service Movement," March 4, 1919, 10, part 2, World War I, box 23, Foster Papers.

64. Foster, "American Expeditionary Forces," 66; "Comrades in Service Is Started at Big Meeting," New York Herald (Paris), January 19, 1919. General Pershing was not present at either event, but he did send his greeting. Both citations in part 2, World War I, box 23, Foster Papers.

65. "Comrades in Service Is Started at Big Meeting"; "Big Initial Meeting of Comrades in Service Has America's President as Guest of Honor," Comrades in Service, January 25, 1919, 1–2.

66. "President Wilson's OK," Comrades in Service, March 8, 1919, 1 (quotes from letter of Wilson to Brent, January 20, 1919), part 2, World War I, box 23, Foster Papers.

67. "Comrades in Service Is Started at Big Meeting."

68. E. C. Carter, speech, typescript, "Comrades in Service Dinner at Hotel Lutetia, Paris," March 14, 1919, part 2, World War I, box 23, Foster Papers.

69. Chaplain Edwin E. Lee speech, quoted in "Big Initial Meeting of Comrades in Service Has America's President as Guest of Honor."

70. E. C. Carter, speech quoted in "Comrades in Service Is Started at Big Meeting."

71. Hyman Enelow, speech quoted in "Comrades in Service Is Started at Big Meeting."

72. Stephen Wise speech, quoted in "Comrades in Service Is Started at Big Meeting."

73. Charles H. Brent speech, quoted in "Comrades in Service Is Started at Big Meeting."

74. "Distinguished Guests Grace Comrades in Service Dinner," *Comrades in Service*, vol. 1, no. 6, March 29, 1919, 1–2, part 2, World War I, box 23, Foster Papers.

75. Charles H. Brent, speech, typescript, "Comrades in Service Dinner at Hotel Lutetia, Paris," March 14, 1919, 1, part 2, World War I, box 23, Foster Papers.

76. Brent, speech, "Comrades in Service Dinner at Hotel Lutetia, Paris."

77. Edward Hearn, speech, typescript, "Comrades in Service Dinner at Hotel Lutetia, Paris," 10–14.

78. S. H. Carroll, speech, typescript, "Comrades in Service Dinner at Hotel Lutetia, Paris," 15–18.

79. E. C. Carter, speech, typescript, "Comrades in Service Dinner at Hotel Lutetia, Paris," 20.

80. Avery Andrews, speech, typescript, "Comrades in Service Dinner at Hotel Lutetia, Paris," 10–14.

81. Edwin F. Lee, speech, typescript, "Comrades in Service Dinner at Hotel Lutetia, Paris," 26–33.

82. Harry Cutler, speech, typescript, "Comrades in Service Dinner at Hotel Lutetia, Paris," 1.

83. Cutler, speech, "Comrades in Service Dinner at Hotel Lutetia, Paris," 4.

84. Cutler, speech, "Comrades in Service Dinner at Hotel Lutetia, Paris," 6–7.

85. Cutler, speech, "Comrades in Service Dinner at Hotel Lutetia, Paris," 6–8.

86. Cutler, speech, "Comrades in Service Dinner at Hotel Lutetia, Paris," 8–9.

87. Brent, speech, "Comrades in Service Dinner at Hotel Lutetia, Paris," 26.

88. Williams, *Torchbearers of Democracy*, 63–72. Williams discusses the profound disillusionment of African Americans related to the denial of respect and rights of citizenship, despite their war service.

89. Carter, speech, "Comrades in Service Dinner at Hotel Lutetia, Paris," 20. O. D. Foster also mentioned the "white man's burden" in an article he wrote for the Comrades' biweekly newspaper: "Comradeship in Reconstruction," *Comrades in Service*, vol. 1, no. 6, March 29, 1919, p. 2, part 2, World War I, box 23, Foster Papers.

90. Avery Andrews, speech, typescript, "Comrades in Service Dinner at Hotel Lutetia, Paris," 24–25.

91. "Education Program Brings Out Comradeship," *Comrades in Service*, vol. 1, no. 6, March 29, 1919, 5, part 2, World War I, box 23, Foster Papers. The article describes how the Comrades education program was teaching the Black soldier "to write his own name" and "was one of a class of illiterates" [which was] "improving the time before their departure for the home land in acquiring the rudiments of an education."

92. "Give Minstrel Show," *Comrades in Service*, vol. 1, no. 9, May 17, 1919, 4, part 2, World War I, box 23, Foster Papers.

93. "Comrades Program Wins Hearty Approval at Bases One and Two," *Comrades in Service*, vol. 1, no. 4, February 22, 1919, 1, part 2, World War I, box 23, Foster Papers.

94. Keene, *World War I*, 114–115.

95. Brent, speech, "Comrades in Service Dinner at Hotel Lutetia, Paris," 8.

96. Cutler, speech, "Comrades in Service Dinner at Hotel Lutetia, Paris," 8.

97. Keene, *World War I*, 115–120, and Jonathan H. Ebell, *Faith in the Fight: Religion and the American Soldier in the Great War* (Princeton: Princeton University Press, 2010), 137–144. Both Keene and Ebell agree that despite the vital and demanding military work of women in the First World War, the Victorian image of women still generally prevailed.

98. "The Comrades in Service Platform," *Comrades in Service*, vol. 1, no. 6, March 29, 1919, 2, part 2, World War I, box 23, Foster Papers.

99. "Purposes Organization and Operation of the Comrades in Service Movement," *Comrades in Service*, January 1919, 2–4, part 2, World War I, box 23, Foster Papers.

100. O. D. Foster, "Report by Executive Secretary," 11–12, 16.

101. Edwin Lee, CIS, Report of the Central Council for the Regular Meeting, April 8, 1919, typescript, 2, part 2, World War I, box 23, Foster Papers.

102. William Pencak, *For God and Country: The American Legion, 1919–1941* (Boston: Northeastern University Press, 1989), 49–62.

103. "Relationship with American Legion Definitely Determined," *Comrades in Service*, vol. 1, no. 7, Paris, April 19, 1919, 1, part 2, World War I, box 23, Foster Papers.

104. Charles H. Brent, "Cooperation of Comrades in Service Accorded to New American Legion," *Comrades in Service*, vol. 1, no. 6, March 29, 1919, 4; Charles H. Brent, "Report of Bishop Brent on Relations with American Legion," April 8, 1919, part 2, World War I, box 23, Foster Papers.

105. Brent, "Report of Bishop Brent; "Relationship with American Legion Definitely Determined."

106. Brent, "Report of Bishop Brent"; "Relationship with American Legion Definitely Determined."

107. O. D. Foster, typescript of Minutes of the Continuation Committee of the Comrades in Service Movement, undated, 1–4, part 2, World War I, box 23, Foster Papers. The Comrades did form an interfaith continuation committee of individuals that functioned for a time after the troops came home. It studied the possibility of cultivating a relationship with Community Services Incorporated, considered a kindred organization and a past member of the CTCA. Another possibility considered was continuing the Comrades in the regular Army and possibly the Navy. A third idea was to have CIS continue to keep up contact with the American Legion. Despite these efforts, no substantive results followed.

108. Brent, "Cooperation of Comrades in Service Accorded to New American Legion."

109. Charles H. Brent, "Report of Bishop Brent on Relations with American Legion," typescript, undated, part 2, World War I, box 23, Foster Papers.

110. Foster, *Memoir*, "Post War Hopes of the Comrades in Service," chap. 16, 2–4, part 2, World War I, box 23, Foster Papers.

111. Foster, "Post War Hopes of the Comrades in Service," 2–7.

112. Foster, "Post War Hopes of the Comrades in Service," 2–7.

113. Foster, "Post War Hopes of the Comrades in Service," 4–5. Foster retyped Pershing's letter to him, dated June 13, 1919, and included it in the *Memoir*. Pershing's letter appeared in the *Chicago Tribune*, June 18, 1919. Part of the money that Pershing awarded to Foster for CIS was set up for a continuation committee chaired by Brent to promote the ideals of the Comrades among veterans in the military establishment. Foster later used part of the money for a "character building" organizations during the Second World War.

114. Foster, "Post War Hopes of the Comrades in Service," 7.

115. Foster, "Post War Hopes of the Comrades in Service," 8.

Chapter 2. Religious Cooperation at State Universities

1. Clarence Prouty Shedd, *The Church Follows Its Students* (New Haven: Yale University Press, 1938), 29.

2. Douglas Sloan, *Faith and Knowledge: Mainline Protestantism and American Higher Education* (Louisville, KY: Westminster John Knox Press, 1994), 24–26. These attempts included engaging student pastors, establishing religious foundations, and implementing Bible classes, among others.

3. Wilson G. Cole, "The Church and the Returning Soldiers," *Methodist Review* 102 (1919): 257–58, cited by Morton Szaz, *The Divided Mind of Protestant America, 1880–1930* (Tuscaloosa: University of Alabama Press, 1982), 87.

4. Shedd, *Church Follows Its Students*, 84.

5. Joseph W. Cochran, "Preparation for Leadership," *Religious Education* 5 (1911): 123.

6. Shedd, *Church Follows Its Students*, 72–75.

7. Foster, *Memoir*, "Developing Inter-Protestant Programs," AAR (with documentation), undated, box 25, Ora Delmer Foster Papers, MsCo211 SCUI (hereafter Foster Papers).

8. Philip Gleason, *Contending with Modernity: Catholic Higher Education in the Twentieth Century* (New York: Oxford University Press, 1995), 143–145.

9. John Whitney Evans, *The Newman Movement: Roman Catholics in American Higher Education, 1883–1971* (Notre Dame, IN: University of Notre Dame Press, 1980), 27–32; Gleason, *Contending with Modernity*, 143–145. Gleason discusses the controversy

between Catholics who supported and those who opposed Newman work in the post–First World War era. See also Shedd, *Church Follows Its Students*, 55–62.

10. Daniel Greene, *Jewish Origins of Cultural Pluralism: The Menorah Association and American Diversity* (Bloomington: Indiana University Press, 2011), 58–62.

11. Foster, *Memoir*, "Developing Interfaith Programs," chap. 19, pp. 3–4, AAR, undated, box 25, Foster Papers.

12. Foster, "Developing Interfaith Programs," chap. 19, p. 4.

13. Foster, "Developing Interfaith Programs," 2, 4. In a letter he wrote to O'Hara on September 27, 1923, Foster refers back to a recent speech he had given in Oregon about how efforts to strengthen religion at the university needed to address the needs of Jewish and Catholic students, as well as Protestant ones. In that letter he invited O'Hara to join the AAR, then in the process of formation.

14. Timothy Michael Dolan, *Some Seed Fell on Good Ground: The Life of Edwin V. O'Hara* (Washington, DC: Catholic University Press, 1992), 35–57, 83–87.

15. Foster, *Memoir*, "The American Association on Religion," 2, AAR, undated, box 25, Foster Papers.

16. Foster, "American Association on Religion," 2–3.

17. Foster, "American Association on Religion," 3–4.

18. Foster, "American Association on Religion," 6–11, letter of Austin Dowling to O. D. Foster, September 17, 1923.

19. Jessica Cooperman, *Making Judaism Safe for America: World War I and the Origins of Religious Pluralism* (New York: New York University Press, 2018), 102, 152. Although Cooperman talks specifically about training Jewish military men to display masculine values, her description of those value, embodies a generally accepted idea of masculinity at the time.

20. Foster, "American Association on Religion," 3–8.

21. Foster, "American Association on Religion," 5.

22. Foster, "American Association on Religion," 5.

23. Foster, "American Association on Religion," 8.

24. Foster, *Memoir*, "The University Council of Church Boards of Education," 24, AAR, undated, box 25, Foster Papers.

25. Foster, "American Association on Religion," 9.

26. Foster, "American Association on Religion," 11.

27. Foster, "American Association on Religion," 12–15.

28. Foster, "American Association on Religion," 15.

29. Foster, "American Association on Religion," 17.

30. A major principle of the AAR was that it should consist of equal number of Protestants, Catholics, and Jews. The early members of each of the caucuses were as follows: Catholic caucus: John G. Agar, prominent corporate lawyer; Parker T. Moon, professor of international law at Columbia University; Edwin V. O'Hara, then a priest whom

Foster had met when speaking at the University of Oregon; and James H. Ryan, from the NCWC. The Jewish caucus included Cyrus Adler, president of the Jewish Theological Seminary and one of the founders of the Jewish Welfare Board; conservative rabbi, scholar, and educator Jacob Kohn, previously associated with the Jewish Theological Seminary; David Philipson, reform rabbi of Ben Israel Congregation in Cincinnati, an author, educator, social reformer, speaker, public figure active in the American Council of Rabbis, a member of the board at Hebrew Union College and chairman of the Commission on Jewish Education; and Abram Simon, the Reform rabbi of the Washington Hebrew Congregation in Washington, DC, president of the Central Council of American Rabbis and an old friend of Ryan who described him as "a scholar, tactful gentleman, and cooperator." Members of the Protestant caucus included Foster; Charles Brent, formerly chief of chaplains in the First World War and an Episcopal bishop; and Matthew Willard Lampe, a Presbyterian student leader and member of the CCBE. They were joined by Livingston Farrand, a physician active in public health, and president of Cornell University. Brent was to choose the fourth. He chose John W. Suter Jr., a member of the Religious Education National Council of the Protestant Episcopal Church. The university/at large caucus included university administrators and public figures. The early members of this group comprised Protestant John H. Finley, who knew Foster from the war. He was a Presbyterian, an associate editor of the *New York Times*, formerly a professor of politics at Princeton University, president of Knox College in Illinois, and president of the City College of New York. He was also formerly the president of the Commission of Education in New York State and a good friend of Catholic archbishop Patrick J. Hayes of New York City. Hayes had served as a member of the National Catholic War Council during the First World War and would become a cardinal in 1924. Finley was able to recruit Adolph Ochs, owner of the *New York Times*, as a Jewish member of the university/at large caucus. Walter A. Jessup, the president of the University of Iowa and a Protestant, was another member. Distinguished Catholic lawyer and Assistant US Attorney General Francis Patrick Garvan, the dean of Fordham University School of Law and a trustee of the Catholic University of America, was the fourth member of the university/at large caucus.

31. Foster, "Schools of Religion at State Universities," paper read at Annual Conference of Church Workers at State Universities, January 11, 1922. The School of Religion at the University of Missouri did offer credit and had two denominations cooperating; the University of Kansas and Ohio State University had interdenominational facilities and planned to offer credit in the future; but none were tri-faith.

32. Pamphlet, *American Association on Religion and Colleges*, 1927. Retyped in Foster, *Memoir,* "Developing Interfaith Programs," 20–21.

33. "Minutes of the General Committee on Religious Instruction in Colleges and Universities, Statement of Principles," January 17, 1924, retyped in Foster, "Developing Interfaith Programs."

34. James H. Ryan, "Meeting of Subcommittee," November 13, 1925, AAR, undated, box 25, Foster Papers; David Mislin, *Saving Faith: Making Religious Pluralism an American Value at the Dawn of the Secular Age* (Ithaca: Cornell University Press, 2015), 151.

35. Lila Corwin Berman, *Speaking of Jews: Rabbis, Intellectuals, and the Creation of an American Public Identity* (Berkeley: University of California Press, 2009), 1–7.

36. Mislin, *Saving Faith*, 63–64.

37. "Minutes of the General Committee on Religious Instruction in Colleges and Universities, Statement of Principles," January 17, 1924.

38. "Minutes of the General Committee on Religious Instruction."

39. "Minutes of the General Committee on Religious Instruction."

40. "Minutes of the General Committee on Religious Instruction."

41. "Minutes of the General Committee on Religious Instruction."

42. "Minutes of the General Committee on Religious Instruction."

43. "Minutes of the General Committee on Religious Instruction."

44. "Minutes of the General Committee on Religious Instruction."

45. "Minutes of the General Committee on Religious Instruction."

46. "Minutes of the General Committee on Religious Instruction."

47. Letter of Archbishop Dowling to O. D. Foster, November 21, 1926, AAR, undated, box 25, Foster Papers.

48. Letter of James H. Ryan to O. D. Foster, November 26, 1926, AAR, undated, box 25, Foster Papers.

49. Foster, "Schools of Religion at State Universities."

50. George M. Marsden, *The Soul of the American University: From Protestant Establishment to Established Nonbelief* (New York: Oxford University Press, 1994), 335–336, 140–146.

51. Foster, "Iowa City Conference," *University of Iowa Extension Bulletin*, no. 188, January 15, 1928, 8–10. Joseph C. Todd, member of the Disciples of Christ and dean of the new school of religion at Indiana University came up with the idea together with Foster. Marcus Bach, *Faith and Learning* (Iowa City: University of Iowa Press, 1952), 145.

52. "Excerpts from Letters from Those Who Attended the Conference on Religious Education at the State University of Iowa," January 2, 3, and 4, 1928, *University of Iowa Extension Bulletin* no. 188, January 15, 1928, AAR, undated, box 25, Foster Papers.

53. Stow Persons, *The University of Iowa in the Twentieth Century: An Institutional History* (Iowa City: University of Iowa Press, 1990), 88, 116. Chairing the committee was George F. Kay, dean of the College of Liberal Arts. Others prominent on the committee included Edwin Starbuck, professor of philosophy and psychology, George W. Stewart, professor of physics, and Carl E. Seashore, professor of psychology, pioneer in education, music, and creative arts research and dean of the Graduate School. Others on the committee included F. C. Ensign, M. A. Shaw, C. A. Phillips. Starbuck and

Seashore were antagonists, and in 1927 Walter Jessup, president of the University of Iowa, divided the Department of Philosophy and Psychology into two departments, Philosophy, chaired by Starbuck and Psychology, chaired by Seashore. None of the members of the university committee were Jewish or Catholic.

54. Letter, Charles Foster Kent to Walter Jessup, December 12, 1922, AAR, undated, box 25, Foster Papers. In the letter Kent responded to a letter from Jessup inviting him to meet with the university committee. Kent wrote that he was involved with a project at the University of Michigan and could not meet with the committee until later. Kent never was interviewed by the university committee at Iowa. He died in 1925, and the Michigan project was discontinued.

55. "The Origin, Organization and Aims of the Council," *Bulletin of the Council of Schools of Religion*, 5, AAR, undated, box 25, Foster Papers.

56. "Origin, Organization and Aims of the Council," 5–7, 10–11.

57. Foster, *Memoir*, "Origin of State Interfaith Religion of School of Religion State University of Iowa," 8–9, AAR, undated, box 25, Foster Papers.

58. Foster, "Origin of State Interfaith," 9–10. Foster states that he helped Kent with the itinerary of his lecture tour and implies that Kent used information Foster had gathered.

59. Foster, "Origin of State Interfaith Religion of School of Religion State University of Iowa," 19.

60. Foster, "Origin of State Interfaith Religion of School of Religion State University of Iowa," 17–19.

61. Foster, "Origin of State Interfaith," 18.

62. Foster, "Origin of State Interfaith," 10.

63. Letter of George F. Kay to Foster, October 2, 1923, typescript, 20–21; "Origin of State Interfaith," 18. Both in AAR, undated, box 25, Foster Papers.

64. Foster, letter of R. H. Fitzgerald to Foster, November 14, 1923, in typescript, "Origin of State Interfaith," 38. When Foster met Fitzgerald during his visit to the Iowa campus, he converted him to "the church point of view."

65. Foster, "Origin of State Interfaith," 22. Kent had some good friends in banking and on Wall Street; one of them was banker Frank Vanderlip.

66. Foster, "Origin of State Interfaith," 24.

67. Letter of Edwin Starbuck to Foster, December 1, 1923, typescript, in "Origin of State Interfaith," 38.

68. Letter of Edwin Starbuck to Foster, December 6, 1923, typescript, in "Origin of State Interfaith," 40–41.

69. Letter of Foster to Starbuck, December 9, 1923, typescript, in "Origin of State Interfaith," 41–42.

70. Letter of Foster to Kay, December 13, 1923, typescript, in "Origin of State Interfaith," 43–44.

71. Foster, "Origin of State Interfaith," 44.

72. G. F. Kay, committee chair, letter to President W. A. Jessup (signed by all six committee members), April 12, 2024, typescript and commentary by Foster, in "Origin of State Interfaith," 56–57.

73. Foster, *Memoir*, typescript, "The Establishment of a School of Religion in the University of Iowa," April 15, 1924, AAR, undated, box 25, Foster Papers, 58–60.

74. Foster, "Establishment of a School of Religion," 58–59.

75. Foster, "Establishment of a School of Religion," 58–59.

76. Typescript, letter of G. F Kay to Foster May 1, 1924, in "Origin of State Interfaith," 62.

77. Foster, "Memo to University Committee of the CCBE and the AAR," May 21, 1924, AAR, undated, box 25, Foster Papers.

78. To be prudent, publicity about the plan had been delayed until granted official approval. Typescript letter of G. F. Kay to O. D. Foster, June 19, 1924, in " Establishment of a School of Religion," 66.

79. Kay to Foster, June 19, 1924, 66.

80. Typescript, letter of Foster to G. F. Kay, July 1, 1924, in "Establishment of a School of Religion," 66–67.

81. Typescript, letter of Foster to G. F. Kay, July 18, 1924, in "Establishment of a School of Religion," 70.

82. Foster, "Establishment of a School of Religion," 6.

83. Foster, "Establishment of a School of Religion," 6–7.

84. Foster, *Memoir*, commentary, typescript, following letter of Foster to Kay, July 18, 1924, 69–71.

85. Foster to Kay, July 18, 1924. This document describes the difficulties with several religious leaders who opposed the interfaith cooperation central to the Iowa project and dragged their feet in supporting it. They included some of the pastors in Iowa City. Foster turned to university leaders Rufus Fitzgerald, members of the Iowa university committee, and members of the AAR to intervene and obtain the support (financial and otherwise) of those who objected to the project.

86. Foster, commentary following letter to Kay, July 18, 1924, 73–75, 93–94.

87. Foster, commentary following letter to Kay, July 18, 1924, 69–71.

88. Typescript of M. A. Shaw, "Minutes of Meeting of Electors at the Old Capitol, Called by Walter Jessup, President of University of Iowa, May 12, 1925," in Foster, "Establishment of a School of Religion," 92–93.

89. Foster, "Establishment of a School of Religion," 94.

90. Marcus Bach, *Of Faith and Learning: The Story of Religion at the State University of Iowa* (Iowa City: University of Iowa, 1952), 101–102; Foster, "Establishment of a School of Religion," 94.

91. Sometimes there was no clerical Catholic faculty member in the ISR, and turnover of clerical faculty members was frequent.

92. Typescript of letter of Foster to Rufus Fitzgerald, November 23, 1924, 87, in Foster "Establishment of a School of Religion," 87–88.

93. Foster, "Establishment of a School of Religion," 94.

94. William Shannahan and Thomas Farrell were the two Catholics on the Board; Eugene Mannheimer and E. P. Adler were the two Jewish members. The Protestants comprised about 74 percent of board membership, Catholic members about 13 percent, and Jewish members about 13 percent. In the 1920 census, these numbers corresponded roughly to the respective proportions of the Protestant and Catholic population in Iowa and overrepresented the Jewish percentage. The representation of the three groups thus was roughly in line with the demographic percentages, although it was not weighted.

95. The University of Iowa paid the salaries of the academic faculty of the Iowa School; the various religious groups of Iowa paid the salary of the clerical faculty member of their religion, but for the director's salary had to come through fundraising. Foster, with the help of the AAR, turned to the Rockefeller Foundation, which awarded a grant of $35,000 dollars payable over three years. The grant was later renewed. Eventually the University of Iowa came to pay the director's salary from its own resources.

96. M. Willard Lampe, *An Autobiographical Sketch of the School of Religion*, appendix, 1957, in Foster, "Establishment of a School of Religion in the University of Iowa," 23.

97. "Origin of University Religious Conference of the University of California at Los Angeles," Project no. 2, AAR, undated, box 27, Foster Papers.

98. Foster, Memo on study of religious programs of the New University of California, Southern Branch, at Westwood, in "Origin of University Religious Conference."

99. Foster, memo on study of religious programs, 7–8, 10.

100. E. C. Moore to Miss Addams and Miss Starr, May 9, 1930, box 6, folder 1930, E. C. Moore Papers 124, University Archives, University of California at Los Angeles.

101. Foster, memo on study of religious programs, 8.

102. E. C. Moore, "Contemporary Ideals in Education," in *What the War Teaches about Education, and Other Papers and Addresses* (New York: Macmillan, 1919), 1–25.

103. Foster, "University Religious Conference at the University of California at Los Angeles," in "Origin of University Religious Conference," 8.

104. Foster, "University Religious Conference," 14.

105. Foster, "University Religious Conference," 14.

106. Edgar F. Magnin, letter to O. D. Foster, May 6, 1927, in "Origin of University Religious Conference."

107. Walter Morris Hart, vice president of the University of California, Berkeley, letter to O. D. Foster, May 30, 1927, and letter of Foster to Walter Morris Hart, June 6, 1927, stating that the California Board of Regents has denied permission for a "Hall of

Religion" to be built on the campus of the University of California at Los Angeles, in "Origin of University Religious Conference."

108. Foster, "University Religious Conference," 10.

109. Foster, "University Religious Conference," 10.

110. Foster, "University Religious Conference," 11, 11a, 11b.

111. Gordon S. Watkins, chair, university committee, letter to E. C. Moore, October 25, 1927, box 8, folder 28, Adaline Guenther Papers 1150.

112. Foster, "University Religious Conference," 11, 11a.

113. E. C. Moore, *I Helped Make a University* (Los Angeles: Dawson's Book Shop, 1952), 5–6.

114. The Baptists, Methodists, and Episcopalians had thought about going their own way, but did not.

115. Foster, *Memoir*, "Minutes of the Meeting of the Provisional Committee of Religious Co-operation of the University of California, Southern Branch, Hotel Alexandria, May 7, 1926, 9 A.M.," in "Origin of University Religious Conference," 11b.

116. Foster, "University Religious Conference," 10–11; according to Foster's account, the DSC and the CCBE were uneasy with having such liberal representation on the committee and appointed J. D. Fox as a counterweight. Kengott and Wadsworth became alternates.

117. Foster, "University Religious Conference," 12–13.

118. Foster, memo on study of religious programs, 3, 12.

119. Foster, memo on study of religious programs, 12.

120. Foster, "Origin of University Religious Conference," 13. Foster was disappointed in the fact that the URC never became the school of religion he had envisioned.

121. Foster, "Origin of University Religious Conference," 4–5. Banker Frank Vanderlip, formerly a backer of Charles Foster Kent, offered the Palos Verde site as a gift to the Board of Regents for the new campus.

122. The first branch of the URC to open was at the new Los Angeles City College in 1930.

123. E. C. Moore, "A Testimonial," in Herman Beimfohr, ed., *History of the University Religious Conference* (1978), 7.

124. Foster, memo on study of religious programs, 16–17.

125. Foster, "Confidential Report to the American Association on Religion," n.d., Chancellor's Files, RSG 261, box 32, folder 11, UCLA University Archives.

126. Foster, "Confidential Report to the American Association on Religion."

127. Charles Conaty to E. C. Moore, January 12, 1929, Chancellor's Files, R.S. 261, box 47, UCLA University Archives.

128. Moore, "Testimonial," 7.

129. The founding religious groups were: Baptist, Episcopal, Church of Jesus Christ of Latter-Day Saints, Jewish, Lutheran, Methodist, Presbyterian, and Roman Catholic.

130. Thomas Gorman, typescript, "A Notable Effort at Cooperation," quoted by Foster, *Memoir,* "My Postlude to Project No. 2," box 27, Foster Papers.

131. Foster, "My Postlude to Project No. 2," 20–21, typescript of Foster's quote from *Christian Education,* November 1928, in "Origin of University Religious Conference at the University of California at Los Angeles."

132. Foster, "My Postlude to Project no. 2," 21, typescript of Foster's quote from *Christian Education,* November 1928.

133. Foster, "My Postlude to Project No. 2," typescript of Foster's quote from *Christian Education,* November 1928, 20, 22.

134. Soon after the URC opened, the CCBE gave Foster an ultimatum: resign from the AAR or resign from the CCBE. He chose to resign from the CCBE and remained with the AAR because of his commitment to building interfaith projects, as well as his loyalty to the interfaith community that made up its membership. With the economic upheavals and without his CCBE salary and connections, however, it proved difficult to keep the AAR afloat, although many of his friends from the AAR and from his other interfaith projects rallied around him. They included: Cyrus Adler, Alphonso Bell, John J. Cantwell, John Finley, Walter Jessup, Jacob Kohn, M. Willard Lampe, Louis Mann, Isaac Landman, Edgar Magnin, Parker T. Moon, David Philipson, Abram Simon, Robert Sproul, and W. Bertrand Stevens. Those friends made up some of his CCBE salary and pitched in to help him found the North American Board for the Study of Religion in Higher Education (NAB). The objectives of the NAB were more modest than those of the AAR. Unlike the AAR, the NAB concentrated on providing services for multifaith education at colleges and universities through research, institutes, conferences, and the creation of literature, rather than by actually founding interfaith institutions at or near universities. Even with these more modest aims, the NAB lasted for only a few years, probably because of the economic depression of the 1930s. After that Foster faded out of the picture, departing from the United States in 1935 for an extended trip to study religious institutions and meet religious leaders in South and Central America. He did not return to the United States until the late 1930s. By then both the ISR and the URC had weathered the uncertainties of the founding years and were on their way to becoming well-established interfaith institutions.

Chapter 3. Building Community at the University Religious Conference

1. Steven J. Ross, *Hitler in Los Angeles: How Jews Foiled Nazi Plots against Hollywood and America* (New York: Bloomsbury, 2017), 2–4, 12–17, 64–68, 71–78, 205; Bradley W. Hart, *Hitler's American Friends: The Third Reich's Supporters in the United States* (New York: Thomas Dunne Books), 39–40; author interview with Gilbert Harrison, March 29, 1998. Former URC student Gilbert Harrison had attended a few weekly luncheon meetings of the community committee, which consisted of Jewish members who worked against Nazi anti-Semitic plots in Los Angeles, especially against Hollywood

figures. Rabbi Edgar J. Magnin and Mendel Silberberg, both supporters of the URC, were active members of the community committee.

2. Thomas Evans to E. C. Moore, March 24, 1933, Chancellor's Files, R.S. 261, box 47, folder 10, UCLA University Archives; E. C. Moore, *I Helped Make a University* (Los Angeles: Dawson's Book Shop, 1952), 63, 73; C. C. McCracken of the Board of Christian Education of the Presbyterian Church to E. C. Moore, November 24, 1928, Chancellor's Files, RS 261, box 29, folder 9, UCLA University Archives.

3. Not only the symbolism but the appearance of the URC building was important to attracting students to its off-campus location. David P. Setran, *The College "Y": Student Religion in the Era of Secularization* (New York: Palgrave Macmillan, 2007), 88–90. Setran argues that the attractiveness of YMCA buildings was important to attracting students. No doubt the same idea was important to the URC.

4. The URC had difficulty getting the advisers to work together. Evans and Guenther devised occasional projects for the purpose, but results were mixed.

5. Herman Beimfohr, *History of the University Religious Conference at U.C.L.A.* (1978), 12.

6. Beimfohr, *History*, 28–33.

7. Beimfohr, *History*, 11.

8. *Los Angeles Times*, November 26, 1948.

9. The URC charter allowed for the organization's expansion to other California colleges and universities. University Religious Conference, incorporation papers and bylaws, July 26, 1928, Article 2, reprinted in Beimfohr, *History*, 52.

10. Unlike the URC at UCLA, the URC branch at the USC, a private university, could offer religious courses for credit. One of several courses on religion offered at USC was "Religion 60: The Church and Its History," organized by USC dean Dr. Carl Knopf. Following the model of the ISR, the USC engaged faculty members of various faiths who taught classes on religion, including a rabbi, a Protestant Episcopal clergyman, an apostle of the Church of Christ of the Latter-Day Saints, and a Protestant minister. Each taught the history and ritual of his own group, usually at the USC Student Union. The USC and the URC had a reciprocal relationship. By and large, the USC borrowed the URC model and participated in URC projects. Although the USC extension had its own branch, the URC occasionally invited USC faculty and staff to give non-credit talks on religion to UCLA students. Like the URC at UCLA, the USC branch had various religious denominations as members. See Margaret King, "In the Beginning," *Religion Today*, tenth anniversary ed., May 1938, 3; "URC Staff to the Board of Trustees," March 22, 1933, Chancellors files, RS 261, box 47, file 10, UCLA University Archives; "Nominations to the URC Board of Trustees for 1933–34," URC annual report, May 1933, URC Files; Adaline Guenther, "History of the Year 1933–34," URC annual report, May 1934, URC Files; Adaline Guenther, "History of the Year 1935–36," URC annual report, May 1936, URC Files; Margaret King, report of the USC

Student Board, May 1938, URC Files; Father John Lavalle, "The Shape of Thing to Come," report on USC advisers and clubs, May 1938, URC Files.

11. The University Religious Conference, "Suggested Procedures at the University of Southern California," undated, manuscript at the URC; report of the secretary of the University of Southern California Student Board, URC annual meeting May 1939, URC Files. The USC and UCLA branches worked together until 1940, when USC started its own separate organization. As early as May of 1939, Jane Cassell suggested that "a separate S.C. program is needed here to establish the Religious Conference as an S.C. activity."

12. Although it had Methodist affiliation from its founding until the 1950s, USC admitted students of all religions. Moreover, it was located on land donated by John G. Downey (Catholic), Isais W. Hellman (Jewish), and Ozro Childs (Protestant).

13. Gordon S. Watkins, former member of the UCLA faculty and dean, later became the provost of UC Riverside and helped found the URC branch there.

14. George M. Marsden, *The Soul of the American University: From Protestant Establishment to Established Nonbelief* (New York: Oxford University Press, 1994), 140–146.

15. Author interview with URC graduate Bill Burke, March 21, 1998, 20.

16. Bill Gray, speech at annual student banquet, May 13, 1953, URC Files.

17. Setran, *College "Y"*, 82–87. Setran argues that at the turn of the twentieth century, the YMCA was responding to the new emphasis on secular extracurricular activities on university campuses by recruiting secular students of status who were popular because of their athletic prowess, social connections, and the like. Such practices were undoubtedly known to Evans and thus to Guenther.

18. Jim Stewart, UCLA Student Board report, URC annual meeting, May 1940, URC Files.

19. Author interview with Luke Fishburn, October 28, 1997.

20. Author interview with Jean Burke, March 21, 1998.

21. Author interview with Robert Hine, October 4, 1998; Robert and Shirley Hine, in Beimfohr, *History*, 20.

22. Irvin Goldring, speech at Uni-Camp dinner, February 6, 1975, 14, URC Files.

23. Author interview with Bill Burke.

24. Robert and Shirley Hine in Beimfohr, *History*, 20.

25. Bill Gray, speech at annual student banquet, May 13, 1953, URC Files.

26. Robert and Shirley Hine, eulogy of Adaline C. Guenther, in Beimfohr, *History of the University Religious Conference at UCLA*, 20.

27. Author interview with Fishburn.

28. Robert and Shirley Hine, eulogy of Guenther.

29. Don Hitchcock, speech, annual student banquet, May 13, 1953, URC Files.

30. Frank Wilkinson, report of the UCLA Student Board, URC annual meeting,

May 1936, URC Files. After graduating from UCLA, Wilkinson traveled around the world and saw poverty more extreme than anything he had seen at home. As a result, his views became too radical for Adaline Guenther, and the two of them had a falling out. Later in life Wilkinson became the director of housing in Los Angeles and founder of the First Amendment Society.

31. Robert and Shirley Hine, eulogy of Guenther, 21.

32. Robert and Shirley Hine, eulogy of Guenther, 20.

33. Author interview with Jean Burke.

34. Robert Hine, in Beimfohr, eulogy of Guenther, 20–21.

35. Author interview with Fishburn; Virginia Brereton, "Women as Subordinated Insiders," in *Between the Times: The Travail of the Protestant Establishment in America, 1900–1960*, ed. William R. Hutchinson (Cambridge, UK: Cambridge University Press, 1990), 154–155. As mentioned earlier, Guenther seems to have seen women like Jane Addams and Lillian Wald as role models rather than the more subordinate wifely model favored by many active church women of the day.

36. Luke Fishburn makes this point about Guenther's overlooking the precedent of Evans at the University of Pennsylvania when she spoke about the origins of Unicamp. Author interview with Fishburn.

37. Stewart, UCLA Student Board report.

38. In the middle 1970s the camp had serious financial difficulties, and at first the URC appointed a commission to take over its operation. The commission consisted of university and community groups, in addition to those from the URC, but thereafter it was recommended that the commission itself appoint the members and require no more than confirmation by the URC board of directors. Final Report of the Committee of Nine, presented November 8, 1976, reprinted in Beimfohr, *History*, 73.

39. Since counselors were unpaid volunteers, most of them, like Frank Wilkinson and John Burnside, were from prosperous families, but some, like Luke Fishburn, were less well off. Fishburn was one of those who managed to get the support he needed to volunteer. Author interview with Fishburn.

40. Bernard Galm, ed., *The Gift of a Mind*, UCLA Oral history transcript of interviews with Adaline Guenther, 1974, 60, 88; pamphlet on Uni-Camp, no title, no date, Adaline Guenther Papers, box 8, folder 28, 114; Ivan Olsen, chairman of LACC Student Board Report, URC annual meeting 1940, URC Files.

41. Author interview with Fishburn.

42. Pamphlet on Uni-Camp, 1935, Uni-Camp papers, URC Files.

43. Pamphlet on Uni-Camp, 1935.

44. Camp pamphlet, 1935.

45. Camp pamphlet, 1935.

46. Robert Hine, in Beimfohr, *History*, 16.

47. Camp pamphlet, 1935.

48. Olsen, report of the LACC Student Board, 1940; Stanley Dickinson, chairman, report of LACC Student Board, URC annual report, May 1941; *Los Angeles Times*, June 29, 1935, URC Files. The article mentions an international Garden Festival benefit put on at Del Amo Gardens to raise money for Uni-Camp. The festival was organized by Joy Mae Parke and Robert McHarge, two prominent members of the URC student board. Students assisting the event also included board members Frank Wilkinson and prospective counselor Frank Dooley. Los Angeles City College also raised money for Uni-Camp.

49. Eventually the camp fund received the proceeds of Mardi Gras, a popular UCLA festival. In 1977 Uni-Camp received ninety thousand dollars from the UCLA Mardi Gras festival, URC Files.

50. In the 1940s, the Joe. E. Brown family gave Uni-Camp a gift of ten thousand dollars to honor Donald Brown, their deceased son. See Beimfohr, *History*, chap. 9, 36; pamphlet on the URC Minutes of URC Executive Committee Meeting, June 1938, URC Files.

51. Report on University Camp for Younger Boys, August 8–18, 1938, URC Files.

52. Bernard Galm, *The Impossible Dream*, interview with Tom Bradley (UCLA Oral History Department, 1978), 37.

53. Report on Uni-Camp for Younger Boys, August 8–18, 1938, URC Files.

54. Author interview with Jean Burke.

55. Report on Uni-Camp for Younger Boys, August 8–18, 1938.

56. Galm, *Gift of a Mind*, 65.

57. Author interview with Jean Burke.

58. Author interview with Bill Burke.

59. Adaline Guenther, "History of the Year, 1939–40"; Stewart, UCLA Student Board report. Both presented at URC annual meeting, May 1940, in URC Files.

60. June Breck, speech, annual student banquet, May 13, 1953, URC Files.

61. Pamphlet on Uni-Camp (probably after 1940, judging from the time of the US entry into the war), 1 (Joe E. Brown donated the funds for renovating the Lodge); Report on Uni-camp, given at URC annual meeting, May 1944, URC Files.

62. Author interview with Jean Burke.

63. History of URC (probably after 1944, judging from the timing of the specialized camps.) According to Jean Burke, these specialized camps had specialized counsellors. For instance, the one for diabetic counsellors had medical personnel and supplied special diets. Author interview with Jean Burke; author interview with Hine.

64. Report on Uni-Camp, given at URC annual meeting, May 1940, URC Files; URC annual report, URC annual meeting, May 1944, URC Files; *The URC and How It Grew*, URC Files.

65. Dickinson, report of LACC Student Board, 1941; URC University Camp Report given at the Annual Meeting, 1944, URC Files.

66. Adaline Guenther, typescript of speech at the URC annual dinner, May 1950, URC Files.

67. *The URC and How It Grew,* "University Camp—A Community Welfare Project," in *Religion Today,* tenth anniversary issue 1938, URC Files.

68. *The URC and How It Grew.* In the 1970s the camp housed special camps for particular demographic groups, including Native Americans, African Americans, Asians, and "exceptional children." See *Unicamp Alumni News,* vol. 2, no. 1, April 1975, URC Files. According to Luke Fishburn, Uni-camp and College Camp together made up the largest camp for economically disadvantaged children in the West. Author interview with Fishburn.

69. Adaline Guenther, "University Camp," *Religion Today,* June 1939, 3, URC Files; Louis Ramos Jr., "From One Camper to His Counselor," in *An America United!* undated, shown to author by John Burnside at interview with author, March 21, 1998.

70. Guenther, "University Camp," 3.

71. Breck, speech, annual student banquet, 1953.

72. Adaline Guenther, speech, Uni-Camp dinner honoring Adaline Guenther, February 6, 1975, 21, Adaline Guenther Papers, box 8, folder 7, UCLA Special Collections.

73. Author interview with Fishburn.

74. Author interview with Fishburn.

75. Robert and Shirley Hine, eulogy for Guenther, 21.

76. Donald Brown, "Memo: To Members of the Student Board, Report of University Camp," July 1938, URC Files.

77. Guenther, "University Camp," 3.

78. Robert Hine uses the term "noblesse oblige" when he described the camp experience. Author interview with Hine.

79. Fragment of a typed manuscript on Uni-Camp in Camp Scrapbook, 2. A comic book that was likely used at Uni-camp and published after the Second World War made a similar point but assumed it was easy to get along with others not of the same color, race, or religion. See Eva Knox Evans, "All about Us," Capitol Publishing, 1947. This was not what the people at Uni-Camp thought; they thought it was difficult.

80. Galm, *Impossible Dream,* 34.

81. Galm, *Gift of a Mind,* 84–86.

82. Upon her death in 1975, Guenther bestowed a bequest of an endowed chair at Ohio Wesleyan University for an African American woman.

83. Adaline Guenther, "History of the Year," URC report, May 1941, URC Files.

84. Robert and Shirley Hine, eulogy for Guenther, 21.

85. Robert Hine, "An Expression of Appreciation to Mr. Thomas Evans on Behalf of His Student Friends at UCLA," May 7, 1945, in Beimfohr, *History,* 16.

86. Robert Hine, speech at URC annual meeting, May 7, 1945, in Beimfohr, *History,* 21.

87. Hine, speech at URC annual meeting, 1945.

88. Jim Taylor, speech, annual student banquet, May 13, 1953, URC Files.

89. Author interview with Fishburn.

90. June Beck, speech, annual student banquet, May 13, 1953, URC Files.

91. Guenther, "University Camp."

92. Author interview with Fishburn. Fishburn also served as URC associate director from 1960 to 1970.

93. Hitchcock, speech, annual student banquet, 1953.

94. Author interview with Fishburn.

95. Robert and Shirley Hine, eulogy for Guenther, 21.

96. Ivan Olson, report of Student Board of Los Angeles City College, 1939, URC Files.

97. "University Camp and Student Social Service," URC pamphlet, undated, URC Files.

98. Bob Jaffee, speech, annual student banquet, May 13, 1953, URC Files.

99. Hanford Files, URC Student Board report, annual meeting, May 1942, URC Files.

100. Hanford Files, URC Student Board report, annual meeting, URC Files.

101. Report of the Social Service Department, annual meeting, May 1944, URC Files.

102. Report of the Social Service Department, annual meeting, 1944.

103. Report of the Social Service Department, annual meeting, 1944.

104. Report of the Social Service Department, annual meeting, 1944. A few months later, at a Christmas Party at the URC, a gang from the Alpine Street district crashed a Christmas dance given at the URC for another group of Mexican youth. Apparently, word of the dance had slipped out. The Alpine gang had weapons such as bicycle chains and knives. Several were injured and there was some property damage. "Fifteen More Youth Hunted after Fracas at Dance Hall," *Los Angeles Times*, Saturday, December 24, 1944.

105. Report of Social Service Department, annual meeting, May 1944.

106. Report of Social Service Department, annual meeting, 1944.

107. "University Camp and Student Social Service," URC Pamphlet, undated, URC Files.

108. "University Camp and Student Social Service."

109. Jaffee, speech, annual student banquet, 1953.

110. Author interview with Fishburn.

111. Jaffee, speech, annual student banquet.

112. Report of the Social Service Department, URC sixteenth annual report, May 1943, URC Files.

113. "University Camp and Student Social Service."

114. Galm, *Gift of a Mind*, 94.

115. Author interview with Jean Burke.

116. "Introduction" to the Catalogue for the Panorama of the American Negro in the Fine Arts, Westwood Hills Press, May 31, 1946, URC Files.

117. Author interview with Jean Burke.

118. Allen Davis and Mary Lynn McCree, eds., *Eighty Years at Hull House* (Chicago: Quadrangle Books, 1969), 77–82.

Chapter 4. Partnership with the NCCJ

1. Guenther later suggested that helping Burnside and the others benefited the reputation of the URC on campus. Bernard Galm, ed., *The Gift of a Mind*, UCLA Oral history transcript of interviews with Adaline Guenther, 1974, 42–44; "UCLA Ousts Five in Anti-Radical Drive," *Los Angeles Times*, October 30, 1934.

2. Adaline Guenther, URC annual report, May 1934, URC Files. Prior to 1938, the NCCJ was known as the National Conference of Jews and Christians; in 1938 it was renamed the National Conference of Christians and Jews. This book uses the later name and abbreviation because that is how the organization is most widely known today.

3. The cooperative arrangement between the URC and the NCCJ ended not long after the death of Thomas Evans in 1945. The relationship between the two organizations deteriorated as various disagreement arose, especially over competition for funds and control of local programs in Southern California.

4. Dr. McNicholas, report of the URC Education Division, URC annual meeting, May 1936, URC Files.

5. Kevin M. Schultz, *Tri-Faith America: How Catholics and Jews Held Postwar America to Its Protestant Promise* (Oxford: Oxford University Press, 2011), 65; Diana Selig, *Americans All: The Cultural Gifts Movement* (Cambridge, MA: Harvard University Press, 2008), 119.

6. Marshall McComb, report of the Extension Council, URC annual meeting, May 1936, URC Files.

7. McComb, report of the Extension Council, 1936.

8. Steven J. Ross, *Hitler in Los Angeles: How Jews Foiled Nazi Plots against Hollywood and America* (New York: Bloomsbury, 2017), 77.

9. Guenther, Executive Committee meeting, December 14, 1936, URC Files.

10. Marshall McComb, report of Extension Council, URC annual meeting, May 1938, URC Files.

11. Marshall McComb, report of Extension Council, URC annual meeting, May 1937, URC Files.

12. McComb, report of the Extension Council, 1938.

13. McComb, report of Extension Council, 1936.

14. McComb, report of Extension Council, 1936.

15. McComb, report of Extension Council, 1936.

16. According to Catholic URC member Bill Burke, Riggs was the only "independently ordained" priest in the United States at the time. He was "not ordained as a member of a religious order or any particular diocese of any bishop. In other words, he would answer only to the apostolic delegate." Author interview with Bill Burke, March 21, 1998.

17. McComb, report of Extension Council, 1937.

18. The primary work of the Women's Division was raising money for various URC projects through such events as teas, garden parties, and luncheons. At this time, the division decided to extend its membership and deal more directly to promote active interfaith fellowship. Clara Reynolds, president of the URC Women's Division, URC annual meeting, May 1937, URC Files.

19. Reynolds, May 1937.

20. Reynolds, May 1937.

21. Reynolds, May 1937.

22. The NCCJ speakers were Clinchy, Rev. Ashby Jones, and Rabbi Morris Lazaron; see Elaine Newport, UCLA Student Board report, May 1938, URC Files. The URC Clergy Council was formed as part of the Clerical Division, which consisted of leading Los Angeles Protestant, Jewish, and Catholic leaders such as Rabbi Magnin and Monsignor Cawley. The division set up the council to combat the increasing anti-Jewish movements in the Los Angeles area by drawing in "more of the ministers, priests and rabbis into a group" in the hope that "the friendly relations of all the religious groups could successfully oppose" intolerance. Leonard Oechshli, report of the Clergy Division, URC annual meeting, May 1938, URC Files. Also see McComb, report of Extension Division, 1938.

23. McComb, report of Extension Division, 1938.

24. Little seems to have resulted from the meeting. McComb, report of the Extension Division, 1938.

25. Alphonso Bell, annual report of the Business Man's Committee, 1938, URC Files.

26. Author interview with Gilbert Harrison, March 29, 1998; Newport, UCLA Student Board report, 1938.

27. McComb, report of the Extension Council 1937; Thomas Evans, report of the Executive Secretary, URC annual meeting, May 1937, URC Files.

28. John Burnside, report of the Extension Council, URC annual meeting, May 1939.

29. Bob Kemp, report of the Student Board at LACC, URC annual meeting, May 1938, URC Files.

30. Adaline Guenther, speech at annual URC dinner, May 7, 1945, URC Files.

31. Evans, URC report of Executive Secretary, 1937.

32. McComb, report of the Extension Council, 1937.

33. Gilbert Harrison, report of the UCLA Student Board, URC annual meeting, May 1937.

34. Adaline Guenther, "History of the Year 1936–37," URC Files.

35. Newport, UCLA Student Board report, 1938.

36. Margaret King, report of the USC Student Board, May 1938, URC Files.

37. A pamphlet of the NCCJ specifically quotes from one of Lincoln's speeches on religious pluralism.

38. Adaline Guenther, "History of the Year," URC annual meeting, May 1941, URC Files.

39. McComb, report of Extension Council, 1938.

40. McComb, report of Extension Council, 1938.

41. McComb, report of Extension Council, 1938.

42. Guenther, "History of the Year 1939–40."

43. Gilbert Harrison, report on the Radio Division, URC annual meeting, May 1941, URC Files.

44. Harrison, report on the Radio Division, 1941.

45. Harrison, report on the Radio Division, 1941.

46. Harrison, report on the Radio Division, 1941.

47. Gene Zubovich, *Before the Religious Right: Liberal Protestants, Human Rights and the Polarization of the United States* (Philadelphia: University of Pennsylvania Press, 2022), 54–57.

48. Gilbert Harrison, report of the Radio Committee, URC annual meeting, May 1940, URC Files.

49. Harrison, report of the Radio Committee, 1940.

50. Harrison, report of the Radio Committee, 1940; Guenther, "History of the Year 1939–40."

51. Harrison, report of the Radio Committee, 1940.

52. Guenther, "History of the Year 1939–40." The national hook up never materialized.

53. Harrison, report of the Radio Committee, 1940.

54. Harrison, report of the Radio Committee, 1940.

55. Harrison, report on the Radio Division, 1941; Marshall McComb, Report on the Radio Division, URC annual meeting, May 1941, URC Files.

56. McComb, report on the Radio Division, 1941.

57. Harrison, report of the Radio Committee, 1941; Joel Gardner, ed., *Liberal Perspectives*, UCLA Oral history transcript of interviews with Gilbert Harrison, 1982, 155.

58. Marshall McComb, report of Extension Committee, URC annual meeting, May 1942, URC Files.

59. McComb, report of Extension Committee, 1942.

60. Author interview with Harrison. Harrison described the trialogue as an autonomous, spontaneous student program without reference to the NCCJ trio.

61. Author interview with Robert Hine, October 4, 1997.

62. Author interview with Bill Burke, March 21, 1998. Burke gives his own opinion here but gives no specifics about the professors who supposedly insulted Catholics. This resentment mirrors what Foster mentions in his account of how certain Iowa Protestant, Catholic, and Jewish leaders had reservations about having university faculty teaching religion, fearful that they would distort it.

63. The URC was occasionally criticized for presenting Mormons and Episcopalians as Protestants. This may have resulted from the tri-faith division of the chaplaincy by the War Department during the First World War, which at first used Protestant chaplains to minister to both groups. Ronit Y. Stahl, *Enlisting Faith: How the Military Chaplaincy Shaped Religion and State in Modern America* (Cambridge, MA: Harvard University Press, 2017), 4, 37.

64. Author interview with Hine.

65. Author interview Marian Hargrave, December 12, 1997.

66. Gardner, *Liberal Perspectives*, 145, 148.

67. Author interview with Hine.

68. Gardner, *Liberal Perspectives*, 1982, 145.

69. Author interview with Burke, March 21, 1998.

70. Gardner, *Liberal Perspectives*, 145.

71. Thomas Evans to E. C. Moore, February 18, 1936, Chancellors Files, RS 261, box 61, folder 9, UCLA University Archives; *Los Angeles Daily Bruin*, February 18, 1936.

72. McComb, report of Extension Committee, 1936.

73. McComb, report of Extension Committee, 1936.

74. E. C. Moore to William Hensey, February 26, 1936, Chancellors Files, RS261, box 61, folder 9, UCLA University Archives.

75. Gilbert Harrison, report of UCLA Student Board, URC annual meeting, May 1937, URC Files.

76. McComb, report of Extension Committee, 1937.

77. Gardner, *Liberal Perspectives*, 145, 147.

78. McComb, report of Extension Committee, 1938.

79. Guenther, "History of the Year 1939–40."

80. Author interview with Burke, March 21, 1998.

81. John Burnside, report of the Extension Division, URC annual meeting, May 1940, URC Files.

82. Guenther, "History of the Year 1939–40."

83. Burnside, report of the Extension Division, 1940.

84. *Religion Today*, November 1941, URC Files.

85. Adaline Guenther, "History of the Year 1940–41," URC annual meeting, May 1941, URC Files.

86. Guenther, "History of the Year 1940–41."

87. Guenther, "History of the Year 1940–41."

88. Marshall McComb, report of the Extension Council, URC annual meeting, May 1941, URC Files.

89. Ivan Olson, chair, report on LAJC Student Board, URC annual meeting, May 1940, URC Files.

90. Jim Stewart, report on UCLA Student Board, URC annual meeting, May 1940, URC Files.

91. John Hessel, chair, report of UCLA Student Board activities during the school year 1940–41, URC annual Meeting, May 1941, URC Files.

92. Guenther, "History of the Year 1940–41."

93. Marshall McComb, report of Extension Council, 1942.

94. Gardner, *Liberal Perspectives*, 148–149.

95. Gardner, *Liberal Perspectives*, 148–149.

96. *Religion Today*, November 1941; author interview with Bill Burke, March 2, 1998.

97. *Religion Today*, November 1941.

98. Author interview with Burke, March 21, 1998. In the interview, Bill Burke discussed the script of the three URC presenters in the trialogue program given at the Army training camps before American entry into the Second World War.

99. Author interview with Burke, March 21, 1998.

100. Author interview with Burke, March 21, 1998.

101. Author interview with Burke, March 21, 1998.

102. Tisa Wenger, *Religious Freedom: The Contested History of an American Ideal* (Chapel Hil: University of North Carolina Press, 2017), 12–13, 143–187. Wenger's book suggests that religious freedom has been used by various groups when pragmatically advantageous for rationalizing racism, empire, or other forms of privilege and exploitation. No doubt this may be true. But my own view, based upon studying Gilbert Harrison and other Jews who have sought to prevent religious persecution, is that the First Amendment of the US Constitution, which protects the right of exercising religious freedom and prohibits the establishment of religion, meant far more to them than just "talk."

103. Guenther was a strong opponent of intermarriage, as were the leaders of the various religious groups that then belonged to the URC. It is interesting to note that nevertheless it seems there were interfaith marriages among URC students, including Harrison, who later married a Protestant woman. Burke, a Catholic, married a Protestant woman who converted to Catholicism and Burnside, a Protestant, married a Catholic woman. He then converted to Catholicism.

104. Thomas Evans, report of the URC executive secretary, URC annual meeting, May 1941, URC Files.

105. Author interview with Burke, March 21, 1998.

106. Trialogue itinerary in *Religion Today*, October 1941, URC Files.

107. Trialogue itinerary in *Religion Today*, October 1941.

108. *Religion Today*, October 1941.

109. Gardner, *Liberal Perspectives*, 176–178, 386–388. Harrison claims that the national tour took place in the fall of 1940, but Burke, the annual reports and other documentation indicate it was in the fall of 1941; *Religion Today*, November 1941. Author interview with Burke, March 2, 1998; Evans, report of Executive Secretary, 1941.

110. *Religion Today*, November 1941.

111. *Religion Today*, November 1941.

112. Bernard Desenberg, report on the Trialogue team tour, *Religion Today*, November 1941.

113. Donald M. Brieland, letter to the URC, n.d., printed in *Religion Today*, November 1941.

114. *Religion Today*, November 1941.

Chapter 5. The University Religious Conference in the Second World War

1. Wendy L. Wall, *Inventing the American Way: The Politics of Consensus from the New Deal to the Civil Rights Movement* (Oxford: Oxford University Press, 2008), 124–138. Here Wall discusses the impact of the Second World War on shaping an American identity of tolerance and unity in diversity as opposed to the identity of the wartime enemies of the United States.

2. Lyman H. Johnson to Bertram Stevens, January 12, 1942, URC Files. The URC chose a more informal role for helping the USO. No center for hospitality was set up at the URC, but it appears likely that the URC made referrals to church and community activities that provided recreational and social activities for the troops in Los Angeles.

3. Charles Posner to Commanding Officer, 203rd Coast Artillery, January 16, 1942, URC Files.

4. Glenn W. Moore to Louise K. Sims and Sol Lesser at the University Religious Conference, April 2, 1942, URC Files.

5. Thomas Evans letter to Andrew W. Gottschall, March 31, 1943, URC Files.

6. Louise K. Sims, CSC chair, report on the Chaplains Service Corps, for the Year May 1943 to May 1944; "We Must Not Fail Them," pamphlet of Chaplains' Aid, 1943, URC Files.

7. Louise K. Sims, report of the Chaplains' Servicer Corps, URC annual report, May 1944, URC Files.

8. "We Must Not Fail Them."

9. "We Must Not Fail Them."

10. "We Must Not Fail Them."

11. "We Must Not Fail Them."

12. Glenn W. Moore, letter to Louise K. Sims and Sol Lesser, April 2, 1942, URC Files.

13. Author interview with Jean Burke, March 21, 1998.

14. "The Role of the University Religious Conference in Civilian Defense," undated, URC Files.

15. Adaline Guenther, letter to Father John Dunn, April 17, 1942, URC Files.

16. Herman Beimfohr, report, URC annual meeting, May 1942, URC Files.

17. Herman Beimfohr, LACC advisers' report, URC annual meeting, May 1942, URC Files.

18. Beimfohr, LACC advisers' report, 1942.

19. E. C. Farnham, Executive Secretary, Church Federation of Los Angeles, letter to Adaline Guenther, May 22, 1942, URC Files.

20. Anne M. Blankenship, *Christianity, Social Justice, and the Japanese American Incarceration during World War Two* (Chapel Hill: University of North Carolina Press, 2016), 30. Blankenship suggests that many mainline Protestant churches refrained from outright condemnation of the internment but expressed regret or concern about the policy. The URC presents a similar pattern.

21. In my view, the moderate approach of the URC, its support for amelioration and support for fellowship with the interred Japanese students, was consistent with the URC's overall moderate approach to social reform.

22. Peggy Lee Roberton, chair, University Community Youth Committee, letter to Glenn Moore, then president of the URC, November 2, 1944, URC Files.

23. "The Role of the University Religious Conference in Civilian Defense," undated, URC Files. The same flyer lists other ways the URC volunteered to aid the war effort: offering secretarial services and rooms for meetings and classes and cooperating with the UCLA Defense Council by providing a URC speakers' bureau to talk about issues related to the war. Adaline Guenther, letter to Herbert L. Seamans, March 4, 1943, URC Files.

24. "Role of the University Religious Conference in Civilian Defense."

25. Bernard Galm, ed., *The Gift of a Mind*, UCLA Oral history transcript of interviews with Adaline Guenther, 1974, 146.

26. Guenther, *Gift of a Mind*, 146.

27. Guenther letter to Seamans, March 4, 1943.

28. Thomas Evans, report of the URC executive secretary, annual meeting, May 1944, URC Files.

29. A collection of the bulletins and many of the letters themselves are now held in Special Collections at the UCLA Charles Young Library. At the request of the

servicemen, Guenther collected and saved the names and addresses of those who wished to be contacted later about postwar plans and organizations. The servicemen had previously published their own newsletter, the *Barometer*, which Guenther had helped edit and for which UCLA faculty had donated research, but the military prohibited it because it was seen as an organization within the military, which was prohibited. As the principal editor and distributor of the privately published *10845 Le Conte Avenue* bulletin, it was considered acceptable to the military. Memo, March 28, 1943, URC Files.

30. Excerpt of letters from unnamed URC graduates to Adaline Guenther, read at the URC annual meeting, May 1943, URC Files.

31. The author of this letter was probably Clyde Johnson, formerly UCLA associate dean of students, who was over age for military service and who during the war worked with the Lockheed Corporation that was building installations in Northern Ireland. Although not actually a former student or a graduate of the URC, Johnson was a friend of Guenther and of the URC. Excerpt of letters from unnamed URC graduates to Adaline Guenther, read at the URC annual meeting, May 1943, URC Files; Galm, *Gift of a Mind*, 150.

32. Excerpt of letter from unnamed URC graduates to Adaline Guenther, 1943.

33. Excerpt of letter from unnamed URC graduate to Adaline Guenther, read at the URC annual meeting, May 1944, URC Files.

34. Adaline Guenther, speech at the annual URC dinner, May 7, 1945, URC Files.

35. Joel Gardner, ed., *Liberal Perspectives*, UCLA Oral history transcript of interviews with Gilbert Harrison, 1982, 208–210, 285–287. Adaline Guenther did, however, invite Charles Bolte to take over the correspondence and take over organizing what later became the AVC. Guenther, speech at the annual URC dinner, 1945.

36. Guenther, speech at annual URC dinner, 1945.

37. Charles G. Bolte, *The New Veteran* (New York: Reynal and Hitchcock, 1945), 37–47. In addition to Charles Bolte, the AVC included others not from the URC, including Sam Spencer Jr., Wadsworth Likely, Edward T. Ladd, Richard Bowling, and Oren Root. Guenther, speech at URC annual dinner, 1945; Galm, *Gift of a Mind*, 153–160.

38. Guenther, speech at URC annual dinner, 1945; Gardner, *Liberal Perspectives*, 285–287.

39. Bolte, *New Veteran*, 47.

40. *Liberal Perspectives*, 305, 308–311; Bolte, *New Veteran*, 37–47, 159–160. Two URC members, Bill Burke and Al Chamie, did join the American Legion and both became commanders within its ranks. They tried to reform the Legion, but according to Guenther, they had little success. Galm, *Gift of a Mind*, 160, 161. O. D. Foster was active during the Second World War and consulted with the military but apparently was not consulted when it came to the AVC.

41. The idea of adult women panelists was revived at the URC after the war when the URC organized a panel of women who could talk about religion, ethnicity, and race from the perspectives of a wife and mother rather than those of a student. Church Women United later sponsored them. Galm, *Gift of a Mind*, 206–207.

42. Adaline Guenther, "History of the Year 1942–43," URC annual meeting, May 1943, URC Files.

43. Occasionally men filled in as speakers or sometimes as moderators. Women had served in trialogue at times too, but most typically the trialogue teams were all male.

44. Guenther, speech at URC annual dinner, 1945.

45. Press release on the Panel of Americans, 1947, URC Files.

46. Author interview with Marian Hargrave, December 12, 1997.

47. Galm, *Gift of a Mind*, 117; author interview with Hargrave.

48. Author interview with Hargrave.

49. Press release on the Panel of Americans, 1947.

50. Author interview with Hargrave.

51. Press release on the Panel of Americans, 1947.

52. The amateur status of the panelists was important. Adaline Guenther wrote to one of the POA speakers, Marguerita Duran, confirming that she would work for the URC for four months, as staff, for $125 per month and that "the [panel] speaking [would only be] incidental." "We want to preserve your amateur standing, as a panel speaker." Letter of Guenther to Doran, June 19, 1945, URC Files.

53. Author interview with Hargrave.

54. Galm, *Gift of a Mind*, 118.

55. Author interview with Hargrave.

56. Galm, *Gift of a Mind*, 116–119, 190–191, 200.

57. URC pamphlet, "Panel of Americans," 1944, URC Files.

58. Author interview with Hargrave.

59. Author interview with Hargrave.

60. Galm, *Gift of a Mind*, 116.

61. Author interview with Hargrave.

62. "Majority" and "minority" were the terms used at the time. Galm, *Gift of a Mind*, 116–119; author interview with Hargrave.

63. Author interview with Hargrave. Adaline Guenther claims that the planes used to transport the panel were C-47s. See Galm, *Gift of a Mind*, 124.

64. Author interview with Hargrave.

65. Author interview with Hargrave.

66. Galm, *Gift of a Mind*, 118.

67. Kevin M. Schultz, *Tri-Faith America: How Catholics and Jews Held Postwar America to Its Protestant Promise* (Oxford: Oxford University Press, 2011), 45–47.

68. Adaline Guenther, URC annual report, May 1945, URC Files.

69. "R.C. B-ology," *UCLA Daily Bruin*, February 5, 1945.

70. URC annual report, May 1945, URC Files.

71. Mrs. Stafford Warren, "Report on the World Student Associates," 3, URC annual meeting, May 10, 1948, URC Files.

72. Mrs. O. Goodwin, "Report on the Intercultural Committee," 3, URC annual meeting, May 10, 1948, URC Files.

Chapter 6. The Panel of Americans in the Postwar Era

1. The Pledge of Allegiance added the words "under God" in 1954. Wendy Wall, *Inventing the "American Way": The Politics of Consensus from the New Deal to the Civil Rights Movement* (Oxford: Oxford University Press, 2009), 168; Mark Brilliant, *The Color of America Has Changed: How Racial Diversity Shaped Civil Rights Reform in California, 1941–1978* (Oxford: Oxford University Press, 2010), 201. The author quotes the following sign: "'Restricted': For Rent—No Jews or Dogs Allowed," from a pamphlet of the Jewish Federation Council of Greater Los Angeles, in the Edmund (Pat) Brown Papers, pamphlet, Prop. 14 box 2, Folder File All Materials.

2. Matthew F. Delmont, *Half American: The Epic Story of African Americans Fighting World War II at Home and Abroad* (New York: Viking, 2022), 156–167.

3. Delmont, *Half American*, 49–59.

4. Delmont, *Half American*, 156–167. In this section, Dumont quotes the poem "Beaumont to Detroit," written by Lanston Hughes in 1943. In it, Hughes asks the following question: "How long I got to fight, BOTH HITLER—AND JIM CROW."

5. H. S. Truman, Civil Rights Message to Congress, February 2, 1948.

6. Executive Order 9980, Regulations Governing Fair Employment Practices within the Federal Establishment, July 2, 1948; Executive Order 9981, Establishing the Presidents' Committee on Equality of Treatment and Opportunity in the Armed Services; Gary A. Donaldson, *Truman Defeats Dewey* (Lexington: University Press of Kentucky, 1999), 101, 108–111.

7. Two examples of cases on the local level that broke new ground in recognizing the rights of Mexican American school children in Southern California, and African American school children in Johnson County, Kansas, were respectively, *Mendez v. Westminster* in 1948, and *Webb v. School District 90* in 1949.

8. When the case was filed in 1942 Endo was at Tule Lake, but by the time it reached the Supreme Court she was in the Topaz Internment Camp in Utah.

9. William O. Douglas, *Ex parte Endo* 323 U.S. 283 (1944). The opinion addresses the issue not of race or ethnicity but of citizen loyalty. It also does not address the issue of whether the abrogation of the Bill of Rights was a military necessity, essential to national safety. These opinions were expressed in the concurring opinions of Justices Frank Murphy and Owen Roberts. Alfred A. Kelly and Winfred A. Harbison, *The American Constitution: Its Origins and Development*, 3rd edition (New York: Norton, 1963), 840–841.

10. In *Korematsu v. United States*, the Supreme Court affirmed the conviction of Fred Korematsu, an American citizen of Japanese ancestry, for refusing to leave a military exclusion zone on the West Coast. *Korematsu* and *Endo* were decided on the same day in 1944. Justice Hugo Black's majority opinion argues that Korematsu was excluded from the area not because he was of Japanese descent but because of military security. There were, however three dissenting opinions. One of them, by Justice Frank Murphy, attacked the decision on constitutional grounds and racism.

11. President Franklin Roosevelt apparently heard about the *Endo* decision before it was made public. He rescinded executive order 6099 and permitted the Issei and Nisei to return to the West Coast beginning in January 1945.

12. Shelley v. Kraemer 334 U.S. 1.

13. Brown 347 U.S. 483; Plessy 163 U.S. 537.

14. Adaline Guenther, draft of speech, 1946, URC Files; press release on Panel program, undated, 2, URC Files.

15. Adaline Guenther, draft of speech, 1946.

16. Joseph McGucken, letter to Dan Dodson, December 20, 1946, URC Files.

17. Joseph T. McGucken to Marian Hargrave, February 8, 1946, URC Files.

18. The overall cost of the tour was just under $11,000. In most places the local arrangements and scheduling were undertaken by the various local school superintendents, but in Philadelphia, the United Nations Council and the *Philadelphia Record* made the arrangements. In Chicago the URC worked with the local office of the NCCJ but was dissatisfied with the results and admitted that there was a "misunderstanding, conflict of purpose and methods for which the Religious Conference and the Panel must take its share of the blame." URC annual report, May 1947, URC Files.

19. URC annual report, 1947.

20. Press release on the Panel of Americans, 1947, URC Files.

21. URC annual report 1947; Bernard Galm, ed., *The Gift of a Mind*, UCLA Oral history transcript of Interviews with Adaline Guenther, 1974, 125–126; Author interview with Marian Hargrave, December 12, 1997.

22. URC annual report, 1947.

23. Typescript for G. Byron Done, "When the Panel Is Introduced, Panel Speeches, at End of Panel," no date, likely 1947, URC Files.

24. Adaline Guenther, "Report of the Secretary to the Members of the Religious Conference," February 21, 1947, URC Files; Panel scrapbook, URC Files.

25. "Mayor Greets Girls on Tolerance Tour," *Philadelphia Inquirer*, February 18, 1947.

26. Kimbrough was a popular journalist, author, fashion and managing editor of the *Ladies' Home Journal*, and later a radio commentator. She had spent time in Hollywood, where she and coauthor Cornelia Otis Skinner wrote a script for a movie version of their best-selling memoir, *When Our Hearts Were Young and Gay* (New York: Dodd Mead, 1942); Emily Kimbrough, *We Followed Our Hearts to Hollywood* (New

York: Dodd, Mead, 1943); Constance Hays, "Emily Kimbrough, 90, Magazine Editor and Popular Author," *New York Times*, February 11, 1989.

27. "Mayor Greets Girls on Tolerance Tour," *Philadelphia Inquirer*, February 18, 1947; Guenther, "Report of the Secretary to the Members," 1947.

28. Emily Kimbrough, "The Story of the Panel," quoted by G. Byron Done, at the URC annual dinner, May 5, 1947, URC Files.

29. "Six Coeds on Panel Tour Given Ovation in New York Schools," *Westwood Hills Press*, March 7, 1947; Nelson Rockefeller, letter to Clarence "Dyke" Dykstra, March 25, 1947, URC Archives. In the letter, Rockefeller writes that he was sorry to have missed Guenther's visit to his office and encloses a check for $500.

30. "Six Coeds on Panel Tour Given Ovation in New York Schools."

31. "6 California Girls Here to Study Bias," *New York Times*, February 24, 1947; "Six Coeds on Panel Tour Given Ovation in New York Schools"; Adaline Guenther, letter to Eleanor Roosevelt, February 11, 1947. Guenther accepts Roosevelt's invitation to meet with the panel at 5 p.m. on February 25, 1947, URC Files.

32. Letter of Frederic Ernst, associate superintendent, Board of Education, City of New York, to the Principals of the High Schools, February 14, 1947, URC Files.

33. Adaline Guenther, "Report to Trustees and Friends on Current Progress of the Panel of Americans, March 10, 1947; "6 California Girls Here to Study Bias."

34. G. Byron Done, notes on tour in New York City, March 7, 1947, in Panel tour scrapbook, URC Files.

35. G. Byron Done, report on Panel trip, annual URC dinner, May 1947, 3, URC Files.

36. Done, report on Panel trip, annual URC dinner, 1947, 3.

37. Underlining and exclamation point are Done's. Done, notes on tour in New York City.

38. Done, report on Panel trip, annual URC dinner, 1947, 3.

39. "Six Coeds on Panel Tour Given Ovation in New York Schools."

40. Anonymous (probably Adaline Guenther), "Three Full Months," report of the tour of the nation, February to May 1947, Panel tour scrapbook, URC Files; "Tolerance Convocation Held Today: 'Panel of Americans' Outline Race Relations," *California Daily Bruin*, May 5, 1947.

41. Marian Hargrave, first report from Pittsburgh, March 14, 1947, Panel tour scrapbook, URC Files.

42. G. Byron Done, telegram to Guenther, in "Report to Trustees and Friends on Current Progress of the Panel of Americans," March 10, 1947, Panel tour scrapbook, URC Files.

43. G. Byron Done, "Third Report on the Progress of the Panel of Americans," March 24, 1947, annual URC dinner, May 5, 1947, URC Files.

44. Done, "Third Report," 3.

45. Dilworth Lupton, "Dilworth Lupton Says: Girl Panel Discusses Bigotry," *Cleveland Plain Dealer*, March 11, 1947.

46. Lupton, "Girl Panel Discusses Bigotry."

47. Lupton, "Girl Panel Discusses Bigotry."

48. Done, report on Panel trip, annual URC dinner, 1947, 3.

49. "Six Coeds on Panel Tour Given Ovation in New York Schools," *Westwood Hills California Press*, March 7, 1947.

50. Done, report on Panel trip, annual URC dinner, 1947, 2; Panel tour scrapbook.

51. G. Byron Done, first report from Pittsburgh, March 14, 1947, URC Files.

52. Roy T. Mattern, letter to G. Byron Done, March 18, 1947, Panel tour scrapbook, URC Files.

53. Done, report on Panel trip, annual URC dinner, 1947, 3, capitals are Dimmick's; Panel tour scrapbook, URC Files.

54. Delmont, *Half American*, 151–156.

55. Done, report on Panel trip, annual URC dinner, 1947, 2.

56. J. J. Powels, letter to Byron Done, April 2, 1947, Panel tour scrapbook, URC Files.

57. Done, report on Panel trip, annual URC dinner, 1947, 2.

58. "We Heard the Panel," Panel tour scrapbook, URC Files.

59. Done, report on Panel trip, annual URC dinner, 1947, 2; Panel tour scrapbook, URC Files.

60. "Building Together," Mayor's Friendly Relations Committee, Cincinnati, Ohio, March 1947 Panel tour scrapbook, URC Files.

61. Done, report on Panel trip, annual URC dinner, 1947, 1–2.

62. Done, report on Panel trip, annual URC dinner, 1947, 1.

63. Done, report on Panel trip, annual URC dinner, 1947, 2.

64. "Six Co-eds Stop Here on Tour to Promote Better Race Relations," *Cincinnati Post*, March 31, 1947.

65. F. F. Carpenter, letter to G. Byron Done, April 11, 1947, Panel tour scrapbook, URC Files.

66. "Better Racial Relations Object of Ohio Tour Begun by Six California Girls: Six Girls from California to Discuss Inter-Racial Problems in Springfield," *Xenia Daily Gazette*, March 30 1947, URC Files.

67. Done, report on Panel trip, annual URC dinner, 1947, 2.

68. Done, report on Panel trip, annual URC dinner, 1947, 2.

69. Report of Extension Program, "National Outreach," URC annual meeting, May 1947, URC Files.

70. "We Heard the Panel."

71. Done, report on Panel trip, annual URC dinner, 1947, 1.

72. C. O Williams, letter to G. Byron Done, April 29, 1947, Panel tour scrapbook.

73. Done, report on Panel trip, annual URC dinner, 1947, 1.

74. Done, report on Panel trip, annual URC dinner, 1947, 1.

75. Student, Westport High School essay, "The Assembly Today," Panel tour scrapbook.

76. "The Assembly Today."

77. "Tolerance Convocation Held Today," *California Daily Bruin*, May 5, 1947; Adaline Guenther, notes on the *Bruin* article, Panel tour scrapbook.

78. "Six Coeds on Panel Tour Given Ovation in New York Schools."

79. Frank E. Cane, letter to Adaline Guenther, May 9, 1947, URC Files.

80. "Tolerance Convocation Held Today."

81. J. M. Ewing was a Presbyterian clergyman from Santa Barbara. East Los Angeles Junior College was also interested in receiving help in establishing a branch of the URC, URC Files.

82. Glenn Moore, "Report of Clergy Division," URC annual meeting, May 5, 1947, URC Files.

83. Adaline Guenther, report of the executive secretary, URC annual meeting, May 9, 1948, URC Files.

84. Rabbi Henry Rabin, "Report of the LACC Advisers," URC annual meeting, May 9, 1949, URC Files. The increase in the student population at LACC was in part the result of the founding of California State University, Los Angeles, on the same campus as LACC.

85. Glenn Moore, "Executive Committee Report," URC annual meeting, May 8, 1950, URC Files.

86. Guenther, report of the executive secretary, 1948.

87. Patricia R. Fisher-Smith, Report on Hollywood High Student Board, URC annual meeting, May 5, 1947, URC Files.

88. Edgar J. Goodspeed, report of Education Division, URC annual meeting, May 5, 1947, URC Files.

89. James Thayer, report of the UCLA Student Board, URC annual meeting, May 10, 1948, URC Files; Rabbi Jacob Kohn, report of the Educational Division, URC annual meeting, May 10, 1948, URC Files.

90. During this time the URC experimented with Veterans' Panels. It seems likely that one of the veterans on those panels was John D. Ehrlichman who attended UCLA as a veteran and was a URC participant. He later became a White House counsel and assistant for domestic affairs in the Nixon administration. He was involved in the Watergate scandal, for which he served about eighteen months in prison.

91. Guenther, report of the executive secretary, 1948; M. J. Karpf, memo to the members of the Education Committee, July 30, 1948, URC Files.

92. Bess Wilson, "UCLA Religious Conference Sets Pattern for the East," *Los Angeles Times*, October 5, 1948.

93. Karpf, memo, July 30, 1948.

94. Mrs. Morris Pfaelzer, report on the Panel of Americans, URC annual meeting, May 9, 1949. URC Files; Barbara Jewkes, Memo to "Old Hands and Prospective Panelists," November 9, 1949, URC Files. The local Panel program used male as well as female panelists.

95. Letter of Edward Goodspeed to Adaline Guenther, August 30, 1948, URC Files.

96. Loyd McCormick, report of the UCLA Student Board, URC annual meeting, May 9, 1949, URC Files.

97. Guenther, report of the executive secretary, 1948.

98. Adaline Guenther, letter to David Danzig, 1948, URC Files.

99. Guenther, letter to Danzig, 1948.

100. Guenther, letter to Danzig, 1948; Barrett, report to Guenther, URC Files.

101. Guenther, letter to Danzig, 1948.

102. Guenther, letter to Danzig, 1948.

103. Guenther, letter to Danzig, 1948.

104. Guenther, letter to Danzig, 1948.

105. The year 1948 is penciled in. Here Guenther is referring to an earlier plan to have a URC panel do the presentations at each site and stay there for several weeks to train local panelists. The AJC would have paid for the travel and lodging of the Panel. URC Files.

106. Guenther, letter to Danzig, 1948.

107. Guenther, letter to Danzig, 1948.

108. Guenther, letter to Danzig, 1948.

109. Guenther, letter to Danzig, 1948.

110. Guenther, letter to Danzig, 1948.

111. Guenther, letter to Danzig, 1948.

Chapter 7. Building Panels Nationwide

1. Mrs. Guy C. Wilson Jr., report of the Intercultural Association, URC annual meeting, May 21, 1951, URC Files.

2. Mrs. Morris Pfaelzer, report of the Panel Advisory Board, URC annual meeting, May 19, 1952, URC Files.

3. B. L. Fox to University of Syracuse dean Charles G. Noble, August 27, 1952, URC Files.

4. Pfaelzer, report of the Panel Advisory Board, 1952, 19. The number of student panels changed from year to year, depending on student interest, university support, and university funding; it ranged from about sixteen to twenty-four.

5. Pfaelzer, report of the Panel Advisory Board, 1952.

6. Pfaelzer, report of the Panel Advisory Board, 1952.

7. Mrs. Henry G. Mosler, report of the Intercultural Associates, URC annual meeting, May 18, 1953, URC Files.

8. The URC Charter provided for the expansion of the URC to other parts of California, but not beyond the state.

9. "The Panel of Americans—Today," in *Panel of Americans: A Program in Intergroup Education*, National Council for the Panel of Americans, 3, March 1954, UMKC University Archives.

10. Wolfgang Saxon, "John McGill Krumm, 82, Episcopal Bishop," October 26, 1995.

11. "Panel of Americans—Today," 3.

12. John M. Krumm, "A Proposal to Foundations for the Expansion of the Panel of Americans," 1954–1955, 2; Dwight Culver, "Status of the Panel of Americans, Inc.," March 15, 1958, Panel Files of Marian Hargrave (hereafter PFMH).

13. "Panel of Americans—Today," 2.

14. Krumm, "Proposal to Foundations," 1, PFMH.

15. John M. Krumm, *The Panel of Americans—Today: A Message from the Chairman of the Executive Board*, National Council for the Panel of Americans, 1–3, March 1954, PFMH.

16. Krumm, "Proposal to Foundations," 1.

17. "Racial Panel in Full Swing," *University News*, University of Kansas City, Wednesday, October 22, 1952.

18. "Panel Gains in Popularity among Community Groups," *University News*, January 29, 1953; *Kansas City Star*, February 8, 1953.

19. "A Panel for Tolerance: Student Groups Hope to Relieve Social Tensions," *Kansas City Star*, March 27, 1953.

20. Letter of Joan Meierseick to Earl C. McGrath, December 5, 1954, UMKC Archives.

21. Meierseick to McGrath, December 5, 1954.

22. Letter of Earl C. McGrath to Joan Meierseick, December 17, 1954, UMKC Archives.

23. Inter-Office Correspondence, University of Kansas City, March 31, 1955, UMKC Archives.

24. Letter of Joan Meierseick to Earl C. McGrath, March 25, 1955, UMKC Archives.

25. Inter-Office Correspondence, University of Kansas City, Wheadon Block, Dean, to Earl McGrath, March 24, 1955, August 15, 1956, UMKC Archives.

26. Beta K. Smith to Marian Hargrave, January 9, 1962, PFMH.

27. Panel of Americans Handbook, part 3, Some Resources, 39–51, undated, PFMH.

28. Panel of Americans Handbook, part 2, 14–16, 18, by NCPA, printed, undated.

29. Panel of Americans Handbook, part 2, 16.

30. Panel of Americans Handbook, part 2, 18–25.

31. Panel of Americans Handbook, part 2, 18–25.

32. Panel of Americans Handbook, part 2, 18–25.

33. Panel of Americans Handbook, part 2, 26.

34. Panel of Americans Handbook, part 2, 26.

35. Panel of Americans Handbook, part 2, 26–28.

36. Panel of Americans Handbook, part 2, 26–30.

37. Panel of Americans Handbook, part 2, 26, 31–32.

38. Panel of Americans Handbook, part 2, 26, 34–35.

39. Panel of Americans Handbook, part 2, 26, 37.

40. Panel of Americans Handbook, part 2, 26, 37–38.

41. Panel of Americans Handbook, part 2, 22.

42. *Some Criteria for Evaluating a Panel Program*, printed, Panel of Americans, Inc., undated, 13–14; Panel of Americans Handbook, part 2, 20–25.

43. First National Training Conference, Panel of Americans, March 15 and 16, 1957, PFMH.

44. First National Training Conference, Panel of Americans.

45. First National Training Conference, Panel of Americans.

46. John Krumm, "Excerpts from the Role of the Protestant Speaker in the Panel of Americans," Panel of Americans, Inc., Eastern Area Training Conference, Columbia University, February 11, 1961, typescript, 1–2, PFMH.

47. Krumm, "Excerpts from the Role of the Protestant Speaker in the Panel of Americans," 1–2.

48. Krumm, "Excerpts from the Role of the Protestant Speaker in the Panel of Americans," 2.

49. Krumm, "Excerpts from the Role of the Protestant Speaker in the Panel of Americans," 2.

50. Panel of Americans, Inc., Eastern Area Training Conference, Columbia University, February 11, 1961, typescript, 2, PFMH.

51. "The Panel of Americans," *American Unity: An Educational Guide*, 13, no. 5 (1955): 16–20, PFMH.

52. "Panel of Americans," *American Unity*, 18.

53. "Panel of Americans," *American Unity*, 19–20.

54. "Panel of Americans," *American Unity*, 20.

55. *Time Magazine*, June 6, 1955, 51; "Kids Who Speak for Brotherhood," *Coronet Magazine*, July 1957.

56. "Teenagers Talk," *Seventeen Magazine*, October,1961, pages 112–113, 182–185.

57. Letter of Barbara Lovett to Dorothy Bauman, October 11, 1961, PFMH.

58. Vance Packard, *The Status Seekers* (New York: David McKay, 1959), 199.

59. Justine Wise Polier, "Closing Address and Summary of National Organization of Women, Conference," Washington DC, February 17–19, 1960, PFMH.

60. "Supplement to the Panel of Americans Brochure," undated, 1–2; Letter of Mary F. Brinig, director of Church Activities, Marble Collegiate Church, to Marian Hargrave, February 2, 1962, PFMH.

61. Dorothy Bauman, memo to Dorothy Height, May 29, 1959, PFMH.

62. "Supplement to the Panel of Americans Brochure," 1–2.

63. "Supplement to the Panel of Americans Brochure," undated, 1, PFMH.

64. William H. Lane, Principal, Public School, 175, Queens, to Marian Hargrave, March 7, 1961, PFMH.

65. William Nosofsky, assistant principal, Junior High School 178, Brooklyn, to Marian Hargrave, October 17, 1960, PCMH; Julius Raskin, principal, Junior High School 178, Brooklyn, to Marian Hargrave, October 17, 1960, PFMH; Bernard Friedman, of Public School 157, Manhattan, to Dorothy Bauman, November 23, 1960, PFMH; Harold G. Walters, acting principal of Public School 77, Queens, to Marian Hargrave, February 7, 1961, PFMH.

66. "Panel of Americans, Inc. Briefing Sheet," February 21, 1962, typescript, PFMH.

Chapter 8. The University Religious Conference Goes to India

1. Eugene Burdick and William J. Lederer, *The Ugly American* (New York: W. W. Norton, 1958); Gene Zubovich, *Before the Religious Right: Liberal Protestants, Human Rights, and the Polarization of the United States* (Philadelphia: University of Pennsylvania Press, 2022), 24–25. Zubovich discusses E. Stanley Jones, a Methodist missionary in India early in the twentieth century, and the "study missions" and tours sponsored by Sherwood Eddy after the First World War to promote "dialogue" and "mutual understanding." G. Bromley Oxnam, a Methodist leader from Los Angeles, was among those who went on Eddy's venture at the time. Whether this had any influence on Adaline Guenther and Project India is unknown.

2. "Color Psychology," *Time Magazine*, April 28, 1952. Cited by Judith Kerr Graven, *Project India: How College Students Won Friends for America 1952–1969* (Minneapolis: Mill City Press, 2014), 1.

3. Lee Nichols, speech at the annual URC student banquet, May 13, 1953, URC Files. Nichols himself never went to India, but he found Robinson and the URC students returning from India to be truly inspiring.

4. Adaline Guenther, "Report on URC Programs," annual report, 1955, URC Files.

5. In 1959 students from the Santa Barbara and Riverside campuses joined UCLA students in traveling to India under the auspices of the URC affiliates at both campuses. Sam Thomsen, the director of the URC at Santa Barbara, was one of the two adult leaders who traveled with the group of fourteen students. Thomsen praised the group, saying that they spoke to 115 Indian groups and to a total of about forty-five thousand people. He also praised the model UN Session that those URC students undertook in cooperation with about forty Indian student leaders from the University of Bombay. The URC developed Project Pakistan in 1959. It was similar in format to Project India, but the URC dropped the program after that one summer.

6. The place names used in this book are the same ones that were used by Americans

in the period from 1950s to the 1970s, the era when PI was in operation. Project Ceylon lasted just one year.

7. The UCLA Counselling Department helped Guenther set the requirements and select the applicants; at times PI alumni participated in the process as well. Guenther continued to help select and train PI applicants until 1963. URC Files.

8. Project India application form, URC Files.

9. The tests were administered and prepared by the California Testing Service, URC Files.

10. Adaline Guenther, "Project India 1957," typescript report, 1, URC Files.

11. Guenther, "Project India 1957," 1.

12. Guenther, "Project India 1957," 3.

13. Lynn Phillips, "Project India," *Pig Skin Review: UCLA Alumni Magazine*, November 1957, 13, URC Files.

14. Adaline Guenther had applied to the Rockefeller Foundation but was turned down. Later, Winthrop Rockefeller gave the URC a gift of fifteen thousand dollars from a special Rockefeller fund on the condition that the source of the gift remain anonymous, so as not to set a precedent. As for the gift from the Episcopal Church, it was made so that an Episcopalian student could be part of the PI Team. Adaline Guenther, minutes of the meeting of the URC Board of Directors, June 19, 1952, URC Files. Students sometimes paid for a portion of their own travel, but PI was to be open to students of limited means.

15. Board of Directors meeting, June 18, 1953, URC Files.

16. Guenther, "Project India, 1957."

17. Project India made efforts to appear separate from the State Department. Guenther, "Project India 1957," 1–2.

18. Guenther, "Project India 1957," 4.

19. Guenther, "Project India 1957," 2.

20. Guenther, "Project India 1957," 5.

21. Phillips, "Project India," 13.

22. Founding principles, quoted in "The University Religious Conference, 1928 to 1958," URC Files.

23. Founding principles, quoted in "University Religious Conference, 1928 to 1958."

24. URC annual report, May 18, 1955, URC Files.

25. David A. Hollinger, *Protestants Abroad: How Missionaries Tried to Change the World but Changed America* (Princeton, NJ: Princeton University Press, 2017), 3; Zubovich, *Before the Religious Right*, 14, 24–25, 65, 165.

26. Over the eighteen summers PI students visited some seventy-five sites in India. The large cities PI visited included Bombay, Calcutta, Madras, as those cities were called at the time, and New Delhi. A few of the more popular of the medium- and small-sized cities included Agra, Ahmedabad, Bangalore, Cochin, Ernakulam,

Hyderabad, Lucknow, Mysore, Patna, Poona, and Udaipur. Graven, *Project India*, 397–402.

27. Typescript of "Report on Project India as stated by the 1952 group and followed by the groups in 1953 and 1954, 1955," URC Files.

28. Phillips, "Project India," 13.

29. Memo on Project India, AR 31148, BR 22000, State Department Document, 1955 URC Files.

30. Guenther, "Project India, 1957," 5.

31. Phillips, "Project India," 13.

32. "U.S. Students in Calcutta: Person-to Person Discussions," *Statesman*, August 6, 1957, Project India, 1957, URC Files.

33. Philips, "Project India," 13.

34. Guenther, "Project India 1957," 2.

35. Guenther, "Project India 1957," 2.

36. Memo on Project India, State Department, 1–3.

37. For instance, Project India encountered cyclones in Puma. Dave Lund came down with polio while in Paris, on his way back from India. Tuberculosis, typhoid, and intestinal upsets also plagued PI travelers, including Guenther.

38. Memo on Project India, State Department, 1–3. Social Service Leagues were set up at colleges and universities to involve students in service work in the community.

39. All India Radio and various newspapers gave Project India favorable publicity. Some examples included "1957 UCLA Project Work at Bansdroni," *Hindustan Standard*, August 14, 1957. Some PI students held interviews on All India radio. The 1952 PI students publicized their cooperative labor projects to other UCLA students after they returned home. URC Files.

40. Phillips, "Project India."

41. "1957 UCLA Project Work at Bansdroni."

42. Project India Team, "Geneva Report," typescript of Evaluation of Project India Trip, 1955, 2, URC Files.

43. Memo on Project India, State Department, 2.

44. US Department of State, Foreign Service Dispatch 466, Bombay Area, November 17, 1960, 2, URC Files; "America and India: Value of Contact an Understanding," *Hindustan Standard*, August 21, 1957, URC Files.

45. Memo on Project India, State Department, 2, URC Files.

46. Phillips, "Project India."

47. "1957 UCLA Project Work at Bansdroni."

48. "1957 UCLA Project Work at Bansdroni."

49. "1957 UCLA Project Work at Bansdroni."

50. "Welfare Centre for Refugees: Commendable Work by UCLA Students," *Sunday Hindustan Standard*, August 25, 1957; "1957 UCLA Project Work at Bansdroni"; "P. C.

Sen Opens DP Welfare Centre: Bldg. Set Up by Students of California Varsity," *Sunday Amrita Bazar Patrika*, August 25, 1957, URC Files. The concept of "One World" that Sen mentioned was the dream expressed by Wedell Wilkie in the 1940s of an international world interconnected by idealism. Samuel Zipp, *The Idealist: Wendell Wilkie's Wartime Quest to Build One World* (Cambridge, MA: Harvard University Press, 2020), 3–14.

51. "U.S. Students in Calcutta: Person-to Person Discussions," *Statesman*, August 6, 1957, URC Files.

52. Guenther, "Project India 1957," 2.

53. Surjyansu Bhattachayya, "Bani Bhaban: A Growing Monument of Indo-U.S. Good Will," *News Feature US Information Service*, October 5, 1976, 1–2 URC Files.

54. Bhattachayya, "Bani Bhaban"; Guenther, "Project India 1957," 2.

55. "Geneva Report on Project India, 1955," 3.

56. "Geneva Report on Project India, 1955," 4.

57. "UCLA Projects for India, by Returning PI Students," typed manuscript, 1955–1957, 2, 3, URC Files. After they returned home, the PI participants held a charity drive on campus and in the community to send gifts to India. Every project was described in detail, including the name of the proposed recipients, the background, the project itself, the need, and the justification.

58. Marty Rosen and Lorraine Stickney, "To Whom It May Concern," February 16, 1953, URC Files. Rosen and Stickney addressed this letter to donors who contributed gifts for India to be sent by the PI participants who had returned to UCLA. Most of the PI participants wrote similar letters as follow-up after they returned home.

59. "UCLA Projects for India," 2–3.

60. "UCLA Projects for India."

61. "UCLA Projects for India."

62. Index numbers 1 and 2, in "UCLA Projects for India."

63. Index numbers 1 and 2, continued, and index number 3, in "UCLA Projects for India."

64. Guenther," Project India 1957, typescript, 4–5.

65. Chester Bowles, letter to Edwin Pauley, May 24, 1956, 1–3, URC Files.

66. Bowles, letter to Pauley, May 24, 1956, 1–3.

67. Guenther, "Project India, 1957," 4.

68. Guenther, "Project India, 1957," 4.

69. Moses Hirschtritt to Adaline Guenther, February 12, 1959, URC Files.

70. Peaceful coexistence and a strong desire for peace were mentioned by PI students in their 1955 evaluation. See N. Marbury Efimenco, acting public affairs officer, USIS Bombay, India, "Project India 1959 Visit to Bombay Consular Area, Dispatch No. 15, May 6, 1960," 3–4, URC Files.

71. Winthrop Brown to Chancellor of UCLA and Provosts of UC Riverside and UC Santa Barbara, August 25, 1959, URC Files.

72. John Lund to (Gram) Adaline Guenther, October 1, 1959, URC Files.

73. Department of State, Dispatch No. 466, November 17, 1960, 1, 2, URC Files.

74. Dispatch from Madras Consular Area, Dispatch No. 466, November 17, 1960, 2, URC Files.

75. Department of State, Dispatch No. 466, November 17, 1960. Arti is a central form of ritual Hindu worship, involving the lighting of candles. Most often it is directed to the deities but can occasionally be directed to individuals of note as an honor and sign of respect.

76. Author interview with Luke Fishburn. Martin Luther King Jr. stayed at the URC because housing for African Americans was still unavailable in Westwood.

77. Beimfohr, *History of the University Religious Conference*, 1978, 25, 43–48.

78. In the 1963 US Supreme Court case of *Abington School District v. Schempp*, Justice Potter Stewart in his sole dissent expressed the idea that Bible readings and other religious practices in the public schools could be permitted by the free exercise clause of the First Amendment. That dissent became the basis for other similar rulings and was later applied to public colleges and universities. This opened the door for religion to be taught at UCLA. Kevin Kruse, *One Nation under God: How Corporate America Invented Christian America* (New York: Basic Books, 2015), 190–201. See also Leigh Eric Schmidt, *The Church of Saint Thomas Paine: A Religious History of American Secularism* (Oxford: Princeton University Press, 2021), 13–14.

79. Beimfohr, *History*, 43–47.

80. Beimfohr, *History*, 39, 42.

81. Beimfohr, *History*, 46–47.

82. Beimfohr, *History*, 69–82.

83. David Hollinger, *Christianity's American Fate* (Princeton: Princeton University Press, 2022), 163–164. Hollinger argues that the line that distinguishes liberal Protestants, liberal Catholics, and liberal Jews from post-Protestants, post-Catholics, and post-Judaic Jews and secularists has become blurred, and that together they constitute "an inclusive national community committed to democracy."

Epilogue: URC Legacies

1. Congressional Record, House of Representative, 114, no. 61, April 10, 1968.

2. An exception was Sister Christine Banta, who was a nun. But other Catholic panelists generally were lay women who were mothers. Author interview with Sister Christine Banta, July 22, 1998, Patricia McCarty, April 22, 1996, and Bernadette Hoyt, April 6, 1996.

3. Lois Mark Stalvey, *The Education of a Wasp* (New York: William Morrow: 1970), 9–10.

4. Shirley Chisholm, "Introduction," in Stalvey, *Education of a Wasp*, ix–x.

5. Beth Ashley, "On the Front Lines of Bigotry Battle," *Marin Independent Journal*, December 16, 1988.

Index

publicity of, 203–207
sponsoring group of, 188–189
training books of, 195–199
See also Panel of Americans (POA)
National Federation of College Catholic
  Clubs, 51
Native Americans, 106, 161
nativism, 19
Nazimova, Alla, 118, 121
Nazism, 84, 109
Nehru, Prime Minister, 213, 234
Newman, John Henry, 51
Newman Clubs, 51, 82, 147
Newman Hall (UCLA), 82
New York City, 165–67, 184, 207–208
New York School of Social Work, 208
New York University, 129, 166, 200, 208
Nichols, James Hasting, 202
Nichols, Lee, 213
Niebuhr, Reinhold, 196
Nisei, 135, 160–162
Nixon, Richard, President 216, 232–233
North, Frank Mason, 9
North American Board for the Study of
  Religion in Higher Education (NAB),
  260n134
Northwestern University, 129, 190
Nosofsky, William, 209
Noyes, Alfred, 115
Nugent, Anthony P., Jr., 194

Oberlin Graduate School of Theology, 6
Obler, Arch, 118
O'Brien, Pat, 117
Ochs, Adolph, 254n30
O'Dwyer, William, 163
Office of Civilian Defense (OCD), 130
Office of Superintendent of Schools of the
  New York City Board of Education,
  166
O'Hara, Edwin V., 53, 61, 253n30
Ohio National Guard, 233
Ohio State University, 200
Olman, Luther, 234
Olson, Ivan, 126
One World concept, 286n50
Operation Crossroads Africa, 235

Oregon Minimum Wage Law, 53
Orozco, Jose Clemente, 105
Oxford University, 51

Packard, Vance, 206–207
Padelford, Frank, 77, 80
Pakistan, 232–233, 234
Panel Advisory Board of the Intercultural
  Associates, 184
Panel Extension Division (URC), 184, 185,
  186, 187
Panel of Americans (POA)
  as catalyst, 190
  description of, 186
  diversity of, 142, 166, 174, 186
  donations for, 169
  flyer of, 159
  goals of, 162
  origin of, 140–147, 237
  photo of, 156, 158
  recommendation regarding, 187
  success of, 149–150, 163, 172
  tour of, 163–175, 178, 179–180, 187
  See also National Council of the Panel of
    Americans (NCPA)
Panel of American Women (PAW), 195,
  237–238
"Panorama of the American Negro in the
  Fine Arts" (exhibition), 106
Paris Caucus, 45
Parke, Joy Mae, 264n48
Parker, A. L., 20–21, 25–26, 27
Parker, James, 20, 25, 26
Pasadena Junior College, 126
Pasadena Round Table Committee, 112
Paseo High School (Kansas City), 192
"The Pastor's Study" (radio program), 119
patriotic pluralism, 4
Pauley, Edwin, 229
Peace Corps, 219, 232
Peale, Norman Vincent, 207
Peekskill High School, 207
Penn, Julius H., 26–27
Pershing, John, 26–27, 31, 47
Philadelphia, Pennsylvania, panel tour, 165
Philipson, David, 59–60, 69–70, 75, 114,
  254n30, 260n134

University of California at Santa Barbara
(UCSB), 87, 175
University of California Los Angeles
(UCLA)
demographics of, 12, 175
discrimination at, 135
expansion of, 175
founding of, 15–16
at NCPA conference, 200
University of Chicago, 6, 74
University of Cincinnati, 180–181, 186, 200,
203
University of Denver, 129
University of Iowa, 58, 62, 63–72, 258n95
University of Kansas City, 200
University of Minnesota, 200
University of Omaha, 203
University of Oregon, 191
University of Pennsylvania, 51, 93
University of Pittsburgh, 190, 200
University of Southern California (USC),
80, 86, 261n10, 262n12
University of Texas, 200
University of Washington, 186
University Religious Conference (URC)
after school program of, 104
alumni of, 238–239
American Jewish Committee (AJC) and,
179
art exhibits of, 105–106
building committee of, 85
Catholics in, 82
challenges of, 175–176, 177–178
changing times and, 233–235
cultural outreach of, 102–107
decline of, 235
denominational clubs of, 88–89
donor contributions to, 103, 114
Education Committee of, 178, 179
expansion of, 86–87
gifts to, 285n14
goal of, 4–5, 87, 139–140, 151, 234
groups joining, 85–86
interfaith cooperation at, 82–83
intermarriage in, 271n103
Iowa School of Religion (ISR) as
compared to, 78

leadership of, 80–81, 234
legacy of, 236
USO and, 272n1
veterans of, 137–140
Veterans' Panels of, 280n90
wartime losses of, 147–150
Women Associates of, 133–134
women panelists in, 274n41, 275n52
Women's Division of, 113, 133–134,
268n18
University Religious Council, 76
UN Security Council model session, 231
US Information Service (USIS), 217
US State Department, 216, 217
US Supreme Court, 191–192
Utah State University, 207

Vagabond Club, 104, 105
Vanderbilt University, 190
Ventura Board of Education, 163
veterans, of University Religious
Conference (URC), 137–140, 157
Vietnam War, 233

Wadsworth, Guy W., 73, 75
Wald, Lillian, 263n35
Walnut Hills High School (Cincinnati), 170
Walters, Harold G., 209
War Camp Community Service, 18
Ward, Edith, 166
War Department, 2, 10, 18
Warner brothers, 75, 114
War Relocation Authority, 162
Washington University, 129, 181–182, 186,
200
Watkins, Gordon, 175
Wayne State University, 186, 193, 194, 200,
203, 205
Weed, Earl D., 133–134
Weifenbach, William, 194
Weiss, Lewis Allen, 117
"Well-You're Wrong" (radio program), 119
Wesleyan College (Ohio), 129
West Bengal Commission on Refugee
Rehabilitation, 224
"West Coast Church of the Air" (radio
program), 119, 120

www.ingramcontent.com/pod-product-compliance
Lightning Source LLC
Chambersburg PA
CBHW020338100426
42812CB00029B/3177/J